Taxation, Wage Bargaining, and Unemployment

Why were European economies able to pursue the simultaneous commitment to full employment and welfare state expansion during the first decades of the postwar period, and why did this virtuous relationship break down during recent decades? This book provides an answer to this question, by highlighting the critical importance of a political exchange between unions and governments, premised on wage moderation in exchange for the expansion of social services and transfers. The strategies pursued by these actors in these political exchanges are influenced by existing wage bargaining institutions, the character of monetary policy, and the level and composition of social policy transfers. The book demonstrates that the gradual growth in the fiscal burden has undermined the effectiveness of this political exchange, lowering the ability of unions' wage policies to affect employment outcomes.

Isabela Mares is Assistant Professor of Political Science at Stanford University. She is the author of *The Politics of Social Risk: Business and Welfare Development* (Cambridge University Press, 2003), which won the Gregory Luebbert Award of the American Political Science Association for best book in comparative politics. Her articles have appeared in *International Organization, World Politics, Comparative Political Studies, Politics and Society, Governance, Journal of Public Policy, Studie Politiczne*, and various edited volumes.

Cambridge Studies in Comparative Politics

General Editor
Margaret Levi   *University of Washington, Seattle*

Assistant General Editor
Stephen Hanson   *University of Washington, Seattle*

Associate Editors
Robert H. Bates   *Harvard University*
Peter Lange   *Duke University*
Helen Milner   *Columbia University*
Frances Rosenbluth   *Yale University*
Susan Stokes   *Yale University*
Sidney Tarrow   *Cornell University*
Kathleen Thelen   *Northwestern University*
Erik M. Wibbels   *University of Washington, Seattle*

Other Books in the Series

Continued after index

Taxation, Wage Bargaining, and Unemployment

ISABELA MARES

Stanford University

CAMBRIDGE
UNIVERSITY PRESS

FLIP

CAMBRIDGE UNIVERSITY PRESS
Cambridge, New York, Melbourne, Madrid, Cape Town, Singapore, São Paulo

Cambridge University Press
40 West 20th Street, New York, NY 10011-4211, USA

www.cambridge.org
Information on this title: www.cambridge.org/9780521857420

First published 2006

Printed in the United States of America

A catalog record for this publication is available from the British Library.

Library of Congress Cataloging in Publication Data

Mares, Isabela.
Taxation, wage bargaining, and unemployment / Isabela Mares.
   p.   cm. – (Cambridge studies in comparative politics)
Includes bibliographical references and index.
ISBN 0-521-85742-2 (hardback) – ISBN 0-521-67411-5 (pbk.)
1. Europe – Economic policy.   2. Europe – Social policy.   3. Manpower policy – Europe.
4. Welfare state – Sweden – History – 20th century.   5. Wages – Sweden – History –
20th century.   6. Labor unions – Sweden – History – 20th century.   7. Welfare state –
Germany – History – 20th century.   8. Wages – Germany – History – 20th century.
9. Labor unions – Germany – History – 20th century.   10. Welfare state – Great Britain –
History – 20th century.   11. Wages – Great Britain – History – 20th century.
12. Labor unions – Great Britain – History – 20th century.   I. Title.   II. Series.

HC240.M244   2005
331.11′094′0904–dc22   2005012019

ISBN-13   978-0-521-85742-0 hardback
ISBN-10   0-521-85742-2 hardback

ISBN-13   978-0-521-67411-9 paperback
ISBN-10   0-521-67411-5 paperback

For Radu

Contents

Contents

List of Figures and Tables

Figures and Tables

List of Abbreviations

DGB	Deutscher Gewerkschaftsbund (Federation of German Trade Unions)
LO	Landsorganisationen i Sverige (Swedish Trade Union Confederation)
OECD	Organization for Economic Cooperation and Development
ÖTV	Gewerkschaft Öffentliche Dienste, Transport und Verkehr (Public Sector, Transportation, and Traffic Union)
SACO	Sveriges Akademikers Central Organisation (Central Organization of Professional Employees)
SAF	Svenska Arbetsgivareföreningen (Swedish Employers' Federation)
SAP	Sveriges Socialdemokratiska Arbetarparti (Social Democratic Party)
SERPS	State Earnings-Related Pension Scheme
SF	Statsanstalldas Forbund (Union of State Employees)
TCO	Tjänstemännens Centralorganisation (Central Organization of Salaried Employees)
TGWU	Transport and General Workers' Union
TUC	Trades Union Congress
VF	Verkstads Förening (Engineering Employers' Union)

Acknowledgments

It is my great pleasure to thank the individuals and institutions that have provided support during the period of research and writing of this book. I have incurred many debts from colleagues and friends in the Stanford political science department, my intellectual home during the past few years. I would like to thank Jim Fearon, Steve Haber, David Laitin, and Mike Tomz for extremely helpful suggestions on early draft chapters. I am also immensely grateful to Beatriz Magaloni and Alberto Diaz-Cayeros for a number of very engaging conversations which helped me tremendously sharpen my criticism of existing studies. At Stanford, Jackie Sargent and Eliana Vasquez have helped me in innumerable ways to move this project along. I owe everybody more than my thanks.

Over the past few years, I have presented several draft chapters at various seminars and conferences. I am grateful to many colleagues who have provided extremely valuable comments on various aspects of the manuscript. For their generous and insightful suggestions, I would like to thank Jim Alt, Carles Boix, Pepper Culpepper, Keith Darden, Karl-Orfeo Fioretos, Peter Gourevitch, Peter Hall, Lane Kenworthy, Herbert Kitschelt, Peter Lange, Kathy Thelen, and Michael Wallerstein. I also thank seminar participants at Duke University, Yale University, the American Political Science Association, and the Conference of the Council for European Studies for helpful feedback.

I would like to acknowledge financial support provided by Stanford University and the German Marshall Fund of the United States. At Stanford, I am especially grateful to Karen Cook and Paul Sniderman for a leave of absence that allowed me to complete the first draft of the book. I have benefited from excellent research assistance from Raluca Boboc, Benjamin Brutlag, Daniel Butler, and Alex Kuo.

I am grateful to many colleagues for their help during the final stages of work on this book. At Cambridge University Press, my thanks go to Lew Bateman for his editorial advice. I am extremely grateful to Margaret Levi for her detailed written comments on the manuscript and for her enthusiasm about the project. Two anonymous reviewers have provided extremely engaging comments. I hope I have answered all their questions in the final version of the manuscript. Many thanks to Ruth Homrighaus and Elise Oranges for helping me prepare the manuscript for publication.

My deepest gratitude goes to my husband Radu. I am grateful to Radu for believing in this project from the very beginning and for encouraging me to leave everything else aside and work on this book. It is my great pleasure to dedicate this book to him, with love.

Introduction

DOES THE WELFARE STATE HURT EMPLOYMENT?

The employment performance of European economies has not fared particularly well in recent years. In most countries unemployment has risen to historically unprecedented levels, in some cases surpassing in relative terms the level of unemployment experienced during the Great Depression. In addition to unemployment, other labor market indicators also show signs of troublesome deterioration. Labor force participation rates of elderly workers have continued to decline in many countries despite policy makers' efforts to reverse the trend toward "early exit" from the labor market. Young workers and first-time job seekers have experienced disproportionately high levels of unemployment, and most policy efforts to integrate this group into the labor market have remained unsuccessful. Long-term unemployment as a percentage of total unemployment has been on the rise in many countries, transforming the long-term unemployed into a group permanently excluded from the labor market. In addition, overall labor force participation rates have stagnated or declined in several economies, despite an increase in the labor force participation rates of women.

In troubled times such as these, it can be hard to distinguish good news from bad news. Even sudden economic recoveries in the midst of decade-long recessions have frequently been characterized by jobless growth. The slow real growth experienced in the mid-1990s did not result in increased employment; unemployment levels continued to rise after each economic recovery. Thus, in the first decade of a new century, it appears that current levels of high unemployment are here to stay.

The political will to address these troubling problems is not in short supply. Labor market reforms and efforts to change the financing of social insurance occupy a prominent place on the policy agendas of European governments. Most reforms initiated in recent years respond to the growing political perception that high levels of income and payroll taxes are one of the causes of the economic malaise experienced by European economies during the last two decades. The diagnosis that high levels of nonwage labor costs are an obstacle to employment growth is now being accepted by many governments in Europe, and even by social democratic governments, the traditional defenders of the welfare state (Leisering 1999; Clasen 2001: 652–3). Consider the following examples: In the past decade, both left- and right-wing governments in France have introduced more than 40 policy measures that have lowered social charges of employers, exempting a number of sectors from social security contributions to family or sickness insurance (Bourguignon and Bureau 1999; De Foucauld 1995; Dehez and Fitoussi 1992; Piketty 1998; Assouline 1998). In recent years, the Belgian and Dutch governments have enacted policies reducing payroll taxes on employers in the manufacturing and service sectors. In Germany, the Red-Green coalition government is considering a broad reform in the mode of financing the social insurance system that would involve a partial shift to taxes that are not employment based, such as ecological taxes, as well as various *Kombilohn* proposals, that is, fiscal transfers that compensate social insurance contributions at low-income levels (Schelkle 2000; Bofinger and Fasshauer 1998; Wanger 1999).

Why were European economies able to reconcile the simultaneous pursuit of full employment and welfare state expansion during the first three decades of the postwar period, and why did this virtuous relationship break down in recent decades? What factors account for the deterioration of employment performance experienced by European economies in recent decades? This book develops a theoretical framework that provides an answer to these questions. The explanation advanced in this study seeks to account for both cross-national and intertemporal variation in the employment performance of advanced industrialized economies. The first part of the question is familiar to students of comparative political economy. What are the most salient factors that account for cross-national differences in the levels of unemployment experienced by European economies? Can we identify systematic differences in institutions and policies that can account for these differences? I also examine changes over time in the employment performance of these economies. Why have most European societies experienced a steady rise in the level of unemployment? What countries have experienced a stronger deterioration of their labor markets and why?

In its simplest form, the book's argument can be formulated as follows: In the first decades of the postwar period, welfare state expansion was premised on a political exchange between unions and governments, whereby governments of all partisan orientations guaranteed increases in social services and transfers while unions delivered wage restraint. The significant wage moderation exercised by unions in exchange for advances in social protection explains how most economies were able to reconcile welfare state expansion with full employment over a long period of time.

The process of welfare state growth and maturation, however, has undermined the effectiveness of this political exchange. We can distinguish two political mechanisms by which the growth of welfare state commitments has constrained the effectiveness of policies of wage moderation in restoring high levels of employment. The first is through a change in the composition of social policy transfers. In recent decades most European economies have experienced sharp increases in their numbers of "labor market outsiders." This heterogeneous category includes persons who enter the labor market only intermittently, the long-term unemployed, workers who retire early, and other labor market groups whose members do not belong to unions. The growth in social policy transfers going to labor market outsiders has reduced the net social policy transfers and services received by union members. This reduction, in turn, lowered unions' willingness to deliver sustained wage moderation. The second mechanism is a consequence of the rise in taxes necessary to finance existing social policy commitments. A higher part of the wage bill is now committed in the form of income or payroll taxes. As a result, the "room for action" of unions' wage policies is severely curtailed. As wages represent a small fraction of total compensation, even high pay cuts accepted by unions are likely to have only a modest impact on lowering employment. In other words, as the fiscal burden rises, the sensitivity of employment to wages declines. The net effect of these political developments is the sharpening of the trade-off between the pursuit of full employment and the commitment to welfare state expansion. The process of welfare state maturation has undermined the effectiveness of a critical political exchange that underpinned social policy expansion in the first decades of the postwar period.

Developments in European Labor Markets: Two Theoretical Perspectives

This book seeks to provide a unified approach that accounts for cross-sectional as well as temporal variations in the employment performance of European economies. For most studies this has remained, so far, an elusive goal. Most political science studies have been relatively successful in explaining cross-sectional variation in a broad range of economic outcomes across European economies. However, they have been unable to provide an answer to the question of why the employment performance of these economies has deteriorated so sharply over time. In contrast, economic approaches have focused on the extensive regulation of European labor markets as an important factor accounting for the rise in the level of unemployment. While these explanations attempt to account for intertemporal changes in the employment performance of advanced industrialized economies, they fail to provide an explanation for cross-national variation. The goal of this section is to identify the most significant limitations of the existing research.

Broadly speaking, we can identify two competing perspectives examining the sources of cross-national variation in the employment performance of advanced industrial democracies. Each of these approaches encompasses internal divergences and disagreements that will be analyzed in more detail in Chapter 1. The first of these perspectives is the neoclassical approach, which derives its conclusions from an extension of competitive labor market models. Most scholars working within this perspective contend that the regulation of labor markets and the dense networks of policies and practices that prevent the "flexible" deployment of labor by firms are at the root of the European unemployment problem. The second theoretical perspective, the corporatist approach, has been elaborated in a vast literature examining the economic consequences of different institutions of wage bargaining. These studies have shown that competitive labor markets do not always produce the best employment performance. Under some conditions, economies characterized by encompassing institutions of wage bargaining have produced employment outcomes superior to those of decentralized labor markets.

Neoclassical approaches contend that extensive measures protecting the employment security of workers are the main factor accounting for the poor employment performance of European economies in recent decades and for the contrast between "sclerotic" European economies and that of the dynamic, employment-generating United States (OECD 1994; Scarpetta 1996; Siebert 1997; IMF 2003). Their studies focus on several institutional features of the European labor market as labor market rigidities and causes for high levels of unemployment. The first is employment security regulations, or rules governing the hiring and firing of workers. These rules are regarded as a barrier to employment creation because they impede the flexible employment adjustment of firms in response to changes in demand.

Because firms operating under these rules can lay off workers only with great difficulty, they are also more reluctant to hire new workers during economic upswings. Other studies also point to the generosity of social policy benefits as a factor that raises the reservation wage of workers and lowers the likelihood that an unemployed worker will accept a job. As a recent report of the International Monetary Fund (IMF) succinctly characterizes the policy implications of this analysis, "countries with high unemployment are urged to undertake comprehensive structural reforms to reduce 'labor market rigidities' such as generous unemployment insurance schemes, high employment protection, high firing costs, high minimum wages, noncompetitive wage-setting mechanisms; and severe tax distortions" (IMF 2003: 125).

These arguments have both theoretical and empirical limitations. Critics of the theoretical logic underpinning this approach have pointed out that the "employment-security-regulations-as-rigidity" hypothesis discounts the positive externalities of these institutions for firms (Estevez-Abe, Iversen, and Soskice 2001; Wood 1998, 2001). Protective employment security regulations increase the long-term horizon of firms and workers and strengthen the incentives of these actors to invest in skills. Similarly, firms in economies with significant provision of training might also favor social policies with generous earnings-related benefits (Mares 2003; Manow 2000). Such benefits raise the reservation wage of high-skilled workers relative to low-skilled workers and further contribute to the incentive for these workers to invest in skills (Manow 2001; Mares 2003). As a result of the institutional linkages between systems of skill protection and social policies, employment security regulations are not always a source of rigidity for firms. In many economies with well-established systems of social protection, employers have embraced policy proposals to deregulate labor markets only reluctantly (Wood 1998, 2001; Thelen 2000, 2001). Most surprisingly, in some countries, such as Germany, firms have not changed their employment practices even after legislation weakening the stringency of employment security regulations has been enacted (Buechtemann 1991, 1993). In recent years, reports of the Organization for Economic Cooperation and Development (OECD) have incorporated these challenges to the neoliberal orthodoxy and have begun to advocate for a more selective reform of European labor markets.

On empirical grounds, the neoclassical perspective fails to account for the divergent employment performance of European economies. Figure 0.1 maps the correlation between a measure of the stringency of employment

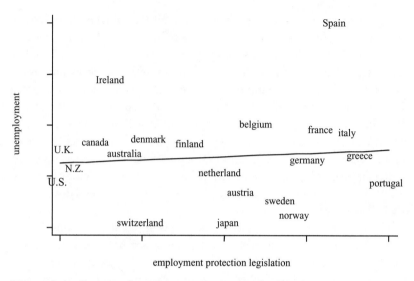

Figure 0.1. Impact of employment protection legislation on unemployment. (*Source:* OECD 1999b: Table 2.5.)

protection legislation developed by the OECD and unemployment in a number of European countries averaged over the period between 1990 and 1999. The employment security regulation index takes values between 1 and 26, with 26 being the economy with the most rigid labor markets. The measure takes into account regulations concerning hiring (such as rules favoring disadvantaged groups, conditions for using temporary labor, or fixed-term contracts) and regulations concerning dismissals (such as procedures for redundancy, mandated prenotification periods, and requirements for collective dismissal) (OECD 1999b: 50). While the correlation between this index and average unemployment rates is positive, the relationship is rather weak. Several countries with stringent employment security regulations, such as Sweden and Norway, have experienced relatively low levels of unemployment. Portugal is an interesting outlier here: It has the most stringent employment security regulations in the sample (the OECD score is 26), yet its average level of unemployment in this period was 6 percent, 3.5 percent below the average for western European economies. In other countries, such as Ireland, the unemployment level has been very high (14.8 percent) despite relatively weak levels of employment protection. The bivariate correlation shown here is, of course, illustrative. However, a number of studies that use more sophisticated estimation methods,

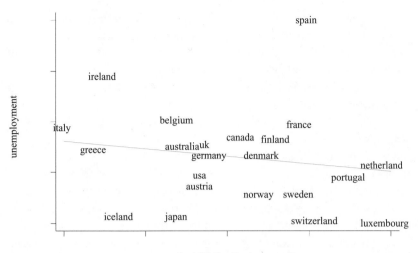

Figure 0.2. Relationship between generosity of social policy benefits and unemployment. (*Source:* OECD 1999b: Table 3.2.)

such as time series or panel data, have reached similar conclusions. It appears that employment security regulations have no effect on unemployment levels (Bertola 1990; Blanchard 1990; Blanchard and Wolfers 2000; Jackman, Layard, and Nickell 1996; Esping-Andersen 2000) and only a modest effect on the *composition* of unemployment.[1] It is important to point out that this explanation also faces difficulties in accounting for temporal change in unemployment. Despite the weakening of employment security regulations and the deregulation introduced by many European governments in recent decades under pressure from international organizations, unemployment has continued to rise.

Figure 0.2 examines the plausibility of a second hypothesis advanced by neoclassical scholars that the generosity of social policy benefits is the primary factor accounting for cross-national differences in unemployment

---

[1] In contrast to these studies, Elmeskov, Martin, and Scarpetta (2000) find that employment protection regulation has a positive impact on structural unemployment. Using 1993 unemployment data for 18 countries, Esping-Andersen (2000) finds that employment protection has a quadratic effect on unemployment. The unemployment level of young workers and of women is high when employment security regulations are either very rigid or very flexible. Other studies, such as Grubb and Wells (1993), find that stringent employment protection legislation increases the percentage of part-time workers.

levels. The horizontal axis of Figure 0.2 maps the net replacement rates of social policy benefits for a married couple working at an average wage. The values for this variable have been computed by the OECD as part of its benefit systems database and include unemployment, family, and housing benefits in the first month of benefit receipt. The surprising result in this case is that while the correlation between replacement rates and unemployment is rather weak, its sign is negative, suggesting that countries with more generous levels of benefits experience lower rates of unemployment. Sweden, Switzerland, and Norway are again outliers, with very high replacement rates and very low levels of unemployment. Switzerland, for example, has an average replacement rate of 78 percent, but its unemployment average during this period was 2.2 percent, 7 percentage points lower than the European average. These findings disconfirm the second hypothesis of neoclassical studies, which regards generosity in the level of social policy benefits as the main cause for high levels of unemployment.

The corporatist perspective has informed a vast political science literature exploring cross-national variation in the economic performance of OECD economies (Schmitter 1979, 1981; Cameron 1984; Goldthorpe 1984; Iversen 1999; Garrett and Lange 1995; Garrett 1998). In contrast to neoclassical scholars, corporatist studies argue that labor market regulations and strong and encompassing trade unions are not always a source of rigidity and a cause of high unemployment levels. The central theoretical proposition of the corporatist approach is that institutional differences among wage bargaining institutions – more specifically, differences in the level of centralization of the wage bargaining authority – explain cross-national variation in a variety of economic outcomes, such as levels of inflation, growth, and unemployment. As will be shown in Chapter 1, corporatist scholars differ in the specification of the functional form of the relationship between labor market institutions and labor market outcomes. One set of studies argues that the relationship is monotonic, where the performance of economies with centralized labor market institutions is strictly superior to the performance of economies with more fragmented institutions of wage bargaining (Cameron 1984; Crouch 1985; Lange 1984). Other scholars argue that the relationship between the centralization of the wage bargaining system and unemployment follows a "hump-shaped" pattern (Calmfors and Driffill 1988; Calmfors 1993). According to these studies, employment performance in economies in which wages are set at the industry level is inferior to employment performance in economies with *either* highly centralized *or* highly decentralized labor market institutions. The theoretical

Developments in European Labor Markets

Table 0.1. *Average unemployment in European political economies*

Period	Decentralized*	Intermediately centralized[†]	Highly centralized [‡]
	Unemployment categorized by wage bargaining system		
1960–1975	3.04	3.135	1.49
1976–1995	6.986	8.4616	3.166

Notes:
See Chapter 2 for a description of the wage bargaining centralization measure used here (computed as an average of existing indices).
* Decentralized economies include those with a wage bargaining centralization score greater than 10: Britain, the United States, and France.
† Intermediately centralized economies include those with a wage bargaining centralization score greater than 4 and less than 10: Belgium, Denmark, Finland, Germany, Italy, The Netherlands, and Switzerland.
‡ Highly centralized economies include those with a wage bargaining centralization score lower than 4: Austria, Norway, and Sweden.

claim common to both approaches is that unions in economies characterized by encompassing institutions of wage bargaining face an incentive to internalize some of the externalities of their wage demands. As a result, the overall level of unemployment will be lower in these economies than in economies with fragmented labor market institutions.

The corporatist approach is more successful than the neoclassical studies in explaining cross-national variation in European economies' employment performance. Its most important limitation is its inability to account for the deterioration in the labor market performance of European economies over the last two decades. To illustrate these trends, consider Table 0.1, which classifies economies into those with "decentralized," "intermediately centralized," and "highly centralized" labor market institutions and computes the average level of unemployment for each type of economy over the periods 1960–1975 and 1976–1999. This presentation of the data reveals the presence of a hump-shaped relationship between labor market institutions and unemployment, as hypothesized by Lars Calmfors and John Driffill (1988) as well as other scholars (Iversen 1999). Economies with intermediate-level centralization of the wage bargaining system, in which wages are set by industry-level unions, have an employment performance inferior to economies with either highly centralized or highly decentralized labor market institutions. The data presented in Table 0.1 suggest that unemployment has risen in all economies over time irrespective of the structure of their labor market institutions. However, in the 1976–1995 period, economies with intermediately centralized wage bargaining systems exhibited the worst employment performance, and the deterioration of their employment performance has been sharper than in economies with either centralized or decentralized labor market institutions. Why has the employment performance of European economies deteriorated so sharply during recent decades? This question, which has received little attention from corporatist studies, is the main object of study of this book.

The Argument

The central theoretical argument of this book explores the conditions under which unions are willing to deliver wage restraint in exchange for the provision of social services and transfers; it also considers the policy constraints on unions' wage moderation that are a consequence of the process of welfare state maturation. In Chapter 1, I develop a formal model of the optimal wage choice of trade unions in different macroeconomic environments and in welfare states characterized by different levels of taxes and transfers. A critical assumption made in this study is that unions care about the provision of social policy benefits and services received by their members. In other words, unions' utility comprises a component that denotes their concern for social policy services and transfers going to union members. This assumption distinguishes my model from the majority of "union monopoly," or bargaining, models, which generally assume "utilitarian" preferences – that is, that unions want to maximize the real wages of their members and minimize unemployment (Farber 1986).

The analysis developed in Chapter 1 explores the employment consequences that follow from unions' choices and the ways in which the various institutional parameters of a political economy magnify or decrease the impact of these choices on the equilibrium level of employment. I examine the effect of three policy parameters: the structure of labor market institutions; the impact of monetary policy; and the influence of existing welfare state arrangements. Let me discuss the impact of these institutions in turn.

In exploring how labor market institutions affect the equilibrium level of employment, my analysis builds on existing corporatist studies. The key results of my model are in agreement with the theoretical results of the Calmfors and Driffill (1988) analysis. More specifically, I show that unemployment is highest in economies with industry-level wage bargaining systems. In this particular setting, the effects of unions' monopoly power outweigh the incentives for unions to internalize some of the costs of their militant behavior. As I have shown elsewhere, the results of the Calmfors-Driffill model are the most general results in a model of the impact of labor market institutions on economic outcomes (Mares 2005, forthcoming). The case of a monotonic relationship between the centralization of the wage bargaining system and unemployment can be obtained as a limit case of the Calmfors-Driffill model and is thus not inconsistent with this framework.[2] The additional assumption about unions' utility made in this book predicts in equilibrium higher levels of wage moderation and hence lower unemployment than in the Calmfors and Driffill model. In other words, unions that care about social policy will demand lower wages than unions that care only about their members' real wage levels. Moreover, the magnitude of the employment effect that follows from this additional wage restraint increases as the centralization of the wage bargaining system increases. This modifies the predicted level of unemployment as compared to the Calmfors-Driffill model, flattening the functional form of the curve that links the centralization of the wage bargaining system to unemployment.

As a recent wave of scholarship has pointed out, the impact of unions' choices on the equilibrium level of unemployment depends not only on the structure of the wage bargaining system, but also on both the macroeconomic policies pursued by the government and the level of central bank independence (Scharpf 1991; Hall and Franzese 1998; Iversen 1999; Soskice and Iversen 1999, 2000). The main insight of this line of analysis is that an independent central bank will "discipline" unions' militancy and will contribute to a moderation of their wage settlements. As Iversen lays out the basic logic of the argument: "If the monetary rule is accommodating (i.e., the monetary authority seeks to avoid a reduction in real demand), the effect on the real money supply of higher wages and prices will be low and there will consequently be little reason for the wage bargainers to endogenize the macroeconomic effects of their actions. By contrast, if the monetary rule is nonaccommodating (i.e., the monetary authority adheres to a low-inflation target), militancy will reduce the real money supply and bargainers will consequently have an incentive to exercise restraint" (1999: 2; for a similar argument, see Soskice and Iversen 1999, 2000). The theoretical model in Chapter 1 incorporates the formal logic developed by Iversen and Soskice

---

[2] The reverse is not true. One can not obtain the Calmfors-Driffill hump-shaped results using the assumptions made in the simpler Soskice and Iversen (2000) setup.

in examining the consequences of monetary policy on the equilibrium level of employment (Iversen 1999; Soskice and Iversen 2000).

In addition to these variables – the centralization of the wage bargaining system and the character of macroeconomic policy – I also examine the effect of the institutional parameters of the welfare state on the equilibrium level of employment. The contribution of this study lies precisely in the addition of the welfare state to existing corporatist models (Calmfors-Driffill) and models of the interaction of wage bargaining agents with monetary authorities (Iversen and Soskice, Hall and Franzese). There are strong theoretical justifications for taking this additional step. The process of wage determination is strongly constrained by the level and structure of taxes that finance existing social policy commitments. The importance of this tax constraint has grown over time; the combination of payroll and income taxes now takes up somewhere between 25 and 50 percent of the total compensation of workers (Svenskt Näringsliv 2002). So far, few studies have systematically explored the economic and political consequences of these fiscal constraints.

I have already discussed the positive effects of the welfare state on the equilibrium level of employment. These effects are the consequence of the wage moderation exercised by unions in exchange for social policy expansion. It is this moderation that explains why the rapid expansion of the welfare state during the first decades of the postwar period came about at a very low cost in terms of unemployment. But welfare states also exercise a negative impact on employment. The present study focuses on two mechanisms by which the growth and maturation of the welfare state affect the equilibrium level of unemployment. The first effect is a consequence of the growth of taxes. Tax increases reduce firms' demand for labor. At the same time, they diminish workers' net income and increase their reluctance to accept a further decline in their wages. Finally, tax increases reduce the overall effectiveness of a policy of wage moderation as an instrument for lowering unemployment: Growth in taxes reduces wages as a percentage of employees' total compensation; thus, when taxes are high, a policy of wage restraint can reduce the total labor costs by only a limited amount and can thereby exercise only a small positive effect on the equilibrium level of employment.

The second mechanism by which larger welfare states can hurt employment identified in this study is through changes in the composition of social policy transfers. The critical assumption made in this study is that unions, as rational actors, will exercise wage moderation only in exchange for benefits and social services that go to union members. Not all social policy benefits go to union members, however, and some transfers go to groups of labor market outsiders. This heterogeneous category includes persons who enter the labor market only intermittently, the long-term unemployed, and other labor market groups that are beyond unions' radar screen. In many European economies, the size of these groups has increased during recent decades as a result of the overall deterioration of the labor market (Esping-Andersen 1999; Alm 2001; Rueda forthcoming). An increase in the share of unemployment, disability, or pension benefits received by labor market outsiders can reduce the share of social policy transfers and services going to union members. This, in turn, can undermine the incentives of unions to exercise wage moderation. As European labor markets become more bifurcated between labor market insiders, who enjoy stable employment, and labor market outsiders, traditional policy instruments that functioned during the period of welfare state expansion no longer function effectively. This remains one of the most significant policy dilemmas faced by contemporary welfare states.

We can now approach the question that serves as the title to this introduction: "Does the welfare state hurt employment?" The answer is, "It depends." Under certain conditions – low levels of taxes, low number of labor market outsiders – the positive employment effects of the welfare state in the form of wage restraint can outweigh the negative employment effects of higher taxes. But welfare states can hurt employment if taxes are too high and unions derive only very small gains in utility from the provision of social services – in other words, when a large subset of total social policy expenditures goes to labor market outsiders. The first proposition explains why welfare state expansion and the pursuit of full employment were compatible policy goals during the first decades of the postwar period. The second proposition characterizes the situation of European labor markets during recent years.

Summing up this discussion, Figure 0.3 presents a graphical display of the predictions of this analysis for the equilibrium level of unemployment. The horizontal axis maps economies based on the level of centralization of their wage bargaining systems. Close to the origin of the axis, we find economies with decentralized labor market institutions, such as the United States and Canada. Movement along the axis represents an increase in the centralization of the wage bargaining system. Along the vertical axis, I map the predicted equilibrium level of unemployment. As discussed previously, the institutional structure of the wage bargaining system affects the optimal

13

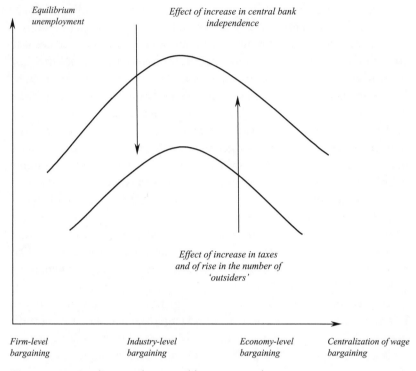

Figure 0.3. Predictions about equilibrium unemployment.

wage strategy of unions. The predicted relationship between the structure
of the wage bargaining system and the equilibrium level of unemployment
is hump-shaped: Unions will exercise the highest levels of militancy in
economies with industry-level wage bargaining but will internalize some
of the consequences of their militancy as the centralization of the wage
bargaining system increases. As predicted by recent studies, an increase
in central bank independence (or, to use the terminology of the existing
studies, in monetary policy nonaccommodation) will shift the equilibrium
employment curve downward. Finally, an increase in the levels of taxes and
social policy expenditures devoted to labor market outsiders will undermine
the effectiveness of wage moderation and will contribute to an upward shift
in the equilibrium level of unemployment. The advantage of this model
as compared to its theoretical alternatives lies in is its ability to generate
predictions about the employment performance of OECD economies that
explain *both* cross-sectional and intertemporal variations in the equilibrium
level of unemployment.

14

The Organization of the Study

Chapter 1 lays out the basic argument of the book. I begin by reviewing the literature on wage determination in advanced industrialized societies. I develop a formal model that extends the Calmfors-Driffill and Soskice-Iversen models by incorporating additional parameters modeling the impact of the welfare state on the equilibrium level of employment. The main part of the chapter presents the logic of the argument in nontechnical terms. The formal derivation of the equilibrium and of the comparative statics results are presented in the appendix.

Chapter 2 presents a quantitative test of the key propositions developed in Chapter 1 using panel data for OECD economies during the period between 1960 and 1998. The measure of the centralization of the wage bargaining system used in this study averages over time eight of the most significant indicators that have been developed. I test the predictions of the model using a broad range of measures of the magnitude of welfare state commitments, including both measures of the tax burden and of transfers devoted to labor market outsiders.

Chapters 3 through 5 present additional tests of the implication of the model through a comparative historical analysis of the evolution of the wage–social policy nexus in Sweden, Germany, and the United Kingdom in the postwar period. These economies take the entire range of values on one of the crucial independent variables of the model: the structure of the wage bargaining system. This approach allows me to examine the employment consequences resulting from unions' choices given different wage setting institutions. As a result of differences in labor markets and demographic developments, the pressures placed by mature welfare states on the choices made by unions have also differed dramatically in these three countries. In these case studies, I rely on a number of union publications and documents to examine whether the key assumption made by the model about unions' willingness to moderate their wage demands in exchange for the expansion of benefits and services to union members is in fact accurate and whether it has informed union behavior. This analysis allows me to identify the particular social policies for which trade unions were in fact willing to forego wage increases. Using time series data on wage and productivity developments, I also test the micro-level implications of the analysis for the conditions leading to wage moderation. In each of the cases, the narrative allows me to contrast policy developments during the "golden age" period to those of recent decades and to examine the ways in which the process of

15

welfare state maturation has undermined the effectiveness of the policy of wage moderation.

In the concluding chapter, I return to a broad comparative context and examine the politics of the "new social pacts" – tripartite agreements among unions, employers, and governments in which the participants attempt to link wage moderation to reforms of the system of taxation and the provision of social policy benefits. Recent years have seen a resurgence of such social pacts, even in economies that initially lacked the institutional preconditions for this corporatist negotiation, such as Italy, Spain, and Ireland (Regini 2000; Fajertag and Pochet 1997, 2000; Berger and Compston 2002; Ebbinghaus and Hassel 2000; Traxler 2000; O'Donnell and O'Reardon 1997, 2000). By drawing on the predictions developed in Chapter 1, I examine the policy choices that may enhance the effectiveness of these new social pacts in lowering unemployment.

1

The Economic and Political Consequences
of Welfare State Maturation

In the introduction I reviewed the main propositions of two competing theoretical approaches to variation in employment performance among advanced industrialized democracies: the corporatist approach and an economic approach that relies on the assumption of perfectly competitive labor markets. The corporatist literature has been more successful than the neoclassical framework in explaining cross-national variation in macroeconomic and labor market outcomes. But corporatist studies fail to account for *both* cross-national *and* intertemporal changes in labor market outcomes across advanced industrialized economies. Most corporatist scholars praise the "institutional advantages" of economies with highly centralized labor market institutions for delivering egalitarian income distribution, high levels of wage moderation, and labor peace. But these studies do not provide an explanation for the deterioration of the labor market performance of these economies in the last two decades. The main theoretical objective of this chapter is to extend and amend the conclusions of the corporatist literature in an effort to explain both cross-national *as well as* intertemporal variation in employment outcomes.

The outline of this chapter is as follows. I begin by reviewing the most significant theoretical developments in the literature that examine the impact of labor market institutions on labor market outcomes. These studies differ in the precise specification of the functional form of the relationship between labor market institutions and economic outcomes. Recent studies have formulated an important qualification of earlier results, suggesting that differences in a government's macroeconomic orientation affect both the optimal wage behavior of trade unions and the equilibrium level of unemployment. Such second-generation corporatist studies attempt to explain differences in economic outcomes, such as inflation or unemployment, by

17

examining the interaction between wage bargaining and monetary institutions. The central part of this chapter will present a theoretical model that extends this approach by adding parameters that capture cross-national differences in the size and structure of welfare state commitments to existing models. The goal of the analysis is to explore the mechanisms by which welfare states characterized by different levels of taxes and different mixes of transfers and services affect the wage behavior of unions and the equilibrium level of employment.

The main implication of the model developed in this chapter is that variation in employment performance among advanced industrialized economies cannot be explained without examining the impact of different social policy arrangements on the wage strategies pursued by trade unions and the resulting employment consequences of these strategies. The massive expansion of welfare states in the first decades of the postwar period was premised on a political exchange between unions and governments, whereby unions delivered wage restraint in exchange for the expansion of social services. Unions' collective wage restraint explains why the growth in taxes and transfers came about at very low costs in terms of employment in the first decades of the postwar period. Previous research on wage determination in advanced industrial democracies has made some implicit references to this political exchange, but no study so far has systematically examined its implications (Cameron 1978; Crouch and Pizzorno 1978; Katzenstein 1985; Crouch 1985; Esping-Andersen 1990). This chapter provides a formal model that integrates these propositions with the economic literature on corporatism.

The model developed in this chapter shows that growth in social policy taxes and transfers undermines the effectiveness of the political exchange. The analysis identifies two consequences of the process of welfare state maturation for union strategies. The most important effect is the result of an increase in the level of taxes necessary to finance existing social policy commitments: Increases in income and payroll taxes are expected to lower both firms' demand for labor and the elasticity of unemployment to wage changes. As the tax burden rises, wages represent an ever-decreasing share of the total wage bill. As a result, even a large reduction in the wage demands of unions is likely to have only a modest impact on employment. Growth in the tax burden thus undermines the importance of a policy instrument that was in the hands of unions, namely, the policy of wage moderation in restoring high levels of employment.

The second mechanism by which the growth in social policy commitments affects the wage strategies of trade unions is through a change in the composition of social policy expenditures. In the model developed in this chapter I assume that there are three categories of social policy benefits: social services, such as education or publicly provided child care; social policy transfers, which include unemployment benefits, pensions, and disability benefits, that are received by individual union members; and social policy transfers that are received by nonunion members, or labor market outsiders. While unions are willing to moderate their wage demands in exchange for both transfers and increases in social services received by their members, they are less willing to exercise wage restraint when a higher share of transfers is received by labor market outsiders. Thus, we expect to see a decline of wage moderation in those economies in which the share of transfers received by labor market outsiders as a proportion of total social policy expenditures has increased.

Both developments suggest that the structural conditions that facilitated the functioning of the political exchange between unions and governments changed dramatically between the early postwar period and recent decades.

Labor Market Institutions and Economic Performance

The literature examining the economic consequences of different wage bargaining institutions is one of the most developed subfields of comparative politics. The strength and vitality of this research tradition has two distinct sources. First, the research agenda has been cumulative. Each new generation of research has refined both the empirical measures and the theoretical specifications of earlier studies. Second, the literature has accommodated a variety of methodological orientations, including qualitative research on the political responses of unions in different political economies, quantitative studies examining the economic consequences of various labor market institutions, and formal models investigating whether the effects of labor market institutions on labor market outcomes differ across institutional settings. Such qualitative, quantitative, and game-theoretic studies have generated a broad range of consistent findings. Overall, the literature has been extremely successful in identifying the conditions under which an increase in the centralization of wage setting institutions can improve both real and nominal economic outcomes.

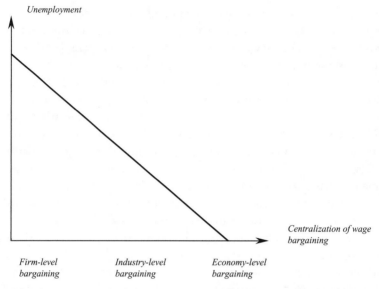

Unemployment

Centralization of wage bargaining

Firm-level bargaining   *Industry-level bargaining*   *Economy-level bargaining*

Figure 1.1. Linear model of effect of wage bargaining centralization on unemployment.

Very early in its theoretical development, the literature examining the impact of labor market institutions on economic outcomes incorporated the insights of Mancur Olson's logic of collective action to model the strategic decisions faced by wage bargaining actors (Olson 1982; Lange and Garrett 1985; Bruno and Sachs 1985). These studies advanced the proposition that economies characterized by corporatist institutions of wage bargaining can achieve both nominal and real wage restraint and thus lower levels of inflation and unemployment (Fig. 1.1). The logic of this argument works as follows: If wage bargaining takes place in fragmented units, unions will ignore the externalities of each settlement and will be likely to demand wage increments to offset increases obtained by other bargainers. Thus, wage bargaining in a decentralized setting might lead to wage demands that are suboptimally high. In contrast, unions in an economy characterized by encompassing institutions of wage bargaining will face an incentive to internalize some of the externalities of their wage demands. Hence, economies characterized by coordinated wage bargaining institutions will achieve lower levels of inflation and unemployment.

The first quantitative tests of these theories produced encouraging results. Schmitter and Cameron developed the first cross-national indicators of the encompassingness of wage bargaining systems and provided the first cross-national tests of these propositions (Schmitter 1979, 1981: 294; Cameron 1984: 164–5; Crouch 1985).[1] Schmitter's index of "societal corporatism" had two distinct components. The first indicator, which measured the "organizational centralization" of a labor movement, assessed the "ability of (con)federal powers to engage in collective bargaining, to support strikes with [their] own funds, to maintain a large staff, and to collect dues from members" (Schmitter 1981: 294). The second component measured the "associational monopoly" of the labor movement and coded labor organizations based on the number of national labor confederations, the presence or absence of stable factions within national union confederations, and the presence or absence of separate organizations for manual and nonmanual workers.

In addition to these two measures of union centralization and associational monopoly, Cameron's index of corporatism considered three additional institutional aspects of the labor movement: union density (union membership as a percentage of the total labor force); the existence of institutions for worker participation in decision making on the plant floor and on company boards; and the "scope of collective bargaining."[2] Cameron regressed his measures against a range of economic variables, such as the level of unemployment, the price level, and measures of changes in nominal and real earnings (Cameron 1984: 169). He found a strong negative relationship between the various measures of the structure and organization of the labor movement and these economic outcomes, thus confirming his theoretical hypothesis that encompassing institutions of wage bargaining produce nominal and real wage restraint and consequently lower levels of inflation and unemployment. Using a sample of 15 OECD countries, Lange and Garrett found that a variable that measured the centralization of wage bargaining in interaction with a measure of the parliamentary strength of left-wing parties explained proportionate changes in economic growth (Lange and Garrett 1985).

---

[1] In fact, both Schmitter and Cameron started from an earlier measure developed in Headey (1970: 407–39).

[2] Cameron's measure of union density averaged figures for 1965 and 1980. See Cameron (1984: 164). The scope of collective bargaining was measured on a seven-point scale that assessed the level of wage bargaining centralization, from highly restricted collective bargaining (as in Spain during the Franco era) and company-level bargaining to industry-wide bargaining with economy-wide negotiated agreements.

In an influential 1988 article, Calmfors and Driffill expressed significant theoretical reservations about the logic of this linear model and formulated an alternative specification of the relationship between labor market institutions and macroeconomic outcomes (see also Calmfors 1993). The important additional consideration brought by Calmfors and Driffill to the analysis was that the degree of centralization of the wage bargaining system affects the relative market power of wage setters. This consideration introduces a significant nonlinearity into the relationship between the centralization of wage bargaining and unemployment. In the Calmfors-Driffill specification, both highly centralized and highly decentralized systems of wage bargaining are likely to produce high levels of wage moderation and low levels of unemployment, while intermediately centralized wage bargaining systems lead to high levels of real wages and hence high levels of unemployment.

Calmfors and Driffill offer the following intuition for this "hump-shaped" relationship between wage bargaining centralization and unemployment: In an economy in which wages are determined at the industry level, unions set wages for all firms that produce similar products. Facing a lower level of competition in their product markets, firms have the option of shifting pay increases to consumers by increasing the relative level of prices. Given their higher capability of externalizing higher labor costs onto consumers, such firms are less likely to resist unions' demands for higher wages. This reinforces unions' incentive to wage militancy in a case in which wages are bargained at the industry level. By contrast, consider a case in which wages are set at the level of the firm. If competition in product markets is intense, individual firms will not be able to raise the relative prices in response to an increase in wage levels. In this context, wage increases are likely to result in a decline in employment. This creates incentives for wage restraint in decentralized labor markets. Similar considerations apply to the case in which labor markets are entirely centralized. In the limit case, if one trade union determines the wage level for the entire economy, an increase in wages leads to a uniform increase in prices for the entire economy. Again, firms will be unable to affect relative prices and will thus respond to higher wage demands by reducing employment. This will reinforce the incentive for unions in very centralized labor markets to internalize some of the consequences of their militancy. Figure 1.2 presents the predictions of the Calmfors Driffill model.

What accounts for the divergence between the predictions of the linear model and those of Calmfors and Driffill? The critical assumption that

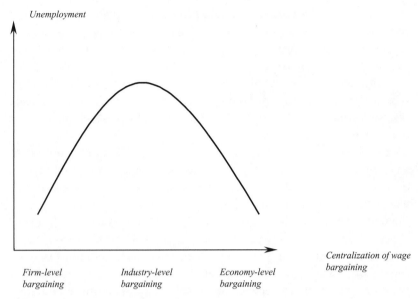

Unemployment

Firm-level bargaining   *Industry-level bargaining*   *Economy-level bargaining*

Centralization of wage bargaining

Figure 1.2. The Calmfors-Driffill model.

distinguishes these models is a highly technical one about the relative wage elasticities of demand. More specifically, the models make different assumptions about the effects of changes in wages in one sector on employment in another sector. In the linear model, the assumption is that changes in wages in one union will have the same effect demand (and thus employment) in the remaining $N - 1$ unions of the economy. In contrast, the Calmfors-Driffill model assumes that changes in wages in one union will have different effects on employment in different unions. Let $\prod_w e$ denote the wage elasticity of employment ($\prod_w e = (\partial e / \partial w)/(e/w)$). $\prod_{wi} e_k$ denotes the elasticity of employment in sector k with respect to the wage demands of unions in sector k. Calmfors and Driffill disagree with all previous studies and assume that $\prod_{wi} e_k$ differs for the remaining $N - 1 \neq k$ unions.

The Calmfors-Driffill approach serves as the baseline model for the analysis developed in this book. Thus, it is important to spell out more clearly the additional assumptions that are necessary to derive the "hump-shaped" relationship between wage bargaining system centralization and the unemployment level. Calmfors and Driffill assume that the wage bargaining system is organized as follows: There are j firms and i sectors in the economy. They distinguish between intrasectoral and intersectoral centralization of wage bargaining. As intrasectoral centralization increases, one union sets the level of wages for a larger number of firms producing goods that are close substitutes; as a result of the intersectoral centralization of wage bargaining, one union sets the wages for different sectors producing less perfect substitutes. In this framework, to study the relationship between $(\partial U_{ij}/\partial w)$ – the marginal gain in utility of union ij from an increase in wages – and the centralization of the wage bargaining system, we need to specify the impact of changes in the wage demand of this union on the wages and employment of other unions.

An increase in the wages of union ij has consequences for both prices and employment. It raises the price level of the goods produced by firm ij, which in turn affects the price levels of goods in other industries for which the goods ij are an input. The impact of the price increase is stronger the more centralized the wage bargaining system. This increase in prices affects adversely the utility of other unions. An increase in wages of union ij can have a positive impact on the employment level in other firms, however, if the firms produce goods that are substitutes. The magnitude of the employment effect depends on the elasticity of substitution among goods and on the level of centralization of the wage bargaining system. Let $\prod_w e_{INTRASECTOR} = \prod_{wij} e_{ik}$ (same i, $j \neq k$) be the intrasectoral wage elasticity of employment and $\prod_w e_{INTRASECTOR} = \prod_{wij} e_{kl}$ ($k \neq i$, $j \neq l$) be the intersectoral wage elasticity of employment. In the Calmfors-Driffill model, the intrasectoral wage elasticity of employment is higher than the intersectoral wage elasticity of employment, because goods within the same sector are closer substitutes. An increase in the wage demands of union ij will have a stronger impact on the utility of another union if the firms are within the same sector. But the sign of the effect is ambiguous and depends on the magnitude of the price and employment effects (that is, $\prod_w U = \underbrace{\prod_w e}_{>0} - \underbrace{\prod_w P}_{<0}$).

How does wage bargaining system centralization affect unions' marginal utility from higher wage demands? In the Calmfors-Driffill model, the relationship between unions' marginal gain from wage increases $(\partial U/\partial w)$ and the centralization of the wage bargaining system depends on the signs of the intrasectoral and intersectoral wage elasticities (the signs of $\prod_w u_{INTRASECTOR}$ and $\prod_w u_{INTRASECTOR}$). Calmfors and Driffill further assume that $\prod_w u_{INTRASECTOR} > 0$ and that $\prod_w u_{INTRASECTOR} < 0$. This assumption leads to the hump-shaped relationship between centralization and unemployment. In the totally decentralized case, in which both i and j are high, unions face incentives for wage moderation, because an increase in wage demands translates immediately into a decline in employment. ($\prod_{w_{ij}} e_{kl}$ is large.) Thus, intrasectoral centralization of wage bargaining reduces the incentives for unions' wage moderation in the sector in question. In contrast, intersectoral centralization of wage bargaining (in other words, a reduction in i, the number of sectors) increases the incentive for wage moderation by reducing the negative externalities of higher price levels. But if the assumptions about the signs of these intrasectoral and intersectoral wage elasticities are not met, the theoretical model does not necessarily lead to a parabolic relationship.[3]

A number of empirical studies have confirmed the predictions of the Calmfors-Driffill model. Calmfors and Driffill regressed a measure of the degree of wage bargaining centralization against a range of macroeconomic variables such as the unemployment, the misery index, and the sum of unemployment and current account deficits as a percentage of the gross domestic product (GDP). Using data for the period between 1974 and 1985, they found a hump-shaped relationship between the centralization of wage bargaining and these economic outcomes. In a 1988 paper, Freeman reported similar results. In contrast to Calmfors and Driffill, Freeman relied on measures of wage dispersion as a proxy for centralization. Rowthorn (1992) confirmed the existence of a hump-shaped relationship between wage bargaining centralization and unemployment for the 1980s but did not find a statistically significant relationship for the 1970s. Mixed empirical results were also reported in a study by Boeri, Brugiavini, and Calmfors (2001).

In an influential article published in 1990, Soskice raised a number of objections to the Calmfors and Driffill findings. He critiqued Calmfors and Driffill for ignoring the "informal coordination" in wage setting practices provided by employers' associations. Soskice objected to the coding of Japan and Switzerland, two countries where wages are set at the firm level but where strong federations of employers ensure a high degree of wage coordination at the level of the economy. After recoding these cases, Soskice found that a linear specification of the relationship between the centralization of wage bargaining and unemployment worked much better than a nonlinear model to explain variation in the employment performance of OECD economies from 1985 to 1989 (Soskice 1990: 40).

---

[3] This raises significant questions, in fact, about how one should empirically test the predictions of the Calmfors-Driffill model.

The contribution of Soskice has generated two important externalities for the literature on the economic consequences of different wage bargaining institutions. The first crucial implication of his analysis is that the resilience or change of corporatist institutions cannot be explained by examining the preferences of labor associations alone: One also has to consider the interests and demands of employers (see also Thelen 1994; Swenson 1991; Pontusson and Swenson 1996). The study of cross-national differences in the preferences and organizational capabilities of employers now occupies center stage both in comparative studies of public policy and in research on the development and change of wage bargaining institutions (Hall and Soskice 2001; Hollingsworth and Boyer 1997; Crouch and Streeck 1997; Kitschelt et al. 1999; Culpepper 2003; Ziegler 2000; Thelen and Kume 1999; Wood 1998; Estevez-Abe 1999; Mares 2003; Swenson 2003). The disagreement between Calmfors and Driffill and Soskice about the functional form of the relationship between the centralization of wage bargaining and unemployment has stimulated efforts to develop additional measures of wage bargaining institutions. At present, any researcher of the political and economic consequences of wage setting institutions can choose among a broad range of measures. (For an overview of these measures, see Kenworthy 2001.) The indicators that are most widely used in cross-national studies have been developed by Calmfors and Driffill (1988); Soskice (1990); Iversen (1999); the OECD (1994, 1997); and Golden, Lange, and Wallerstein (1998). These "second-generation" measures of corporatism differ from the earlier measures in two important ways. First, taking the objection of Soskice seriously, they also incorporate information about the involvement of employer confederations in the wage bargaining process. Second, both the Iversen and the Golden, Lange, and Wallerstein measures vary over time and are measured annually. This is an important development given the significant formal and informal changes in wage setting practices experienced in some countries.

Can these advances in measurement allow us to distinguish between the linear model, which predicts a negative relationship between the centralization of wage bargaining and unemployment, and the Calmfors-Driffill model, which predicts a hump-shaped relationship between labor market centralization and unemployment? Soskice argued that the Calmfors-Driffill results were driven by measurement errors. If the Calmfors-Driffill index was biased, as Soskice claims, the new empirical indicators have removed any measurement errors. But, as the above discussion has pointed out, the linear model and the Calmfors-Driffill model also differ in their assumptions about the relative demand elasticities faced by unions. In the linear model all unions face the same relative demand elasticities, while in the Calmfors-Driffill framework relative demand elasticities differ across unions. This suggests that this controversy cannot be resolved by simply employing better cross-national measures of wage bargaining system centralization; rather, a resolution will require testing the two competing models' assumptions about relative demand elasticities using sector-level wage and employment data.

Labor Market Institutions and Monetary Policy

An important theoretical development of the last decade has been the effort to integrate the findings of the literature examining the consequences of labor market institutions with those examining the consequences of different monetary arrangements (Scharpf 1991; Hall 1994; Hall and Franzese 1998; Iversen 1999; Soskice and Iversen 2000). The motivation for this theoretical synthesis was straightforward: Neither monetary policy makers nor wage bargainers affect monetary and real outcomes in isolation, but only in interaction with the other actors. A number of studies have attempted to develop predictions about the levels of unemployment and inflation that result from different combinations of monetary regimes and labor market institutions. As formulated by Soskice and Iversen, the core result of this theoretical synthesis is that, "even under the assumption of rational expectations, complete information, credible precommitment and a finite number of price and wage setters, . . . monetary rules affect the equilibrium level of employment" (Soskice and Iversen 2000: 279). The findings of these studies dispute the proposition that monetary policy does not affect real outcomes (Barro and Gordon 1983; Kydland and Prescott 1977). They also agree that the specific impact of monetary policy on unemployment depends on the structure of labor market institutions. While agreement exists on these propositions, disagreement continues about the magnitude of the impact of monetary policy in economies with different labor market institutions. The tension in the theoretical predictions of the models parallels previous disagreements among studies predicting a linear and a hump-shaped relationship between labor market institutions and unemployment. The goal of this section is to illuminate the sources of the theoretical disagreement.

Soskice and Iversen (2000) study the strategic interaction between monetary authorities and wage setters that have some monopolistic power.

They distinguish between nonacommodating monetary authorities – the equivalent of independent central banks – in which the monetary authority fixes the nominal money supply, and accommodating monetary authorities, in which the central bank fixes the real money supply. Their analysis generates the result that an increase in monetary nonaccommodation leads to an increase in equilibrium employment. In other words, central banks that are more independent can improve the employment performance of economies with a small number of independently acting unions. In the Soskice-Iversen framework, the real effects of monetary policy are a consequence of the fact that independent central banks can alleviate coordination problems among unions. Soskice and Iversen offer the following explanation for this "apparently counterintuitive" result: In an economy in which the central bank fixes the real money supply (that is, in the case of an accommodating monetary policy), unions have no incentive for wage moderation, because the wage choices of unions cannot affect real demand and thus the equilibrium level of employment. In contrast, if an independent central bank fixes the nominal money supply, an increase in sectoral prices or wages will translate into a reduction in real demand and thus a reduction in output and employment. In this environment, unions face an incentive to lower their wage demands relative to the wage demands of other sectors, contributing to an increase in production and employment. The ability of unions to affect real wages improves as the number of wage bargaining actors in the economy declines. As Soskice and Iversen argue, in the case of a nonaccommodating monetary policy, "the standard trade-off between the real wage and the employment level along the sectoral demand curve is...altered: greater real wage restraint lowers the relative price of the sector and this raises the real money supply (given wage price-setting elsewhere)" (Soskice and Iversen 2000).

Figure 1.3 presents a graphical interpretation of the most important predictions of the Soskice-Iversen model. The key result of the analysis is that the impact of monetary nonaccommodation on unemployment varies with the number of trade unions in the economy. An increase in monetary policy nonaccommodation (an increase in the conservatism of the central bank) contributes to a reduction in the unemployment level. The magnitude of the effect of monetary policy on unemployment increases as the number of trade unions in the economy declines.

The Soskice-Iversen model is extremely elegant and logically compelling, yet it has two significant limitations. First, as Franzese has pointed out, "Real demand elasticity is fixed, exogenous and, in particular[,] assumed

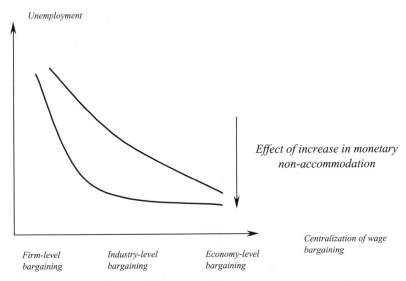

Unemployment

Effect of increase in monetary non-accommodation

Centralization of wage bargaining

Firm-level bargaining   *Industry-level bargaining*   *Economy-level bargaining*

Figure 1.3. The Soskice-Iversen model.

independent of N in the comparative statics results" (Franzese 1999). It is this assumption that distinguishes the Soskice-Iversen from the Calmfors-Driffill setup: In the Calmfors-Driffill framework, not all sectors face the same relative demand elasticities. Second, and most problematic, the theoretical implications of the model are at odds with labor market developments in Europe. The main prediction of the model is that an increase in monetary nonaccommodation will have substantial benefits for long-term employment (Soskice and Iversen 2000: 280). Given that in the last two decades most European economies have actually shifted from accommodating to nonaccommodating monetary policies, the level of unemployment experienced by these economies should have declined from the 1960s and 1970s to recent decades. Thus, the model is unable to account for the rise in unemployment experienced by European economies over time.

Soskice and Iversen do not test the empirical predictions of their model, because "the purpose of the article is analytic rather than empirical" (Soskice and Iversen 2000: 267). Their paper marshals some (albeit weak) evidence in support of the model. Table 1.1 presents their cross-tabulation of wage bargaining centralization and the character of monetary policy for 17 OECD economies during the period between 1973 and 1993. The results support their prediction that monetary nonaccommodation leads to superior employment outcomes only for economies with intermediately

Table 1.1. *Soskice-Iversen predictions: Average unemployment in 17 OECD countries, 1973–1993*

	Unemployment in terms of wage bargaining centralization			
	Very high	Intermediate	Very low	Mean (N)
Monetary rule*				
Accommodating	3.9 (Finland, Norway, Sweden)	7.6 (Australia, Belgium, Italy)	7.1 (United Kingdom, France, New Zealand)	6.2 (9)
Nonaccommodating	5.6 (Austria, Denmark)	3.6 (Germany, Japan, Netherlands, Switzerland)	7.4 (Canada, United States)	5.0 (8)
Difference	1.7	4.0†	0.3	5.6 (17)

Notes:

* Monetary rule refers to the independence of the central bank, except in the case of Japan, where a dependent bank has followed a nonaccomodating rule.

† Difference is significant at a 0.001 level (one-sided test).

Source: Soskice and Iversen 2000: 268, Table 3.

centralized institutions of wage bargaining; such economies' employment performance is shown to be superior to the performance of economies with similar labor market institutions but accommodating monetary policy. In the case of economies with either decentralized or highly centralized institutions of wage bargaining, monetary nonaccommodation is associated with poorer employment results than is monetary accommodation. Thus, in both of these cases, the findings disconfirm the theoretical predictions of the model.

Iversen (1998, 1999) has taken a different approach to the study of the interaction of trade unions and monetary policy regimes. An important difference between his theoretical setup and that of Soskice-Iversen is that in the former, unions' utility comprises a term that shows their concern for wage equality as well as a quadratic term for unemployment. More specifically, Iversen assumes that unions' objective function takes the form

$$U_i = \alpha(w_i - \pi) - (1 - \alpha)U_i\overline{U} - \beta(r^i - r^e)^2,$$

where w_i denotes the increase in nominal wages, π is the percentage increase in consumer prices, U_i is the level of unemployment among the members of union i, and $\overline{U}$ is the average unemployment rate. Thus, unions' utility increases as real wages $(w_i - \pi)$ increase, but it falls as unemployment increases.

Iversen's specification of the effect of unemployment on the utility of trade unions suggests that what matters to unions is not only unemployment in a particular union (U_i), but also aggregate unemployment in the economy $(\overline{U})$. Unions dislike an increase in the level of unemployment of the economy because it increases competition for scarce jobs and thus potentially lengthens the duration of unemployment spells. The third term in the utility of unions denotes unions' concern for wage equality, r^i, denotes the ideal relationship between the wage increases of high-earning and low-earning workers, and r^e represents the actual ratio of wage increases. Thus, any discrepancy between the desired and realized levels of wage equality enters the utility of trade unions with a negative sign. Parameters α and β denote the relative weights attached by unions to these different objectives.

In the Iversen model, unions encounter a monetary authority that cares about both price stability and unemployment. The objective function of the monetary authority takes the form

$$U_m = -\iota^2 - (1 - \iota)\,\overline{U}^2,$$

where π denotes the percentage increase in consumer prices and U denotes unemployment. The parameter ι denotes the relative weight placed by the monetary authority on the policy objectives of maintaining price stability and full employment. Thus, following Iversen's terminology, if ι takes high values, we are in the presence of a nonaccommodating (anti-inflationary) monetary regime. Conversely, if ι takes low values, monetary policy is described as accommodating. In this model, the game proceeds as follows: First, at each level of centralization, low-wage and high-wage unions Nash bargain over wage equality. Next, all unions simultaneously announce their wage demands and choose a nominal wage rate. In the final stage of the game, monetary authorities choose the level of inflation and unemployment.

Using this setup, Iversen formulates a number of propositions that stand in partial contrast to the results derived in Soskice and Iversen. The main implications of the analysis can be summarized as follows: In the case of an accommodating monetary policy (as $\iota \to 0$), the results parallel the findings of the Calmfors-Driffill model. In this context, the model predicts a hump-shaped relationship between the levels of wage bargaining system centralization and unemployment. For low to intermediately centralized wage bargaining systems, an increase in the centralization level leads to an increase in unemployment. In intermediately centralized wage bargaining systems, both market forces and the internalization effects are too weak to restrain unions' demands for higher wages. As wage bargaining centralization increases, the ability of large wage setters to internalize the effects of militancy also increases and begins to offset the monopoly power of trade unions, contributing to a decline in unemployment.

The predictions of the model are reversed in the case of nonaccommodating monetary policy (as ι becomes very large). In this case, the predictions for the equilibrium level of unemployment depend on the values of the parameter β, which denotes unions' concern for wage equality. If β is very small, the predictions of the model are in agreement with Soskice and Iversen. In this case, monetary policy has positive effects on employment that increase as the centralization of the wage bargaining system increases. As Iversen formalizes the intuition accounting for this result, "The collective action problem facing unions in intermediately centralized systems – which can lead to excessive wage demands and unemployment – is thus 'solved' (or at least dissipated) by an agent that is deliberately nonaccommodating to unions' objectives" (Iversen 1999: 34). If β is very large, unions will attempt to forge more egalitarian wage compromises, which can have adverse effects on the employment performance of the economy. Thus, Iversen argues that, for highly centralized wage bargaining systems, there exists a point at which monetary nonaccommodation produces employment outcomes superior to those produced by monetary accommodation. These findings are summarized in Figure 1.4.

The tension between the theoretical predictions of Iversen (1998, 1999) and Soskice and Iversen (1999, 2000) raises a few interesting questions. First, it appears that some of the ambiguity in the predictions about the functional relationship between wage bargaining system centralization and unemployment levels that characterized first-generation corporatism carried over to this second-generation of research, which introduced monetary policy into the analysis. It is important to point out, however, that the theoretical ambiguity has two different sources. One of its sources is the critical assumption about the relationship between the real and relative price elasticities of product demand and the centralization of the wage bargaining system. If the model assumes that elasticity of demand with respect to prices is fixed, exogenous, and independent of the number of wage bargaining agents, then it predicts a linear relationship between wage bargaining

Labor Market Institutions and Monetary Policy

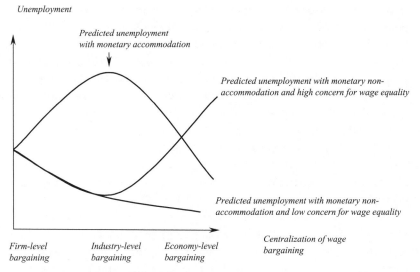

Unemployment

Predicted unemployment with monetary accommodation

Predicted unemployment with monetary non-accommodation and high concern for wage equality

Predicted unemployment with monetary non-accommodation and low concern for wage equality

Firm-level bargaining

Industry-level bargaining

Economy-level bargaining

Centralization of wage bargaining

Figure 1.4. The Iversen model.

system centralization and the unemployment level – we are in the linear model and in the world of Soskice and Iversen. If the model assumes, however, that the price elasticity of demand declines as the number of firms that are subject to the same wage agreement increases, then we are in the Calmfors-Driffill world.

The ambiguity in the theoretical implications of these models also stems from different assumptions about the utilities of trade unions. In the Soskice-Iversen models (1999, 2000), the utility of unions has only two terms: the real wages and the level of employment of union members. In contrast, Iversen's model differs in important ways in its assumption about the utility of trade unions: unemployment enters the utility of unions as a quadratic term, which causes the similarity *in results* between the Iversen case of monetary nonaccommodation and the Calmfors-Driffill case; an additional concern of trade unions is the relative level of wage equality of their members. More transparency in spelling out all the empirical implications that follow from different assumptions about the utilities of these actors is clearly desirable, but the diversity in underlying assumptions about the policy objectives of trade unions is also a strength of this literature: It is an example of a positive interaction between the more formal game-theoretic literature and the vast amount of qualitative research about the objectives and practices of trade unions in different societies.

So far, efforts to test the theoretical models of the influence of monetary policy on employment have produced ambiguous empirical results. Iversen (1998, 1999) has tested the empirical predictions of his model in a sample of 15 OECD countries between 1973 and 1993 using 4-year averages. The results support the theoretical implications of his model: An increase in monetary nonaccommodation leads to lower levels of unemployment in economies with low or intermediate levels of wage bargaining centralization and to higher unemployment levels in economies with highly centralized wage bargaining institutions. The analysis produces similar results with respect to inflation: Monetary nonaccommodation lowers inflation. The effects are stronger (but only weakly so) in economies with encompassing institutions of wage bargaining (Iversen 1999: 70).

However, other empirical analyses reach different conclusions. Hall and Franzese (1998) regress various measures of wage bargaining centralization and central bank independence on measures of inflation and unemployment. Their data set includes 18 OECD economies for the period between 1955 and 1990 and uses annual and decade-level data as well as postwar averages. They find a negative relationship between central bank independence and the unemployment level but a positive relationship between the interactive term of wage bargaining centralization and unemployment. With respect to inflation, Hall and Franzese find a negative relationship between wage bargaining centralization and central bank independence and a positive (but statistically weak) relationship between the interaction term of the two institutional measures (Hall and Franzese 1998: Table 2). Hall and Franzese's findings are thus in conflict with Iversen's results. While Iversen suggests that monetary nonaccommodation leads to lower levels of unemployment in economies with a low or intermediate level of wage bargaining centralization, Hall and Franzese's findings suggest that central bank independence leads to a higher level of unemployment, but that the increase in unemployment is smaller in economies with more centralized institutions of wage bargaining.

Cukierman and Lippi (1999) also regress various measures of wage bargaining centralization and central bank independence on both inflation and unemployment, using a sample of 19 OECD countries at three points in time: 1980, 1990, and 1994. They find that central bank independence reduces unemployment in economies with high- or intermediate-level wage bargaining centralization but that it increases unemployment in economies with decentralized labor markets (Cukierman and Lippi 1999: 1422).

A Theoretical Synthesis: Labor Market Institutions, Monetary Policies, and the Welfare State

The literature of the last decade has attempted to provide an explanation for the employment performance of OECD economies by examining the policy consequences of wage bargaining institutions and monetary policy. The key result discussed in the previous section is that the impact of one particular institution on economic outcomes is conditional on other institutions. The shape of the function linking the centralization of the wage bargaining system to unemployment also depends on other institutions – in this particular case, on monetary policy. A related literature examining "varieties of capitalism" reformulates this theoretical insight as a proposition about institutional complementarities. "Two institutions can be said to be complementary," Hall and Soskice argue, "if the presence (or efficiency) of one increases the returns from (or efficiency) of the other" (Hall and Soskice 2001: 17). To understand economic outcomes such as inflation or unemployment, one has to analyze the consequences of "bundles" of institutions that form a coherent ensemble. However, this raises important questions: How do we know whether we have specified the entire institutional bundle that "matters" correctly? What institutions are a necessary part of this "coherent whole"? What institutions can be omitted from the analysis? Returning to this particular example, there is no a priori theoretical reason to focus on wage bargaining and monetary institutions alone while excluding other institutions of the political economy.

As the previous discussion has indicated, the exclusive focus of the recent literature on monetary and wage bargaining institutions has been problematic for another reason. While unemployment continues to be the favored dependent variable for all studies, existing studies are unable to provide an explanation for the deterioration of the employment performance of OECD economies in recent decades. While the literature examining the interaction between wage bargaining institutions and monetary policies has been extremely successful in explaining *cross-national* patterns in the employment performance of advanced industrialized democracies, it has been less successful in accounting for intertemporal changes in unemployment. Recall the key comparative statics result that is common to both the Soskice-Iversen (2000) and Iversen (1999) models: An increase in monetary nonaccommodation leads to a decline in unemployment. In the last two decades, most advanced industrialized economies have experienced a dramatic macroeconomic shift, either by increasing the independence of the central bank or by explicitly following the strict macroeconomic policies of the Bundesbank. Yet this increase in monetary nonaccommodation has not been associated with the decline in unemployment predicted by the theoretical models. It follows that variables that were not included in these models must have counteracted the positive employment effects associated with the transition to a macroeconomic regime characterized by monetary nonaccommodation.

Finally, looking back on the theoretical progression of the literature over the last three decades, it seems odd that most formal models of the relationship between wage bargaining institutions and economic performance have omitted the welfare state from their analyses. Policy parameters such as the level of taxes and nonwage labor costs, as well as institutional differences across welfare states, clearly affect both the wage behavior of unions and the employment choices of firms, and hence they also affect the equilibrium level of employment. The omission of the welfare state by these studies is even more surprising given that a vast qualitative literature argues that social policy considerations have been important to trade unions and have affected the wage demands of labor associations. Examining union behavior during the period of welfare state expansion, such studies suggest that a political exchange between unions and governments was in place, whereby unions were willing to deliver wage restraint in exchange for the expansion of social policy benefits. This political exchange can partially explain why the massive expansion of taxes and transfers during the first years of the postwar period came about at a very low cost in terms of employment. Formal models of the relationship between wage bargaining institutions and economic performance have so far not captured this political exchange, because they have focused only on the negotiation of wages.

The model developed in this chapter proposes an extension of existing studies that adds a range of social policy parameters to the models of wage bargaining. The goal of this theoretical exercise is to investigate the consequences of welfare states characterized by different levels of taxes and different mixes of transfers and services on the determination of wages and hence on the equilibrium level of employment. The model also seeks to uncover a number of institutional and policy variables that affect the sensitivity of employment to taxation in different political economies.

To explore these questions, I will start from a setup that parallels the basic framework of Calmfors and Driffill. I assume union monopoly wage setting, where unions make wage demands and employers respond by choosing

A Theoretical Synthesis

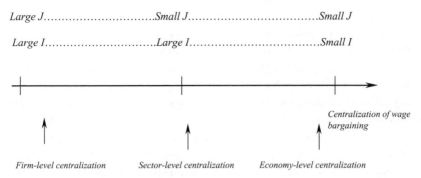

Large J...............................Small J....................................Small J

Large I...............................Large I....................................Small I

Centralization of wage
bargaining

Firm-level centralization   *Sector-level centralization*   *Economy-level centralization*

Figure 1.5. Model of wage bargaining system centralization, given different numbers of firms and sectors in the economy.

prices for the goods they produce. The optimal decision of employers is determined by the resulting consumer demand, which is in turn a function of the level of prices and of the elasticity of substitution among goods produced in different sectors. In equilibrium, the level of demand determines the level of employment in each sector of the economy.

The economy consists of I sectors, with J firms in each sector. Therefore, there is a total of $N = IJ$ unions in the economy. I assume that either the entire workforce is fully unionized or that unions' contracts are binding even for those workers who are not union members. (This assumption is standard in the literature and follows Calmfors and Driffill.) For simplicity, I also assume that all the unions are the same size; if n denotes the total labor force, then the number of members in each union is n/N.

Cross-national variation in wage bargaining centralization is at the core of the Calmfors-Driffill model. Their classification of decentralized, intermediately centralized, and fully centralized wage bargaining systems is modeled as follows by the parameters I (the number of sectors) and J (the number of firms in each sector): The case of a totally decentralized political economy can be characterized as an economy in which both I and J are high. Intrasectoral centralization of wage bargaining can be modeled as a decline in J. Thus, in economies with intermediate centralization, wages are determined by sectoral-level trade unions. Finally, in an economy with national-level institutions of wage bargaining, both J and I take very low values. The limit case of this process of intersectoral wage bargaining centralization is the case in which one union determines the level of wages for all firms in the economy. Figure 1.5 summarizes these distinctions.

37

As discussed previously, the distinction between intrasectoral and inter-sectoral wage bargaining centralization makes it possible to capture more systematically the mechanisms through which the actions of one trade union affect income and employment levels in other firms or sectors. Assuming that goods produced within one sector are close substitutes for one another, higher wage demands by one union would increase demand for the goods produced by other firms in the sector, thereby providing an incentive for wage moderation. Conversely, coordinated higher wage demands in one sector may shift the equilibrium toward higher prices for the goods in that sector, with the costs being borne by the other sectors. Consequently, Calmfors and Driffill argue that equilibrium wage levels exhibit a hump-shaped dependence on centralization, which implies a U-shaped dependence of employment on centralization. I will elaborate on this point of the formal model in Section 3 of the appendix.

Wage bargaining occurs in an exogenous macroeconomic environment in which governments specify taxes (τ) and the monetary policy regime (β) before wage bargaining occurs. These parameters are known to the players and are assumed to be fixed throughout the game.

The Impact of Social Policies: Labor Market Outsiders and Social Services

The main objective of this model is to study how social policy arrangements affect the outcomes of wage bargaining. In contrast to the existing models of wage bargaining, the model accounts for the fact that social policies are a crucial objective for trade unions, which influence their optimal wage demands and consequently employment outcomes.

Before analyzing the maximization problem faced by trade unions, it is important to lay out the assumptions about the structure of social policy benefits made in this model. There are two key dimensions that are relevant to the analysis: the identities of the recipients of social policy benefits and the structure of benefits.

The population of an economy can be roughly divided into two major groups: workers who are currently employed or seeking employment (the size of the labor force being n) and the inactive population, whose total size will be denoted by m. This latter part of the population, which is sizeable in many European economies, comprises pensioners, early retirees, and persons who choose not to enter the labor market. The total population is thus $m + n$, and the active labor force ratio is $n/(m + n)$. I will denote by π the "dependency ratio" of the economy, defined as

$\pi = m/n$, which represents the ratio of labor market outsiders to the labor force.

Building on an important distinction introduced by the comparative literature on social protection, the model distinguishes among social *services* (such as education and child care) and social *transfers* (such as unemployment benefits, pensions, and disability benefits). To simplify notations, I will assume that the individual level of generosity is the same across all major welfare state transfer programs, and I will denote this level of benefits by b. In particular, the same level of benefits is available to both labor force outsiders and insiders. Total social transfers to union members are equal to bn, whereas total transfers to outsiders equal bm.

Social transfers and services are financed through taxation. The model assumes that the level of publicly provided social services (denoted by S) is endogenously determined. I will assume in equation (6) that the level of services (S) is chosen after the existing transfers to union members and to the nonactive population are financed. Another reformulation of this assumption is that passive social policy expenditures are already committed due to their entitlement-based character, while services are more discretionary in nature.

This discussion can be summarized in a budget constraint equation determining the balance between total social policy expenditures and tax receipts. The left-hand side of the equation comprises the three main categories of welfare state expenditures: transfers to the nonactive population, unemployment benefits to union members who are out of work, and social services. The right-hand side of the equation summarizes the taxes that are available to finance these expenditures:

$$bm + b \sum_{i=1}^{I} \sum_{j=1}^{J} \left(\frac{n}{N} - a_{ij} \right) + S = (\tau_U + \tau_E) \sum_{i=1}^{I} \sum_{j=1}^{J} a_{ij} w_{ij}. \tag{1}$$

In this equation, a_{ij} denotes the equilibrium employment level for members of union ij, and w_{ij} denotes the equilibrium wage. Social policy expenditures are financed by two broad categories of revenues: income taxes (paid by union members) and payroll taxes (paid by unions and employers). The model does not take into account the importance of corporate taxes, as corporate taxes play only a modest role in the financing of social policy expenditures in OECD countries. The right-hand side of equation (1) accounts for the fact that both union members and employers pay taxes

$(\tau = \tau_U + \tau_E)$. It will be assumed that the ratio of taxes paid by capital and labor is fixed throughout the game.

From equation (1), the tax balance equation, we can derive the level of services available in the economy as

$$S = (\tau_U + \tau_E) \sum_{i=1}^{I} \sum_{j=1}^{J} a_{ij} w_{ij} + b \sum_{i=1}^{I} \sum_{j=1}^{J} a_{ij} - b(m + n). \tag{2}$$

Social services play an important role in the overall demands of trade unions. As a number of studies have argued, a political exchange between unions and governments in which unions exercised wage restraint in exchange for the expansion of social policy programs was at the basis of social policy expansion during the early decades of the postwar period (Crouch and Pizzorno 1978; Cameron 1984; Katzenstein 1985; Esping-Andersen 1985).

To model this political exchange, I will assume that the objective function of trade unions comprises not only wages and social policy transfers to union members but social services as well. For the sake of simplicity, I assume that services are divided equally among all members of the population. Given that each union has a total of n/N members and that the total size of the population is $m + n$, it follows that the social services received by the individual union are $(1/N)(n/n + m)S$. This implies that the ability of trade unions to internalize the provision of services and collectively exercise wage restraint is influenced by the degree of labor movement centralization and by the share of active labor force participants in the total population. The higher the number of trade unions in the economy (N) and the higher the share of the inactive population (m) receiving social policy transfers, the more circumscribed will be the ability of the trade unions to internalize the provision of services.

We can now fully specify the unions' utility function. As discussed previously, the key assumption of the model is that three broad objectives enter the calculation of the trade unions: the net (that is, after tax) level of wages, passive transfers to union members, and the level of public services available to union members.

Because unions care about the real level of wages and social policy benefits, it is important to divide the net utility derived by union members by the aggregate price level in the economy. Following Soskice and Iversen, I will assume that the aggregate price level of the economy is a function of the degree of the accommodation of the monetary authority.[4] Let the parameter β denote the level of monetary nonaccommodation. The parameter β takes values between 0 and 1. In the case of a totally nonaccommodating monetary regime, $\beta = 1$; β decreases as the level of monetary nonaccommodation decreases.[5] Dividing by the aggregate price level of the economy, the utility of trade unions becomes

$$
U_{ij}^{U} = \frac{1}{P^{\beta}} \left[\underbrace{(1 - \tau_U) w_{ij} a_{ij}}_{NET.WAGES} + \underbrace{\left(\frac{n}{I\tilde{J}} - a_{ij} \right) b}_{TRANFERS.TO.UNION.MEMBERS} + \underbrace{\frac{1}{I\tilde{J}} \frac{n}{m+n} S}_{SOCIAL.SERVICES} \right].
$$

(3)

Equilibrium Employment and Wages

Unions' optimal wage demands can be derived through a standard backward induction argument. Detailed computations are given in the appendix, so here I will focus on the main steps.

Optimal consumption (given prices) is derived from a constant elasticity of substitution (CES) utility function, as in Calmfors and Driffill. Once optimal output is determined, firms' optimal prices are easily computed, and the choice of a simple technology function determines the resulting employment. In fact, I closely follow the approach in Mas-Collell (1995) for this part (see Section 1 in the appendix).

The final key step is finding the unions' optimal wage demands. Given that the wage demands of trade unions are conditional on the level of services provided by the government, we need to substitute equation (2), which expresses the level of services provided by the government, into the unions' utility function (3). The complete derivation of the equilibrium wage is presented in Section 2 of the appendix. Note that, for the sake of simplicity,

[4] See Soskice and Iversen (1999: 5). To make the comparison of the results easier, I use the same notation.

[5] Iversen and Soskice reformulate this assumption as follows: Assume $M = P^{1-\beta}$, where M is the nominal money supply, P is the aggregate price level, and β is the parameter measuring the degree to which the central bank follows a nonaccommodating policy rule. "If the central bank it completely accommodating," they write, "the central bank fixes the real money supply by setting M equal to the price level, whereas if the central bank is completely nonaccommodating, it fixes the nominal money supply and sets M equal to unity" (1999: 5). In other words, in the case of nonaccommodating monetary policy ($\beta = 1$), the money supply is independent of the price level, while in the case of accommodating monetary policy ($\beta = 0$), the money supply is set equal to the price level.

I only consider symmetric equilibria, in which all unions make the same wage demand. The result is the following proposition.

Proposition 1. (A) In a symmetric equilibrium, the total level of employment is given by

$$a^{SYM} = \frac{E(\sigma - 1)}{b\sigma} \frac{\left[I((\mathcal{J} - 1)\sigma - \mathcal{J}) + (I - 1)\rho + 1 + \beta \frac{\pi}{1+\pi}\right] \frac{1-\tau_U}{1+\tau_E} + \frac{\beta}{1+\pi}}{I(\mathcal{J} - 1)\sigma + (I - 1)\rho + (1 + \beta)\frac{\pi}{1+\pi}}.$$

(4)

(B) The optimal wage demand of trade unions is given by

$$w^{SYM} = b \frac{I(\mathcal{J} - 1)\sigma + (I - 1)\rho + (1 + \beta)\frac{\pi}{1+\pi}}{[I((\mathcal{J} - 1)\sigma - \mathcal{J}) + (I - 1)\rho + 1 + \beta \frac{\pi}{1+\pi}](1-\tau_U) + \frac{\beta}{1+\pi}(1+\tau_E)}.$$

(5)

Before exploring the implications of the result, it is important to go back to the assumption by which this model differs from existing models of wage bargaining. The main difference lies in the assumption about the utility of trade unions. Existing models assume that unions care about wages (Iversen and Soskice)[6] or wages and unemployment benefits for union members who are out of work (Calmfors and Driffill). In contrast, this study assumes that social policy considerations are also an important component of the utility of trade unions. Thus, in addition to wages and social policy benefits for their members, the objective function of trade unions used in this model comprises a third component denoting unions' concern for social policy. More formally, the difference between this model and the Calmfors and Driffill model can be written as follows: The utility of a trade union that cares only about wages and unemployment benefits (denoted by U^{CD}) equals

$$U_{ij}^{CD} = \frac{1}{P^\beta}\left[(1 - \tau_U)w_{ij} + \left(\frac{n}{I\mathcal{J}} - a_{ij}\right)b\right].$$

(6)

In contrast, this study assumes that trade unions also derive utility from social services, as modeled in the last term of equation (3). How does this additional assumption about the utility of trade unions affect the predictions about unemployment? To answer this question, we need to study the impact

---

[6] For example, Iversen and Soskice assume that the union in sector i is $U_i = w_i^\alpha \cdot e_i$, where w_i^α is the average wage for the union members in this sector and e_i is the employment rate in sector i. See Soskice and Iversen (1999: 7, n. 13).

of the additional term on the utility of trade unions on wages (and then employment). If we denote the additional term by U_S (shorthand for the social services component), I prove the next proposition in Section 2 of the appendix.

Proposition 2. (A) $\partial U_S/\partial w < 0$. *Consequently, the wage demands of unions that internalize concerns about the provision of social services are lower than the wage demands of unions that care only about the real wages and unemployment benefits of their members.*

(B) $\partial^2 U_S/\partial w\, \partial I > 0$ *and* $\partial^2 U_S/\partial w\, \partial \mathcal{J} > 0$. *The effect in (A) is more pronounced in economies with more centralized systems of wage bargaining (for both intrasectoral and cross-sectoral centralizations).*

The result formalizes an observation of the "neocorporatist" literature, which has argued that an important political exchange between unions and governments underpinned welfare state expansion in the first decades of the postwar period (Cameron 1984; Esping-Andersen 1990). In exchange for the expansion of social programs – the expansion of the social wage – unions delivered wage restraint. The institutional structure of the wage bargaining system affects the employment consequences of this collective wage restraint: Employment is highest in economies with the most centralized levels of wage bargaining. (Because $\partial U_S/\partial w$ becomes more negative as N decreases, the wage restraint effect is more pronounced.) Note also that in the limit case of extremely decentralized labor markets (where N is very large), the provision of social services has no impact on the equilibrium level of employment as $U_S \to 0$ due to the presence of $N = I\mathcal{J}$ in the denominator. In this case, the model proposed here reduces to the Calmfors-Driffill model. Summarizing these results, Figure 1.6 contrasts the employment predictions of this model to those of Calmfors and Driffill.

Comparative Statics

We are now ready to explore some of the implications of the equilibrium results of Proposition 1. Why has the employment performance of European economies deteriorated so strongly during recent decades? What factors explain cross-national variation in the levels of unemployment? To answer these questions, one has to consider changes in the structure of welfare state commitments as well as trends in macroeconomic policy. I will

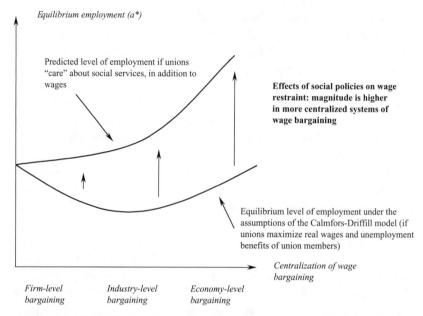

Figure 1.6. Wage bargaining system centralization and equilibrium employment given different assumptions about trade unions' utility.

focus on three aspects: the increase in the number of labor market outsiders, the increase in taxes, and the shift toward less accommodating monetary policies.

The comparative statics of the model can be summarized as follows:

Proposition 3. (A) $\partial a^{SYM}/\partial \pi < 0$. An increase in the number of labor market outsiders (dependency ratio) lowers the equilibrium employment. (B) $\partial a^{SYM}/\partial \tau < 0$. An increase in taxes hurts employment. (C) $\partial a^{SYM}/\partial \beta > 0$. An increase in monetary nonaccommodation promotes employment.

The results in Proposition 3 explore the determinants of unemployment in OECD economies. The implications of Proposition 3(C) are in agreement with the Soskice-Iversen finding, suggesting that the transition to a nonaccommodating monetary regime has a beneficial impact on the equilibrium level of unemployment. The underlying theoretical logic is the same as in the Soskice-Iversen setup: Unions have a stronger incentive to moderate their wage demands if the monetary authority does not accommodate price increases by a lax policy. The results in Proposition 3(A) and (B) point to the existence of mechanisms that work in the opposite direction, leading to an increase in the equilibrium level of unemployment. Unemployment rises as a consequence of higher taxes and the larger share of social policy expenditures going to labor market outsiders. The key result of the model is that the process of welfare state maturation gradually undermines the effectiveness of the political exchange between trade unions and governments based on wage restraint in exchange for social policy expansion.

To explore the precise mechanism by which the change in the composition of the welfare state mix undermines unions' capacity to deliver wage restraint, consider again the budget constraint equation (1) and equation (3), which specifies the utility of trade unions. The worsening of the dependency ratio and the increase in the number of labor market outsiders are modeled as an increase in the parameter m. As a result, the first term in equation (1), (bm), which models the level of passive social policy expenditures, increases. As a consequence of this increase in social policy commitments devoted to labor market outsiders, the level of social policy expenditures devoted to the public provision of social services (S) declines. Returning now to equation (3), the decline in the level of publicly provided social services contributes to a reduction of the third component of the utility of unions. Proposition 2 has shown that unions' concern for the provision of social services promotes wage restraint. It follows that a reduction in the level of social services (as a result of an increase in the level of transfers to labor market outsiders) undermines unions' ability to deliver wage moderation.

Growth in taxes has a similar effect on the optimal wage strategy of trade unions. An increase in the level of taxes has two consequences. First, higher taxes reduce the net wages of union members. The rational wage strategy of trade unions is to demand higher wages to compensate for the loss in income. Second, the increase in the level of taxes decreases the employment consequences of a policy of wage restraint. Given a high level of taxes, unions' wage choices affect only a very small fraction of the total wage bill. Thus, a policy of wage moderation is less effective in lowering unemployment if the share of taxes is higher. The joint effect of these developments is that the virtuous cycle between wage moderation and welfare state expansion becomes more difficult to sustain in mature welfare states.

What is the impact of the centralization of the wage bargaining system on the equilibrium level of unemployment? I have deliberately set this aspect aside, as there are competing views in the literature about the shape of the unemployment curve as a function of centralization. As discussed previously, a number of studies describe a monotonic dependence, with totally centralized systems performing best, whereas the Calmfors-Driffill paper supports the idea of a hump-shaped dependence. It is important to point out that, from the point of view of the formal model, even the Calmfors-Driffill model allows both possibilities: The hump-shaped dependence is only present under certain conditions, which require at least the distinction between intrasectoral and intersectoral centralizations modeled in our two-level economy. The technical details are elaborated in Section 3 of the appendix, so here I will only summarize the key ideas in the following proposition:

Proposition 4. (A) Under suitable technical conditions, $\partial a^{SYM}/\partial I < 0$ and $\partial a^{SYM}/\partial \mathcal{J} > 0$; that is, equilibrium employment is a U-shaped function of centralization. (B) The U shape is less pronounced than in the Calmfors-Driffill approach; that is, if we denote the corresponding quantities in the Calmfors-Driffill model by $()^{CD}$, then

$$\frac{\partial a^{SYM}}{\partial I} < \left(\frac{\partial a^{SYM}}{\partial I}\right)^{CD} \quad \text{and} \quad \frac{\partial a^{SYM}}{\partial \mathcal{J}} < \left(\frac{\partial a^{SYM}}{\partial \mathcal{J}}\right)^{CD}.$$

The objective of this chapter is not to resolve the existing theoretical and empirical controversy about the functional specification of the relationship between wage bargaining centralization and unemployment. As explained previously, most of the theoretical disagreement can be traced back to highly technical assumptions about the relative wage elasticities of demand. This chapter has relied on the Calmfors-Driffill model as the baseline model because it is the more general case. By using its technical assumptions, one can obtain the linear case predicting a monotonic relationship between the centralization of the wage bargaining system and unemployment as a limit case. The reverse, however, is not true: One cannot obtain a nonmonotonic relationship between the centralization of the wage bargaining system and unemployment by starting from the assumptions made by proponents of a linear model about constant wage elasticities, such as that proposed by Soskice and Iversen. The main point of the analysis, however, is to demonstrate that the employment consequences of the process of welfare state maturation (increase in the level of taxes, increase in the number of labor market outsiders) are dependent on the structure of the wage bargaining system. The shape of the Calmfors-Driffill curve itself depends on institutional parameters of the welfare state, such as the level

Looking Ahead

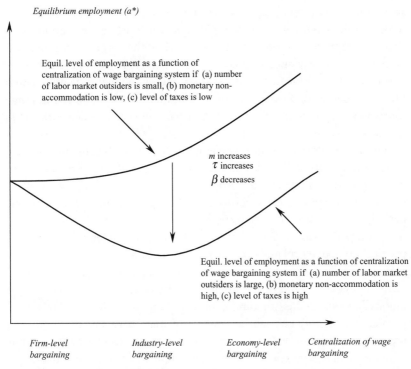

Equilibrium employment (a*)

Equil. level of employment as a function of centralization of wage bargaining system if (a) number of labor market outsiders is small, (b) monetary non-accommodation is low, (c) level of taxes is low

m increases
τ increases
β decreases

Equil. level of employment as a function of centralization of wage bargaining system if (a) number of labor market outsiders is large, (b) monetary non-accommodation is high, (c) level of taxes is high

| *Firm-level bargaining* | *Industry-level bargaining* | *Economy-level bargaining* | *Centralization of wage bargaining* |

Figure 1.7. Predicted employment as a function of wage bargaining system centralization, macroeconomic policy, taxation, and labor market outsiders.

of taxes and the mix of social policy expenditures devoted to labor market insiders and outsiders. Cross-national and intertemporal variations in the employment performance of OECD economies can be predicted by considering the impact of (a) wage bargaining institutions, (b) monetary policy, and (c) the welfare state. Figure 1.7 summarizes the implications of the analysis.

Looking Ahead

I began this chapter by noting that both economic and corporatist theories fail to provide an account of the variations in the employment performance of OECD economies that captures both cross-national and temporal variations in levels of unemployment. Generally, corporatist studies, which highlight the critical role of wage bargaining institutions, have been more successful than economic approaches at explaining cross-national variation in economic outcomes across OECD economies. But as the summary of the most significant theoretical developments of the corporatist studies has pointed out, this explanatory success has not been matched by a similar success in accounting for temporal variation in employment outcomes across OECD economies. The answer to the question of why permanent, long-term unemployment has risen in OECD economies has eluded corporatist scholars.

The model developed in this chapter attempts to fill this explanatory gap in the literature. It elaborates the micro-logic of a political exchange between trade unions and governments that was at the basis of welfare state expansion during the early decades of the postwar period. During this period, unions delivered wage restraint in exchange for the expansion of the social wage (Crouch 1995; Cameron 1984; Esping-Andersen 1990). This political exchange explains why the massive welfare state expansion of the period came about at very low costs in terms of employment. The magnitude of the employment effects resulting from the collective wage restraint of unions depends on the structure of the wage bargaining system. The model predicts that highly centralized systems of wage bargaining magnify the positive employment effects associated with the collective wage restraint of unions and generate lower levels of unemployment than intermediately centralized wage bargaining systems (given similar levels of taxes and similar mixes of transfers and services).

At the same time, the model generates a number of predictions about the factors that account for deterioration in the employment performance of European economies in recent decades. Two factors constrain the ability of trade unions to deliver similar levels of wage restraint as welfare states mature. The first of these factors is growth in taxes. Higher taxes reduce the take-home pay of union members and constrain the ability of unions to deliver wage restraint. Second, a change in the mix between social services and social transfers that go to labor market outsiders can also affect unions' ability to deliver wage restraint. If the level of social policy benefits received by union members declines, unions' incentive to deliver wage moderation also declines. This suggests that the process of welfare state maturation gradually undermines the effectiveness of the political exchange among unions and governments based on wage restraint in exchange for social policy expansion.

The following chapters will test the empirical predictions of this model. I begin in Chapter 2 by testing the macro-level implications of the analysis using panel data for OECD economies. Chapters 3 to 5 will then examine the implications of the model for the wage policies pursued by unions.

Appendix

The goal of the appendix is to provide a formal derivation of the results of the model developed in this chapter. As described, the basic setup is as follows: Unions choose wages. Employers move next by choosing the level of prices. Consumers move next, choosing goods based on the level of prices and on the elasticity of substitution among goods produced in different sectors. In equilibrium, the level of consumption (x) determines the equilibrium level of employment (a). Wage bargaining occurs in an exogenous macroeconomic environment in which governments have established the tax rate (t) and the monetary policy regime before wage bargaining occurs. These parameters are known to the players and assumed to be fixed throughout the game.

Recall that the budget constraint equation determining the balance between social policy expenditures and tax receipts is

$$b_m + b \sum_{i=1}^{I} \sum_{j=1}^{J} \left(\frac{n}{N} - a_{ij} \right) + S = (\tau_U + \tau_E) \sum_{i=1}^{I} \sum_{j=1}^{J} a_{ij} w_{ij}. \tag{1}$$

In this equation, a_{ij} denotes the equilibrium employment level for members of union ij and w_{ij} denotes the equilibrium wage. From this equation, the tax balance equation, we can derive the level of services available in the economy as

$$S = (\tau_U + \tau_E) \sum_{i=1}^{I} \sum_{j=1}^{J} a_{ij} w_{ij} + b \sum_{i=1}^{I} \sum_{j=1}^{J} a_{ij} - b(m+n). \tag{2}$$

Social services play an important role in the overall demands of trade unions. Thus, in contrast to existing models, unions' utility has three components:

$$U_{ij}^U = \frac{1}{P^\beta} \left[\underbrace{(1 - \tau_U) w_{ij} a_{ij}}_{NET.WAGES} + \underbrace{\left(\frac{n}{IJ} - a_{ij} \right) b}_{TRANFERS.TO.UNION.MEMBERS} \right.$$

$$\left. + \underbrace{\frac{1}{IJ} \frac{n}{m+n} S}_{SOCIAL.SERVICES} \right] \tag{3}$$

This stands in contrast to the utility function of the Calmfors-Driffill model, which assumes that unions want to maximize real wages and unemployment benefits for their members:

$$U_{ij}^{CD} = \frac{1}{P^\beta}\left[(1 - \tau_U)w_{ij} + \left(\frac{n}{I\mathcal{J}} - a_{ij}\right)b\right].\tag{4}$$

1. Equilibrium Prices and Consumption

This section summarizes the derivation of equilibrium prices and demand for goods along the lines of Mas-Colell (1995: Chap. 3). The only modification is the use of a two-level CES utility function, in line with the Calmfors-Driffill approach to modeling differences within and across sectors resulting from the wage choices made by unions. The utility function of consumers is

$$U^C = \left(\sum_{i=1}^{I}\left(\sum_{j=1}^{\mathcal{J}} x_{ij}^{\frac{\sigma-1}{\sigma}}\right)^{\frac{\sigma}{\sigma-1}\frac{\rho-1}{\rho}}\right)^{\frac{\rho}{\rho-1}}.\tag{5}$$

Recall that the double index ij denotes the j-th firm in sector i. In equation (5), x_{ij} denotes the consumption of good ij, σ denotes the elasticity of substitution among goods produced within one sector (assumed to be the same for all sectors), and ρ is the elasticity of substitution among sectors. Because goods produced in the same sector are closer substitutes for one another than goods produced in different sectors, it is natural to assume that $\sigma > \rho$. In order to have a well-posed maximization problem for the firms, it is necessary to assume that $\sigma, \rho > 1$.

Consumers' utility function is constructed through a two-step aggregation process: First, goods produced in sector i are combined into a CES basket in the form

$$\left(\sum_{j=1}^{\mathcal{J}} x_{ij}^{\frac{\sigma-1}{\sigma}}\right)^{\frac{\sigma}{\sigma-1}}.$$

This consumption basket can be thought of as an aggregate or synthetic good produced in sector i. In the second stage, aggregate goods produced in each sector are combined into a basket according to the CES rule.

Appendix

If E denotes the total spending in the economy (or total wealth) and p_{ij} denotes the price of good j in sector i, it follows that consumers maximize their utility, U^C, subject to the budget constraint

$$\sum_{i=1}^{I}\sum_{j=1}^{J} p_{ij}x_{ij} = E. \tag{6}$$

Prices are set by the firms in order to maximize total revenue minus labor costs. In other words, employers maximize

$$U_{ij}^E = p_{ij}x_{ij} - w_{ij}(1 + \tau_E)a_{ij}, \tag{7}$$

where w_{ij} represent wages (chosen by trade unions) and a_{ij} is the level of employment in firm ij. I will use a linear technology function, $x_{ij} = \alpha a_{ij}$, with the same productivity factor α for all firms.

The aggregate price level of the economy can be defined as the weighted average of the prices of each sector i. Thus, if the price level in sector i is

$$P_i = \left(\sum_{j=1}^{J} p_{ij}^{1-\sigma}\right)^{\frac{1}{1-\sigma}}, \tag{8}$$

the aggregate price level of the economy becomes

$$P = \left(\sum_{i=1}^{I} P_i^{1-\rho}\right)^{\frac{1}{1-\rho}}. \tag{9}$$

We now summarize the optimal choices for consumers and firms, which follow from the first-order conditions for their utility functions. Equilibrium demand for goods is given by

$$x_{ij} = \frac{E}{P}\left(\frac{P_i}{P}\right)^{-\rho}\left(\frac{p_{ij}}{P_i}\right)^{-\sigma}. \tag{10}$$

Substituting equation (10) into firms' utility function and maximizing with respect to p_{ij} leads to

$$p_{ij} = \frac{\sigma}{(\sigma - 1)\alpha}(1 + \tau_E)w_{ij}. \tag{11}$$

By substituting equation (11) into equations (8) and (9) we can determine the price level in the economy and the level of demand for the goods produced at each firm:

$$P = \frac{\sigma(1 + \tau_E)}{(\sigma - 1)\alpha} \left(\sum_{i=1}^{I} \left(\sum_{j=1}^{J} w_{ij}^{1-\sigma} \right)^{\frac{1-\rho}{1-\sigma}} \right)^{\frac{1}{1-\rho}}, \tag{12}$$

$$x_{ij} = \frac{E(\sigma - 1)\alpha}{\sigma(1 + \tau_E)} \frac{w_{ij}^{-\sigma} \left(\sum_{j=1}^{J} w_{ij}^{1-\sigma} \right)^{\frac{\sigma-\rho}{1-\sigma}}}{\sum_{i=1}^{I} \left(\sum_{j=1}^{J} w_{ij}^{1-\sigma} \right)^{\frac{1-\rho}{1-\sigma}}}. \tag{13}$$

Because the level of employment for firm j in sector i is equal to $a_{ij} = x_{ij}/\alpha$, it follows from equation (13) that

$$a_{ij}(w) = \frac{E(\sigma - 1)}{\sigma(1 + \tau_E)} \frac{w_{ij}^{-\sigma} \left(\sum_{j=1}^{J} w_{ij}^{1-\sigma} \right)^{\frac{\sigma-\rho}{1-\sigma}}}{\sum_{i=1}^{I} \left(\sum_{j=1}^{J} w_{ij}^{1-\sigma} \right)^{\frac{1-\rho}{1-\sigma}}}. \tag{14}$$

Note that equation (14) represents the level of employment in firm ij resulting from the firms' optimal choice of prices once the trade unions' wage demands w_{ij} are known. (The notation on the left-hand side emphasizes the fact that employment in firm ij depends on the wage demands in all other firms.) The final step in the backward induction argument, that is, unions' optimal demands, is developed in the next section.

2. Derivation of Trade Unions' Optimal Wage Demands

Equation (14) specifies the employment outcome for each trade union as a function of the wage demands w_{ij}. In order to solve the unions' maximization problem, it is necessary to express the level of social services S defined in equation (2) in terms of wages and then substitute into equation (3). As a result of this substitution, and after rearranging some terms, the utility

52

Appendix

function of unions becomes

$$
U_{ij}^U = \frac{1}{P^\beta} \left[\left(1 - \tau_U + \frac{1}{I\bar{J}} \frac{1}{1+\pi} (\tau_U + \tau_E) \right) a_{ij}(w) w_{ij} \right.
$$
$$
+ \left(-b + b \frac{1}{I\bar{J}} \frac{1}{1+\pi} \right) a_{ij}(w) + \frac{1}{I\bar{J}} \frac{1}{1+\pi} (\tau_U + \tau_E)
$$
$$
\left. \times \sum_{k,l \neq i,j} a_{kl}(w) w_{kl} + b \frac{1}{I\bar{J}} \frac{1}{1+\pi} \sum_{k,l \neq i,j} a_{kl}(w) \right]. \tag{15}
$$

Note that equation (15) uses the dependency ratio π rather than the total sizes of the active and inactive populations n, m through the relation $(n/m + n = 1/1 + \pi.)$ Also note that using the notation $a_{ij}(w)$ signifies that equation (14) has to be substituted into equation (15) before solving the unions' optimization problem.

The next step is to maximize equation (15) with respect to the unions' wage demand w_{ij}. For reasons of analytical tractability, I will restrict to symmetric equilibria, that is, to equilibria in which $w_{11}^* = w_{12}^* = \cdots = w_{I\bar{J}}^* = w^{SYM}$. In order to derive the optimal wage demand – equation (5) – from the utility function of trade unions – equation (15) – we have to solve for the first-order condition and check the second-order conditions. Equation (15) can be rewritten as

$$
U_{ij}^U = C_1 \frac{a_{ij} w_{ij}}{P^\beta} + C_2 \frac{a_{ij}}{P^\beta} + C_3 \frac{\sum\limits_{k,l \neq i,j} a_{kl} w_{kl}}{P^\beta} + C_4 \frac{\sum\limits_{k,l \neq i,j} a_{kl}}{P^\beta}, \tag{16}
$$

where the employment levels a_{ij}, a_{kl} ($kl \neq ij$) and the aggregated level of prices P depend on w_{ij}, as described in equations (12) and (14). The constants $C_1 \ldots C_4$ are given by

$$
C_1 = 1 - \tau_U + \frac{1}{I\bar{J}} \frac{1}{1+\pi} (\tau_U + \tau_E),
$$

$$
C_2 = b \left(-1 + \frac{1}{I\bar{J}} \frac{1}{1+\pi} \right),
$$

$$
C_3 = \frac{1}{I\bar{J}} \frac{1}{1+\pi} (\tau_U + \tau_E),
$$

$$
C_4 = b \frac{1}{I\bar{J}} \frac{1}{1+\pi}.
$$

To compute the derivative of each of the terms in equation (16) with respect to w_{ij}, it is easier to work with elasticities and rely on the formula

$$\frac{\partial f}{\partial w} = \prod_w f \bullet \frac{f}{w}, \tag{17}$$

where f is a function of w and $\prod_w f$ denotes its elasticity with respect to w.

The computation of elasticities is made simpler by the usual product/quotient rules, for instance,

$$\prod_{w_{ij}} \left(\frac{a_{ij} w_{ij}}{P^\beta} \right) = \prod_{w_{ij}} a_{ij} + 1 - \beta \prod_{w_{ij}} P,$$

$$\prod_{w_{ij}} \left(\frac{a_{kl} w_{kl}}{P^\beta} \right) = \prod_{w_{ij}} a_{kl} - \beta \prod_{w_{ij}} P \, (kl \neq ij),$$

$$\prod_{w_{ij}} \left(\frac{a_{kl}}{P^\beta} \right) = \prod_{w_{ij}} a_{kl} - \beta \prod_{w_{ij}} P, \quad \text{and}$$

$$\prod_{w_{ij}} \left(\frac{1}{P^\beta} \right) = -\beta \prod_{w_{ij}} P. \tag{18}$$

Therefore the calculation requires the elasticities $\prod_{w_{ij}} a_{ij}$, $\prod_{w_{ij}} a_{kl}$, $kl \neq ij$, and $\prod_{w_{ij}} P$. These elasticities are quite complicated in general, but major simplifications occur in the case of symmetric equilibria, that is, when the calculated elasticities are restricted to the case of equal wages. Denoting by $\prod_{w_{ij}}^{SYM}$ the elasticity restricted to the situation in which $w_{ij} = w^{SYM}$ for all ij, equations (12), (14), and (18) lead to

$$\prod_{w_{ij}}^{SYM}(a_{ij}) = -\frac{1}{I\mathcal{J}}[I(\mathcal{J}-1)\sigma + (I-1)\rho + 1],$$

$$\prod_{w_{ij}}^{SYM}(a_{il}) = \frac{1}{I\mathcal{J}}[I\sigma - (I-1)\rho - 1]\,(l \neq j),$$

$$\prod_{w_{ij}}^{SYM}(a_{kl}) = \frac{\rho - 1}{I\mathcal{J}}(k \neq i),$$

$$\prod_{w_{ij}}^{SYM}(P) = \frac{1}{I\mathcal{J}}. \tag{19}$$

In the symmetric case, equations (12) and (14) reduce to

$$P^{SYM} = \frac{\sigma(1 + \tau_E)}{(\sigma - 1)\alpha} I^{\frac{1}{1-\rho}} \mathcal{J}^{\frac{1}{1-\sigma}} w^{SYM}$$

$$a_{ij}^{SYM} = \frac{E(\sigma - 1)}{\sigma(1 + \tau_E)} \frac{1}{I\mathcal{J}} \frac{1}{w^{SYM}} \quad \text{for all } ij. \tag{20}$$

Equation (20) is consistent with the intuition that employment levels are decreasing in wage demands. Moreover, equation (20) clarifies the effect of

Appendix

taxes on the relationship between wages and employment. Namely, if w_{NET} denotes net wages, or $w_{NET} = w(1 - \tau_U)$, equation (20) can be rewritten as

$$a_{ij}^{SYM}(w_{NET}) = \frac{E(\sigma - 1)}{I\mathcal{J}\sigma}\frac{1 - \tau_U}{1 + \tau_E}\frac{1}{w_{NET}^{SYM}}. \tag{21}$$

From equation (21), it follows that

$$\frac{\partial a_{ij}^{SYM}}{\partial w_{NET}} = -\frac{E(\sigma - 1)}{I\mathcal{J}\sigma}\frac{1 - \tau_U}{1 + \tau_E}\frac{1}{\left(w_{NET}^{SYM}\right)^2}, \tag{22}$$

which shows that the higher the total taxes – that is, the smaller the fraction $(1 - \tau_U)/(1 + \tau_E)$ – the less sensitive the employment level is to wages.

After substituting equations (17), (19), and (20) into (16), it follows that in the symmetric case,

$$\frac{\partial U_{ij}^U}{\partial w_{ij}} = K_1(w^{SYM})^{-2-\beta} - K_2(w^{SYM})^{-1-\beta}$$

$$= (w^{SYM})^{-2-\beta}(K_1 - K_2 w^{SYM}), \tag{23}$$

where

$$K_1 = \frac{b}{I\mathcal{J}}\left[I(\mathcal{J} - 1)\sigma + (I - 1)\rho + (1 + \beta)\frac{\pi}{1 + \pi}\right] \quad \text{and}$$

$$K_2 = \frac{1}{I\mathcal{J}}\left[(I(\mathcal{J} - 1)\sigma + (I - 1)\rho + (1 + \beta) - I\mathcal{J})(1 - \tau_U)\right.$$

$$\left. + \frac{\beta}{1 + \pi}(\tau_U + \tau_E)\right]. \tag{24}$$

Equation (23) shows that the unique symmetric solution for the first-order conditions is

$$w^{SYM} = \frac{K_1}{K_2},$$

which is equivalent to equation (5). The second-order condition (for a maximum) is also satisfied, because $K_1 - K_2 w > 0$ for $w < w^{SYM}$ and $K_1 - K_2 w < 0$ for $w > w^{SYM}$.

The total level of employment a^{SYM} – equation (4) – can now be found by substituting w^{SYM} into the second equation in (20), as $a^{SYM} = I \mathcal{J} a_{ij}^{SYM}$.

We turn now to the proof of Proposition 2. Recall that $U_S = S/(I \mathcal{J} (1 + \pi))$, so it suffices to look at $\partial S / \partial w_{ki}$ (where kl denotes one of the unions in the economy). Given the wage demands w_{ij}, the resulting level of services S (which is assumed to be the same for all unions) can be computed from equation (2) after substituting the implied employment levels in equation (14):

$$S(w_{kl}) = (\tau_U + \tau_E) \frac{E(\sigma - 1)}{\sigma(1 + \tau_E)} + \frac{Eb(\sigma - 1)}{\sigma(1 + \tau_E)} S_2(w_{ij}) - b(m + n),$$

where

$$S_2(w_{ij}) = \frac{\sum_{i=1}^{I} \left(\sum_{j=1}^{\mathcal{J}} w_{ij}^{-\sigma} \right) \left(\sum_{j=1}^{\mathcal{J}} w_{ij}^{1-\sigma} \right)^{\frac{\sigma - \rho}{1 - \sigma}}}{\sum_{i=1}^{I} \left(\sum_{j=1}^{\mathcal{J}} w_{ij}^{1-\sigma} \right)^{\frac{1-\rho}{1-\sigma}}}.$$

Note that only the middle term in the above equation depends on the wage demands w_{ij} and on the variables modeling the centralization of the wage bargaining system $(I, \mathcal{J})$. Therefore, it is sufficient to restrict to this term when checking the assertions of Proposition 2.

For part (A), differentiating the above expression with respect to w_{kl} and restricting to the symmetric case $w_{ij} = w^{SYM}$ for all i, j leads to

$$\left(\frac{\partial S_2}{\partial w_{kl}} \right)^{SYM} = - \frac{1}{I^2 \mathcal{J}^2 (w^{SYM})^2} < 0,$$

which shows that $\partial U_S / \partial w < 0$. Note that the absolute value of $(\partial S_2 / \partial w_{kl})^{SYM}$ is decreasing in both I and $\mathcal{J}$, therefore proving part (B) of the proposition.

3. Proofs of Comparative Statics Results

This section contains the proof of Proposition 3. When computing the sensitivity of a^{SYM} to the various parameters in the model, the following observation will be used repeatedly: If $f(x)$ is a function of the form $f(x) = (k_0 x + l_0)/(k_1 x + l_1)$, then $f'(x) = (k_0 l_1 - k_1 l_0)/(k_1 x + l_1)^2$, so the sign of

Appendix

its derivative with respect to x is given by

$$\text{sgn}\, f'(x) = k_0 l_1 - k_1 l_0. \tag{25}$$

We start with part (A) of Proposition 3. Because $\pi/(1+\pi)$ is a strictly increasing function of π, it is enough to prove that $\partial a^{SYM}/\partial(\pi/(1+\pi))$ is negative. Note that the equilibrium employment a^{SYM} – equation (4) – can be rewritten as

$$a^{SYM} = \frac{1-\tau_U}{1+\tau_E}\left[1 + \frac{(1+\beta(1+\tau_E)/(1-\tau_U))(1-\pi/(1+\pi)) - I\mathcal{J}}{I(\mathcal{J}-1)\sigma + (I-1)\rho + (1+\beta)\pi/(1+\pi)}\right]; \tag{26}$$

hence, remark (25) applies. Namely, if $t = (1+\tau_E)/(1-\tau_U) \geq 1$, then

$$\text{sgn}\left(\frac{\partial a^{SYM}}{\partial(\pi/(1+\pi))}\right) = -\text{sgn}\left((1+\beta t)(I(\mathcal{J}-1)\sigma + (I-1)\rho\right.$$
$$\left. + ((1+\beta)(1+\beta t - I\mathcal{J}))\right). \tag{27}$$

The aim is to show that the expression on the right-hand side of equation (27) is positive (so that the overall sign is negative). A simple argument can be given by looking at limit cases and the sign of the various coefficients. First, note that the coefficient of t equals $\beta(I(\mathcal{J}-1)\sigma + (I-1)\rho + 1 + \beta)$, which is strictly positive, because $1 + \beta > 0$ and $I(\mathcal{J}-1)\sigma + (I-1)\rho \geq I(\mathcal{J}-1)\rho + (I-1)\rho = (I\mathcal{J}-1)\rho \geq 0$, due to the fact that $I, \mathcal{J} \geq 1$ and $\sigma > \rho$. (The intrasectoral elasticity of substitution of goods is higher than the intersectoral elasticity of substitution.) Therefore, it is enough to check positivity for $t = 1$, which is the minimum possible value of t, because tax rates are nonnegative. In this case, the right-hand side of equation (27) reduces to

$$(1+\beta)\left[I(\mathcal{J}-1)\sigma + (I-1)\rho + 1 + \beta - I\mathcal{J}\right]. \tag{28}$$

The coefficient of $\mathcal{J}$ in equation (28) equals $I(\sigma - 1)$, which is positive because $\sigma > 1$, so it suffices to prove that equation (28) is positive for $\mathcal{J} = 1$. In this case, equation (28) reduces to

$$(1+\beta)((I-1)\rho + 1 + \beta - 1)$$
$$= (1+\beta)(I(\rho-1) + 1 - \rho + \beta) \geq (1+\beta)\beta \geq 0,$$

where the first inequality uses the facts that $\rho > 1$ and $I \geq 1$, and the second one follows from $\beta \geq 0$. This proves that the right-hand side of equation (27) is positive and completes the proof of part (A) of Proposition 3.

57

Part (B) of the proposition follows immediately from equation (4) if we notice that equilibrium employment is an increasing linear function in $1/t = (1 - \tau_U)/(1 + \tau_E)$; an increase in taxes (either in τ_U or in τ_E) increases t and therefore reduces a^{SYM}.

Part (C) of Proposition 3 is proved by using equation (25) once again, in this case for the derivative with respect to β:

$$\text{sgn}\left(\frac{\partial a^{SYM}}{\partial \beta}\right) = \text{sgn}\left(\frac{t}{1+\pi}\left(I(\mathcal{J}-1)\sigma + (I-1)\rho + \frac{\pi}{1+\pi}\right.\right.$$
$$\left.\left. - \frac{\pi}{1+\pi}\left(\frac{1}{1+\pi} - I\mathcal{J}\right)\right)\right) > 0,$$

because $I \geq 1$, $\mathcal{J} \geq 1$, and $1/(1+\pi) - I\mathcal{J} \leq 1 - I\mathcal{J} \leq 0$.

4. Centralization of the Wage Bargaining System: A Comparison with the Calmfors-Driffill Approach

This section focuses on the impact of centralization (as modeled by I and $\mathcal{J}$) on equilibrium wages and employment levels. I briefly summarize the logic of the original Calmfors and Driffill argument in the context of the two-level economy introduced in Section 1 of this appendix.

The predictions of the Calmfors-Driffill model can be recovered by replacing the trade unions' utility function (3) with the "utilitarian" form (6) and repeating the argument in Section 2. The analog of equation (26) is

$$\left(a^{SYM}\right)^{CD} = \frac{1-\tau_U}{1+\tau_E}\left[1 - \frac{I\mathcal{J}}{I(\mathcal{J}-1)\sigma + (I-1)\rho + 1 + \beta}\right]. \qquad (29)$$

Remark (25) shows that

$$\text{sgn}\left(\frac{\partial a^{SYM}}{\partial I}\right)^{CD} = \text{sgn}(\rho - 1 - \beta)$$

$$\text{sgn}\left(\frac{\partial a^{SYM}}{\partial \mathcal{J}}\right)^{CD} = \text{sgn}(I(\sigma - \rho) + \rho - 1 - \beta). \qquad (30)$$

The significance of the quantities of the right-hand side of equation (30) can be understood in terms of cross-elasticities of union-level real incomes to wage demands. Namely, it follows from the second and third relations

Appendix

in equation (19) that

$$\prod_{w_{ij}}^{SYM} (a_{il}w_{il}/P^\beta) = [I(\sigma - \rho) + \rho - 1 - \beta]/I\mathcal{J}, \qquad l \neq j$$

$$\prod_{w_{ij}}^{SYM} (a_{kl}w_{kl}/P^\beta) = [\rho - 1 - \beta]/I\mathcal{J}, \qquad k \neq i. \tag{31}$$

The expressions on the left-hand side of equation (31) represent the elasticities to wage demands by union ij of total real incomes for other trade unions in the same sector and trade unions in different sectors, respectively. Let us denote these quantities by $\prod_i$ (intrasectoral) and $\prod_c$ (intersectoral). It follows from equation (30) and (31) that the slope of the employment curve in terms of centralization depends on the signs and of $\prod_i$ and $\prod_c$ as

$$\text{sgn} \left(\partial a^{SYM}/\partial I \right)^{CD} = \text{sgn} \left(\prod_c \right) \text{ and sgn} \left(\partial a^{SYM}/\partial I \right)^{CD} = \text{sgn} \left(\prod_i \right). \tag{32}$$

The assumption that goods produced within one sector are closer substitutes than those produced in different sectors $(\sigma > \rho)$ implies that $\prod_i > \prod_c$. However, the sign of $\prod_i$ and $\prod_c$ depends on the values of the elasticities themselves, which may be very hard, if not impossible, to determine in practice, especially in interaction with the other parameters of the model. In fact, Calmfors and Driffill provide examples in which the signs change in order to emphasize the idea that the theoretical model does not necessarily lead to a U-shaped relationship. In order to have a U-shaped relationship, it is necessary, according to equation (30), that

$$\prod_i > 0 > \prod_c. \tag{33}$$

The assumptions needed to satisfy equation (33) have a very natural interpretation based on equation (31): If goods produced within one sector are close enough substitutes for each other, higher wage demands by one union shift demand away from the goods it produces to other goods produced by unions in the same sector. If this increase exceeds the resulting rise in the general level of prices, then the first inequality in equation (33) holds. A similar assumption leads to the second inequality in equation (33): The lower the cross-sectoral elasticity of substitution, the more likely it is that a (coordinated) higher wage demand in one sector will lower the real income in other sectors through a rise in the general level of prices. These stylized assumptions can in fact be regarded as the minimal set of conditions that guarantee a U-shaped dependence of employment on centralization.

Returning to our model, remark (25) applied to equation (26) yields

$$\text{sgn}\left(\frac{\partial a^{SYM}}{\partial I}\right) = \text{sgn}\left(\mathcal{J}(\rho - 1 - \beta) + \frac{1}{1+\pi}\left(\mathcal{J}(1+\beta)\right.\right.$$
$$\left.\left. - \left((\mathcal{J}-1)\sigma + \rho)(1+\beta t)\right)\right)\right)$$

$$\text{sgn}\left(\frac{\partial a^{SYM}}{\partial \mathcal{J}}\right) = \text{sgn}\left(I(\sigma - \rho) + \rho - 1 - \beta + \frac{1}{1+\pi}\left((1+\beta)\right.\right.$$
$$\left.\left. - \sigma(1+\beta))\right)\right).$$

In a more compact form, these can be rewritten as

$$\text{sgn}\left(\frac{\partial a^{SYM}}{\partial I}\right) = \text{sgn}\left(I\mathcal{J}\prod_c - \Lambda_c/(1+\pi)\right)$$
$$\text{sgn}\left(\frac{\partial a^{SYM}}{\partial \mathcal{J}}\right) = \text{sgn}\left(I\mathcal{J}\prod_i - \Lambda_i/(1+\pi)\right), \qquad (34)$$

where Λ_c and Λ_i are easily seen to be positive, because $\sigma > \rho > 1, t \geq 1$, and $\beta \geq 1$. Equations (34) prove part (B) of Proposition 4 and offer some additional insights into the predictions of the model. Namely, in extremely decentralized systems, the terms $I\mathcal{J}\prod_c$ and $I\mathcal{J}\prod_i$ dominate the right-hand sides of equation (33), and therefore the model converges with the Calmfors-Driffill one. The same is true if the number of outsiders π is large, as then the second terms on the right-hand sides of equation (34) approach zero. These implications are in agreement with the basic intuition that the share of social services allocated to each trade union becomes smaller in a totally decentralized system or in a system with significant social transfer commitments to the population outside the labor market.

2

A Quantitative Analysis

The theoretical model developed in Chapter 1 generates a number of empirical predictions about cross-national and intertemporal variations in the employment performance of OECD economies. This chapter tests the macro-level implications of the analysis using time series, cross-section data for OECD economies for the period 1960–1995.

Existing studies seek to explain the variation in the employment performance of advanced industrialized democracies by examining the effects of wage bargaining institutions and monetary authorities (Iversen 1998, 1999; Hall and Franzese 1998; Franzese 2002). This study qualifies their results by suggesting that the optimal wage choices of unions, and thus the equilibrium level of employment, also depend on the structure and magnitude of welfare state commitments: Unions will deliver wage moderation if a large share of social policy expenditures goes to union members, but their incentive to do so declines as the share of social policy transfers received by labor market outsiders increases. Moreover, increases in payroll and income taxes undermine the *effectiveness* of wage moderation in lowering unemployment. In mature welfare states, which are characterized by high levels of taxes, unions and employers effectively bargain over a small part of the total wage bill. Under these conditions, even dramatic levels of wage moderation have only a modest impact in lowering unemployment. In combination, these two factors – the increase in the number of labor market outsiders and the growth in taxes – contribute to a rise in equilibrium unemployment.

Several predictions of the model are consistent with the empirical implications of earlier studies. First, in agreement with several corporatist studies, the model predicts a nonlinear, hump-shaped relationship between labor market institutions and the unemployment level, suggesting that the employment performance of economies with either highly centralized or highly decentralized labor market institutions will be superior to that of economies with intermediately centralized labor market institutions. Moreover, in agreement with recent studies by Soskice and Iversen, the model predicts that an increase in monetary nonaccommodation will lower the equilibrium level of unemployment (Soskice and Iversen 2000). Building on and departing from these studies, however, the analysis developed in Chapter 1 suggests that an increase in taxes and transfers to labor market outsiders shifts the Calmfors-Driffill curve upward, contributing to a rise in unemployment.

The empirical analysis presented in this chapter will begin with a discussion of the measurement of its key independent variables: wage bargaining centralization, monetary nonaccommodation, and the magnitude and composition of welfare state commitments. The second section will present the most important findings of my statistical analysis of panel data for 14 OECD economies from the period between 1960 and 1995. I rely on several empirical measures of the variable measuring growth in welfare state commitments. I begin by discussing several possible ways in which outsiders can be classified and transfers to outsiders can be estimated, and I present a preliminary analysis of the impact of the growth of expenditures devoted to these labor market groups on unemployment. In a richer set of models, I test the robustness of these initial results to the inclusion of a number of additional political and economic variables. The final set of models analyzed in this chapter examines the joint impact of changes in the tax burden and increases in expenditures going to labor market outsiders on the level of unemployment.

Testing the Model: Measurement of the Central Explanatory Variables

Wage Bargaining Centralization

A key independent variable in the analysis is wage bargaining system centralization. Building on the Calmfors-Driffill results, the model in Chapter 1 suggests that cross-national differences in employment performance will depend on the structure of labor market institutions. As hypothesized, economies with intermediately centralized wage bargaining systems will have an employment performance inferior to that of economies with highly centralized or highly decentralized labor market institutions.

Testing the Model

The development of quantitative measures of wage bargaining institutions is an extremely active area of research in comparative politics (Kenworthy 2001: 93; Golden 1993; Flanagan 1999; Iversen 1999; Traxler, Blaschke, and Kittel 2001). In recent years, a number of studies have developed increasingly sophisticated measures that capture cross-national differences in the centralization of the wage bargaining authority, the involvement of the state in the wage bargaining process, the concentration of union membership, and union density, to name just a few dimensions by which wage setting institutions in advanced industrialized democracies differ. Despite the intense scholarly activity, however, both theoretical and empirical disagreements persist about the coding of individual countries. As Lane Kenworthy's excellent survey of existing measures concludes: "None of the existing measures is without flaws. . . . In some respects, [the field] is still in its infancy" (Kenworthy 2001: 93).

Rather than develop a new measure of wage bargaining centralization, I have opted to average eight of the most widely used measures that are currently available. These are the measures developed by Schmitter (1981); Cameron (1984); Calmfors and Driffill (1988); Iversen (1999); Hall and Franzese (1998); the OECD (1997); Traxler, Blaschke, and Kittel (2001); and Golden, Lange, and Wallerstein (1998). This strategy has a number of advantages. First, it incorporates the expertise that has accumulated in the literature over the past 20 years. The index used in my analysis combines some of the earliest measures of labor market institutions – developed by Schmitter (1981) and Cameron (1984) over two decades ago – with measures developed in very recent years. Second, as Golden has pointed out, existing differences in measurement reflect differences in expert judgment among the various individuals and teams responsible for the coding efforts (Golden 1993: 444). By averaging these measures, one can remove some of the measurement bias from individual scores.

The index measuring wage bargaining centralization has been constructed as follows: For each of the individual indices I order the individual economies from those coded as having the most centralized wage bargaining systems, which take low values on the centralization score, to those coded as having the most decentralized labor market institutions, which take high values. Table 2.1 presents the separate rankings and the aggregate score for each economy. Based on the aggregate ranking, Norway is the country with the most centralized labor market institutions, with an average centralization score of 1.5, while the United States has the most decentralized wage setting system, with an average centralization score of

13.25. As Table 2.1 indicates, the individual indices show a relatively high level of correlation. Some disagreement persists, however, about the coding of individual countries. The strongest disagreement in expert opinion concerns Italy, for which the standard deviation of the individual expert scores is 3.28. While most of the studies (Schmitter, Cameron, Hall and Franzese, Iversen, and OECD) code the Italian economy as having relatively decentralized labor market institutions, studies by Golden, Lange, and Wallerstein and by Traxler, Blaschke, and Kittel attribute a high centralization score to Italian labor market institutions.[1] Disagreement also exists with respect to the coding of Switzerland. Wage setting takes place there at the firm level, and most of the rankings (Schmitter, Cameron, and Calmfors and Driffill) reflect this feature of the Swiss wage bargaining system. The OECD annual survey of Switzerland reports the existence of about 800 to 1000 collective agreements with firm-specific provisions (Danthine and Lambelet 1987: 168–9). As Soskice has pointed out, however, effective coordination of wage setting takes place via employers' associations (Soskice 1990: 41).[2] The rankings of Hall and Franzese and of Traxler, Blaschke, and Kittel capture some of this informal wage bargaining coordination by attributing a relatively high centralization score to Switzerland.

Monetary "Nonaccommodation"

The model developed in Chapter 1 predicts that the wage strategies of unions (and, consequently, the level of unemployment) are also influenced by the character of the macroeconomic policy of the government. Its empirical predictions are in agreement with Soskice and Iversen and suggest that unions are more likely to exercise wage moderation in the presence of a monetary authority committed to an anti-inflationary policy (Soskice and

---

[1] According to the Golden, Lange, and Wallerstein (1998) overall wage setting centralization score, Italy is coded (depending on the period) as a country that has either centralized wage setting without sanctions or centralized wage setting with sanctions. These are the two highest categories on the scale. As a result, Italy's overall centralization score is much higher than that of Finland, Austria, or even Germany.

[2] Traxler, Blaschke, and Kittel (2001) describe the informal coordination of wage setting in Switzerland as follows: "Every summer, the ZSAO (SAV) initiates a survey of 800 member firms, asking them to report what wage increases they are willing to accept. For a long time, internal circulation of these data was the only coordinating mechanism. Since 1985–1986, the ZSAO has formulated recommendations for lower-level bargaining on this basis. As regards labour, the SGB organizes an annual meeting in autumn to coordinate the bargaining of its affiliates" (Traxler, Blaschke, and Kittel 2001: 173).

Table 2.1. *Wage bargaining centralization index*

	Schmitter	Cameron	Calmfors-Driffill	Iversen	Hall-Franzese	OECD	Traxler-Kittel	Golden et al.	Average
Austria	1	3	1	5	1	1	6	8	3.25
Belgium	7	4	8	8	8	7	11	7	7.5
Canada	11	12	13	13	12	14	14	13	12.75
Denmark	4	6	4	3	4	5	5	2	4.125
Finland	4	5	5	4	4	6	2	6	4.5
France	12	14	9	12	10	10	10	9	10.75
Germany	8	8	6	7	4	3	8	10	6.75
Italy	15	11	11	10	10	9	4	5	9.25
Norway	2	2	2	1	1	2	1	1	1.5
Netherlands	6	7	7	6	8	10	8	4	7.00
Sweden	4	1	3	2	1	4	3	3	2.625
Switzerland	9	10	12	10	4	10	6	10	8.75
United Kingdom	13	9	10	11	12	8	12	12	10.875
United States	11	13	14	14	12	14	14	14	13.25

Sources:
Schmitter 1981: 284; Cameron 1984: 165; Calmfors and Driffill 1988: 52–3; Iversen 1999: 56; Hall and Franzese 1998: 530; Traxler and Kittel 2000: 1164–7; OECD 1997: 71; Golden, Lange, and Wallerstein 1998.

Iversen 2000). To test these predictions, I rely on the measure of monetary nonaccommodation developed by Torben Iversen (Iversen 1999).

A first step by which governments can establish a stronger commitment to price stability is by delegating authority over the formulation of monetary policy to an independent central bank. To reflect this institutional precondition of monetary nonaccommodation, Iversen's index starts from existing measures of central bank independence (Bade and Parkin 1982; Cukierman 1992; Cukierman, Webb, and Neyapti 1992). These studies have coded two separate issues. A number of scholars have examined the institutional rules that guarantee the independence of central bankers from political pressures, such as rules concerning the appointment and dismissal of central bankers, rules of policy formulation, and constraints on the ability of the central bank to lend to the government (Cukierman et al. 1992: 358–9). Based on an examination of legal statutes regarding various central banks, Bade and Parkin developed one of the first indices of the independence of monetary policy that coded cross-national differences in the independence of monetary authorities (Bade and Parkin 1982). By contrast, other scholars have examined the goals and actual behavior of monetary authorities – in other words, whether monetary authorities pursue anti-inflationary policies or whether they show any concern for policy goals that might interfere with the pursuit of price stability. The index developed by Grilli, Masciandaro, and Tabellini measures "the final goals pursued by monetary authorities," coding central bank independence based on whether a central bank pursues the goal of low inflation (Grilli, Masciandaro, and Tabellini 1991: 357). An index developed by Cukierman combines the two methods by considering both the legal characteristics of central banks and the specific objectives pursued by monetary authorities (Cukierman 1992).

As Iversen has pointed out in a criticism of these measures, "central bank independence is neither a necessary nor a sufficient condition for a commitment to a conservative monetary policy" (Iversen 1999: 58) Even dependent central banks can establish credible commitments to nonaccommodating monetary policies, by participating in international monetary institutions, such as the European Monetary System (EMS). Alternatively, the policy intentions of the most conservative and independent central banks can also be defeated politically. This suggests that, under some conditions, existing indices measuring central bank independence may be unable to capture the parameter that is of theoretical interest in the model, namely, monetary nonaccommodation. To measure monetary

Table 2.2. *Measuring monetary nonaccommodation*

Country	Bade and Parkin	Grilli et al.	Cukierman	Iversen average
Austria		3	0.5806	0.52
Belgium	2	1	0.188	0.47
Canada	2	4	0.456	0.35
Denmark	2	3	0.449	0.42
Finland			0.235	0.38
France	2	2	0.337	0.39
Germany	4	6	0.657	0.60
Italy	1.5	4	0.232	0.29
Norway	2		0.115	0.40
Netherlands	2	6	0.422	0.54
Sweden		2	0.272	0.29
Switzerland	3	2	0.531	0.67
United Kingdom	2	1	0.308	0.15
United States	3	5	0.501	0.47

Sources:
Iversen 1999: 56, based on Bade and Parkin 1982, Grilli et. al 1991, and Cukierman 1992.

nonaccommodation more accurately, one needs to combine these legal and institutional measures with some measure of policy output of the monetary authorities.

Iversen's "monetary regime" index attempts to overcome these problems, by combining an institutional measure of central bank independence with a measure of actual policy outcomes. Iversen's index is constructed in two steps. First, he averages the most widely used indices of central bank independence, namely, those developed by Bade and Parkin (1982); Cukierman (1992); and Grilli, Masciandaro, and Tabellini (1991). Next, Iversen multiplies the resulting number with an index measuring relative movements in a currency. Lower values of the currency score reflect a relatively depreciating currency, while higher values reflect a currency that experiences a relative appreciation. The underlying justification for this additional step is that "credible domestic commitments to a nonaccommodating strategy will raise the medium to long-run confidence in the currency, while the reverse is true if domestic economic policies are perceived to be accommodating" (Iversen 1999: 59). Table 2.2 presents descriptive statistics on the most commonly used indices of central independence in the computation of the measure of monetary nonaccommodation. The final column of the table presents Iversen's monetary regime index. Switzerland takes the highest values on the monetary regime index (with a score of .67), followed by Germany (with a score of .60). By contrast, the countries with the most nonaccommodating monetary regimes are the United Kingdom (0.15), followed by Italy (0.29) and Sweden (0.29).

The Magnitude and Composition of Welfare State Commitments

The model developed in Chapter 1 suggests that the equilibrium level of unemployment depends not only on the structure of labor market institutions and the macroeconomic policy pursued by the government, but also on the level and composition of welfare state commitments. The process of welfare state maturation exerts "feedback effects" on the optimal wage choices made by unions and on the equilibrium level of employment. The political exchange of wage moderation for social policy expansion is more difficult to sustain in mature welfare states. As Chapter 1 hypothesizes, the significant causal variable is not the overall level of social policy expenditures but the distribution of welfare state commitments across programs. Given an equal level of taxes and aggregate spending, welfare states that devote a larger share of their benefits to labor market outsiders will hurt employment more than welfare states that devote a larger share of services and transfers to union members.

Developing empirical estimates of transfers received by labor market outsiders poses some challenges. To meet the definition of labor market outsiders presented in Chapter 1, two separate criteria have to be met. First, members of the group have to draw on some social policy benefits, such as long-term disability benefits, means-tested social assistance benefits, and unemployment benefits. The second criterion ascribing groups to these different categories is intrinsic to unions' choices. A labor market group can be classified as labor market insiders if unions are willing to forego increases in their wages and benefits in exchange for an increase in the benefits received by the group. In ideal terms, the identification of labor market insiders and outsiders also requires some information about the internal decision-making process within unions and the various criteria used by unions in their determination of wage policy choices. Systematic cross-national research that addresses these questions is only in its infancy.

While the precise distinction between labor market insiders and labor market outsiders is difficult to establish empirically, a second-best empirical strategy is nevertheless available. This strategy seeks to estimate the upper and lower bounds of the number of labor market outsiders. As an upper bound, one can consider persons who are currently employed or seeking employment to be labor market insiders and code the remaining part of the population as labor market outsiders. Under this coding rule, pensioners would be classified as labor market outsiders. Lower bound estimates, on the other hand, disaggregate the total number of outsiders into various subgroups, based on criteria such as age, duration of dependence on social policy benefits, and so on. A first distinction that can be made disaggregates total labor market outsiders into "demographic outsiders," on the one hand, and "labor market outsiders," on the other hand. The former are persons aged over 65, while the latter are persons who fulfill the age requirement for participation in the labor market (i.e., they are between 18 and 65 years of age), but who are not currently in the labor force.

Using this classification, I compute the following measures of transfers to outsiders. All these measures attempt to capture empirically the parameter *bm* of the model. The upper bound estimate is a measure of transfers going to all outsiders (*TRANSFERS TO ALL OUTSIDERS*) and is computed as follows. First, I have subtracted total employment and unemployment from the population and divided by total employment. Next, I have multiplied the resulting number by the level of pension expenditures. The main sources for constructing this variable have been OECD statistics.

The narrower, lower bound estimates of transfers to outsiders have been computed as follows. As an estimate of the transfers received by demographic outsiders (*TRANSFERS TO DEMOGRAPHIC OUTSIDERS*), I have computed the ratio of persons over age 65 to the total working age population and multiplied the resulting number by the level of pension expenditures.

In contrast to demographic outsiders, labor market outsiders are persons who fulfill the age requirement for participation in the labor market but are not in the labor force. This heterogeneous labor market group includes, among others, "discouraged workers" (who give up seeking employment) and early retirees, that is, workers aged less than 65 who are neither employed nor unemployed but are drawing on a combination of disability and unemployment benefits. As numerous studies have shown, over the last two decades, the number of early retirees has risen dramatically in many economies (Kohli et al. 2001; Mares 2003). The variable measuring transfers received by labor market outsiders (*TRANSFERS TO LABOR MARKET OUTSIDERS*) is computed as follows. I divide the number of persons aged between 18 and 65 who are neither employed nor unemployed to the working age population, and I multiply the resulting number by the level of expenditures on unemployment benefits.

The final hypothesis examined in this chapter explores the consequences of the growth in the level of taxes on the level of unemployment. In recent years, a number of empirical studies have examined this question. These studies differ in their specifications and in the scope of their empirical analyses. Nickell and Layard (1999) have examined the impact of the tax rate and a variety of additional policy measures on unemployment in OECD economies during the period between 1983 and 1994. Blanchard and Wolfers (2000) have also explored the employment effect of higher taxes, relying, however, on a different model specification that uses an average tax rate and interacts this measure with time-specific dummies. Finally, in a recent study, Daveri and Tabellini (2000) examined the impact of taxes on both unemployment and growth without exploring the impact of the governments' macroeconomic policy orientations. All studies concur in finding a positive relationship between taxes and the equilibrium level of unemployment.

To assess the consequences of the growth in taxes, I use a measure of the labor tax burden. Generally, the calculation of tax ratios poses immense methodological problems due to the complexity of the tax codes in most economies (Volkerink and de Haan 2000; Volkerink, Sturm, and de Haan 2001; Eurostat 1997). The most widely used measures of marginal effective tax rates have been developed by Mendoza, Razin, and Tesar (1994) and serve as the basis of tax measures used by the European Commission (1997) and the OECD (2000a, 2000b). The measure that is of interest to this study is the labor income tax ratio. Mendoza, Razin, and Tesar (1994) derive the latter in a two-step process. First, they define the personal income tax ratio ($T\ Per$) as the ratio of revenues from taxes on individuals' income, profits, and capital gains to the tax base. The latter consists of wages and salaries, the operating surplus of unincorporated enterprises, and the property and entrepreneurial income of households. The labor income tax ratio is defined as the product of the personal income tax ratio, wages and social security contributions, and taxes on payroll and workforce divided by the sum of wages and salaries and employers' social security contributions (Volkerink and de Haan 2000: 15). In other words,

$T\ Per$ = revenues from taxes on income, profits, and capital gains/wages + operating surplus + property and entrepreneurial income of households.

The Dependent Variable

Labor income tax ratio = $T\,Per * $ wages + total social security contributions + taxes on payroll and workforce/wages + employers' social security contributions.

To assess the impact of changes in taxes on employment, I use a time series that updates Mendoza et al's. (1994) measure. The series has been developed and generously provided by Tom Cusack of the Wissenschaftszentrum Berlin. To avoid potential endogeneity problems, I have lagged the tax measures by one period ($TAX\,RATE_{i,t-1}$).

The Dependent Variable: The Employment Performance of OECD Economies

The main goal of this study is to explain both cross-national and intertemporal variations in the employment performance of advanced industrialized democracies. I begin by displaying some simple cross-tabulations, which describe some of the patterns in the data. Table 0.1 presents data on unemployment in economies that feature different levels of wage bargaining coordination.[3] Countries with decentralized labor markets have a centralization score higher than 10 and include Canada, the United Kingdom, the United States, and France. Countries with a centralization score lower than 2.5 (Austria, Sweden, and Norway) are ranked as highly centralized. The remaining seven cases (Belgium, Denmark, Finland, Germany, Italy, The Netherlands, and Switzerland) are classified as intermediately centralized.[4] The figures in Table 0.1 provide initial support for the hypotheses of the model. The employment performance of economies with intermediately

---

[3] In recent years a number of authors have argued that the employment rate might be a better indicator of the overall labor market performance of an economy than the level of unemployment (Scharpf 1998: 125–6; John Stephens, personal communication). The justification for their objection to the use of unemployment as a dependent variable in cross-national research is that the actual level of unemployment can be hidden by various active labor market programs or by low labor force participation rates. The use of employment rates as an indicator of labor market performance, however, is in itself problematic. Cross-national variation in employment rates is primarily determined by variation in the labor force participation rates of women, which is a consequence of various social programs, such as the availability of child care. This variation is thus unrelated to actual labor market circumstances. As a result, despite its problems, unemployment remains a preferable indicator (Nickell 1997; Kenworthy 2002: 372).

[4] Denmark and Finland are, of course, borderline cases. For a discussion of "organizational fragmentation and the conflictual labour relations" in Finland, see Ebbinghaus and Visser (2000: 201).

centralized wage bargaining institutions is inferior to that of economies with either extremely centralized or extremely decentralized labor market institutions. While long-term unemployment has risen in all economies, those with intermediately centralized institutions of wage bargaining have experienced the strongest deterioration in economic performance: Average levels of unemployment rose by 1.67 percent in economies with highly centralized labor markets, by around 4 percent in economies with firm-level wage bargaining, and by 5.33 percent in economies with intermediately centralized wage bargaining institutions. This pattern provides preliminary support for the Calmfors-Driffill hypothesis of a hump-shaped relationship between wage bargaining system centralization and the equilibrium level of unemployment. It also provides support for the hypothesis of an upward shift in the Calmfors-Driffill curve, affecting all economies and not just economies with centralized wage bargaining institutions.

Regression Analysis

I test the implications of the model using pooled cross-sectional time series analysis. The data include 14 OECD countries for the period 1960–1995. Temporally, the sample size was limited by the availability of data on taxes (see Daveri and Tabellini 2000), while cross-nationally, it was limited by the availability of indicators necessary to construct the independent variables of interest. Adopting a recent approach to this type of analysis, I use ordinary least-squares (OLS) regression with lagged dependent variables and panel-corrected standard errors (Beck and Katz 1995). This is a superior estimation method to OLS, when the errors show three common problems: panel heteroskedasticity, contemporaneous correlation, and unit-specific serial correlation. Omitting all controls, the basic regression model estimating the impact of the degree of wage bargaining centralization, monetary policy, and existing welfare state commitments on unemployment is

$$U_{i,t} = a_i + b_1 U_{i,t-1} + b_2 CWB_i + b_3 CWB_i^2$$
$$+ b_4 TRANSFERS.TO.OUTSIDERS_{i,t-1}$$
$$+ b_5 MONETNONACC_i + TIMETREND + b_5 \varepsilon_{i,t},$$

where $U_{i,t}$ is the unemployment rate for country i at period t, CWB_i is the index measuring the level of centralization of the wage bargaining system, CWB_{it}^2 is its squared value, $TRANSFERS.TO.OUTSIDERS_{i,t-1}$ is a measure of social policy transfers to outsiders (lagged by one period), $MONETNONACC_i$ is a measure of the monetary nonaccommodation, and

$\varepsilon_{i,t}$ is an error term. The predictions about the impact of the structure of wage bargaining systems on the unemployment level imply that the signs of the coefficients b_2 and b_3 should be $+$ and $-$, respectively. All specifications also include a time trend (*TIMETREND*) that attempts to capture the effect of variables that are not directly observable but that are correlated with time and might affect the dependent variable. In the concluding section of this chapter, I examine the joint effect of higher taxes and higher transfers going to labor market outsiders on the level of unemployment.

In addition to the variables discussed previously, I also examine the impact of additional political and economic variables. Two additional political variables have been added as control measures. The first variable (*LEFT CAB*) is a measure of the percentage of cabinet seats held by left-wing parties as a percentage of all cabinet portfolios. The variable was developed by Swank, using data compiled by Browne and Dreijmanis and by Keesings' Contemporary Archives (Swank 2000). A vast body of research has shown that left-wing parties show more concern for unemployment than conservative parties, and the theoretical and empirical results are robust even under assumptions of rational expectations (Hibbs 1977, 1992; Alesina 1989). Thus, I expect a negative relationship between this variable and the equilibrium level of unemployment.

The second political control variable is a measure of the ideological position of various governments. This variable (*COGRAVITY*) is a measure of the "center of gravity of the government." It is computed by multiplying the share of seats of parties in the government with an expert ranking of their ideological positions. The "ideological scale" that positions various parties along a left–right dimension was constructed by Francis Castles and Peter Mair based on evaluations of the parties made by a panel of experts (1984: 83–8). The scale ranks from 5 (parties on the extreme right) to 1 (parties on the extreme left). Thus, low values for this variable denote the strong presence of left-wing parties in the government. As the summary presentation of the data reported in Table 2.3 shows, the variable takes the lowest values for Sweden (2.3) and Austria (2.4) and the highest values for the United States (3.6).

The additional economic controls test whether the deterioration in the employment performance of these economies can be attributed to higher levels of integration in capital and goods markets. The first variable (*OPEN*) measures trade exposure and is computed as the sum of exports and imports as a percentage of the GDP using data reported in the IMF International Financial Statistics. The second variable (*CAPFLOWS*) measures

Table 2.3. Descriptive statistics of explanatory variables

COUNTRY	UNEM	CWB	MONETNONACC	TAX RATE	TRANSFERS.TO OUTSIDERS	LEFT CAB	COGRAVITY	OPEN	CAPFLOWS
Austria	2.4	3.25	.52	38.14	0.38	67.9	2.4	65.9	13.60
Belgium	7.4	7.5	.47	40.10	1.26	30.6	2.9	108.1	46.21
Canada	7.6	12.75	.35	23.4	0.75		3.4	48.4	11.68
Denmark	6.1	4.125	.42	33.55	0.53	52.3	2.9	63.2	18.76
Finland	5.0	4.5	.38	28.8	0.13	37.4	2.7	52.5	14.29
France	5.4	10.75	.39	39.36	0.65	27.5	3.5	37.3	11.47
Germany	4.4	6.75	.60	36.95	0.50	34.2	3.2	51.5	10.79
Italy	7.9	9.25	.29	34.5	0.34	14.2	2.8	38.2	13.77
Norway	2.4	1.5	.40	38.55	0.06	66.3	2.5	81.9	18.66
Netherlands	5.3	7	.54	47.1	1.91	17.9	3	98.2	21.98
Sweden	2.4	2.625	.29	47.65	0.1	72.5	2.3	55.8	19.60
Switzerlands	0.7	8.75	.67	29.1	0.07	29.3	3.4	66.6	15.96
United Kingdom	6.4	10.875	.15	25.7	0.21	30.1	3.4	48.9	22.94
United States	6.1	13.25	.47	27.2	0.38		3.6	15.9	5.03
Mean	4.77	7.34	0.44	33.22	0.47	32.11	3.06	57.04	16.87
Standard Deviation	3.48	3.63	0.147	9.12	0.54	33.96	0.643	26.43	17.33

the exposure of an economy to capital movements. It is calculated as the percentage of cross-border capital flows of the GDP. One expects both measures to be positively associated with unemployment.

The empirical analysis will proceed as follows: I begin by estimating a series of models that examine the impact of various measures of transfers to labor market outsiders on the equilibrium level of employment, controlling for the structure of the wage bargaining system and monetary nonaccommodation. Next, I test the robustness of these initial findings in a fuller set of models that includes additional political and economic control variables. In a final set of models, I examine the joint effect of increases in the level of taxes and transfers to labor market outsiders on the level of unemployment.

The models reported in Table 2.4 examine the impact of transfers to labor market outsiders on unemployment, using the three different measures of transfers to outsiders discussed previously. The key hypothesis investigated in these regressions is whether changes in the transfers going to these labor market groups affect unions' wage demands in different ways, leading to different levels of unemployment. Model 1 examines the impact of transfers to all labor market outsiders on the level of unemployment while controlling for labor market institutions and the level of central bank independence. Models 2 and 3 explore the impact of transfers to labor market outsiders and demographic outsiders, respectively. To avoid potential endogeneity problems, all measures of transfers to labor market outsiders have been lagged by one period. The results of these analyses suggest that only increases in expenditures to labor market outsiders are associated with an increase in the level of unemployment that is statistically significant. By contrast, transfers to all outsiders and transfers to demographic outsiders have the predicted sign, but the variables fail to reach statistical significance at conventional levels. These findings suggest that unions approach labor market and demographic outsiders in different ways. This is consistent with results reported in qualitative studies analyzing linkages between pension reforms and unions' wage strategies that point to a higher willingness of unions to exercise wage moderation in response to higher transfers to demographic outsiders (Baccaro 1998; Lynch and Anderson 2004).

The results reported in Table 2.5 allow us to rule out the hypothesis that an increase in transfers to demographic outsiders is a factor accounting for the deterioration of the employment performance of OECD economies over this period. By contrast, the increase in benefits going to labor market outsiders has strained the political exchange between unions and

Table 2.4. *Who are the outsiders? Estimating the impact of transfers to labor market outsiders, demographic outsiders, and total number of outsiders on equilibrium level of unemployment*

Variables	Predicted sign	Regression estimates and standard errors		
		Model 1	Model 2	Model 3
CONSTANT		−4.16	−3.13	−2.21
		3.99	2.13	2.77
$UNEM_{i,t-1}$		0.85***	0.90***	0.75***
		0.09	0.12	0.15
CWB_i	+	0.51*	0.41**	0.45**
		0.28	0.17	0.22
CWB_i^2	−	−0.02**	−0.02**	−0.02**
		0.11	0.11	0.01
$MONETNONACC_i$	−	−1.14	−1.67**	−2.38**
		0.80	0.74	1.11
$TRANSFERS.TO.ALL.OUTSIDERS_{i,t-1}$	+	0.03		
		0.05		
$TRANSFERS.TO.DEMOGRAPHIC.OUTSIDERS_{i,t-1}$	+		0.22	
			0.72	
$TRANSFERS.TO.LABOR.MARKET.OUTSIDERS_{i,t-1}$				0.86***
				0.27
TIMETREND		0.47	0.37	0.33
		0.49	0.28	0.34
N		79	73	73
$Adj.R^2$		0.83	0.89	0.83

Note: ***$p < 0.01$, **$p < 0.05$, *$p < 0.1$. Period effects are included but not reported.

Table 2.5. *Estimation results for impact of labor market outsiders on equilibrium unemployment*

Variables	Predicted sign	Regression estimates and standard errors				
		Model 1	Model 2	Model 3	Model 4	Model 5
$CONSTANT$		-2.21	-1.95	-2.73	-2.72	-2.11
		2.77	2.93	2.56	2.72	2.85
$UNEM_{i,t-1}$		0.75***	0.74***	0.73***	0.79***	0.74***
		0.15	0.16	0.15	0.15	0.15
CWB_i	+	0.45**	0.45**	0.45**	0.44*	0.47**
		0.22	0.22	0.22	0.23	0.23
CWB_i^2	−	-0.02**	-0.02**	-0.02**	-0.02*	-0.02**
		0.01	0.01	0.01	0.01	0.01
$MONETNONACC_i$	−	-2.38**	-2.45**	-2.65**	-2.16*	-2.56*
		1.11	1.09	1.19	1.10	1.39
$TRANSFERS.TO.LABOR.MARKET.$ $OUTSIDERS_{i,t-1}$	+	0.86***	0.86***	0.91***	0.52*	0.96**
		0.27	0.26	0.31	0.31	0.41
$LEFTCAB_{i,t}$			-0.00			
			0.00			
$COGRAVITY_{i,t}$				0.28		
				0.49		
$OPEN_{i,t}$	−				0.08*	
					0.00	
$CAPFLOWS_{i,t}$						-0.00
						0.00
$TIMETREND$		0.33	0.33	0.32	0.30	0.33
		0.34	0.34	0.34	0.33	0.35
N		73	73	73	73	73
$Adj.R^2$		0.83	0.83	0.83	0.83	0.83

Note: ***p < 0.01; ** $p < 0.05$; * $p < 0.1$ Period effects are included but not reported.

governments. In models 2, 3, 4, and 5, I subject the initial results identifying a positive relationship between the increase in transfers to labor market outsiders and an increase in the level of unemployment to further empirical tests. Models 2 and 3 examine the additional impact of differences in the partisan composition of the government on the level of unemployment. Model 2 introduces the measure of participation of left-wing parties in government, while model 3 employs a measure of the ideological composition of the government. We expect a negative correlation between these measures of political partisanship and the level of unemployment. While the variable measuring the participation of left-wing parties in government has the predicted sign, it fails to reach statistical significance at conventional levels. By contrast, the ideological composition of government is positively correlated with unemployment but remains statistically insignificant. Models 4 and 5 examine the additional impact of changes in the level of trade and the openness of capital markets on the level of unemployment. An increase in the level of trade openness is positively associated with unemployment. By contrast, changes in the level of capital mobility have no impact on unemployment that is statistically different from zero.

To assess the magnitude of the impact of an increase in the number of labor market outsiders on the unemployment level, Figure 2.1 presents a simulation based on the regression results reported in Table 2.5. These results represent the predicted level of unemployment for high and low levels of expenditures on labor market outsiders. ("High" and "low" refer to the highest and lowest empirical values of the variable measuring transfers to labor market outsiders.) The results provide strong support for the theoretical hypothesis advanced in Chapter 1. First, they demonstrate the existence of a hump-shaped relationship between wage bargaining system centralization and the equilibrium level of unemployment. Economies with intermediately centralized wage bargaining systems have an employment performance inferior to that of economies with highly centralized or highly decentralized labor market institutions. Second, the results provide support for the hypothesis that an increase in the magnitude of transfers to labor market outsiders has adverse employment consequences, pushing the Calmfors-Driffill curve upward. A change in the variable measuring transfers to labor market outsiders from its average to its maximal value contributes to an increase in the equilibrium level of unemployment by 1.4 percent.

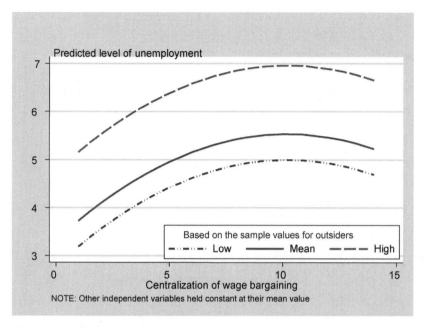

Figure 2.1. Impact of changes in transfers to labor market outsiders on equilibrium unemployment. (*Note*: Other independent variables held constant at their mean value.)

A final set of models reported in Table 2.6 examines the joint impact of tax increases and increases in the transfers going to labor market outsiders on the equilibrium level of unemployment. The results of the baseline model reported in the first column of Table 2.6 support the hypothesis suggesting that the deterioration in the employment performance of OECD economies can be attributed both to an increase in the tax burden and also to an increase in the level of transfers received by labor market outsiders. By contrast, an increase in the level of central bank independence has a positive impact on the equilibrium level of unemployment. As in the models reported in Table 2.5., we also find evidence that the impact of wage bargaining institutions on employment outcomes is U-shaped, whereby economies with intermediately centralized wage bargaining systems have the worst employment performance. The results of the initial model are robust to the introduction of additional political control variables. Surprisingly, none of the political control variables (the measure of left participation

Table 2.6. *Impact of growth in taxation and expenditures on labor market outsiders on equilibrium unemployment*

Variables	Predicted sign	Regression estimates and standard errors				
		Model 1	Model 2	Model 3	Model 4	Model 5
$CONSTANT$		-3.35	-3.38	-3.97	-3.67	-2.84
		2.68	2.73	2.72	2.92	2.92
$UNEM_{i,t-1}$		0.71***	0.70***	0.70***	0.72***	0.66***
		0.17	0.17	0.16	0.19	0.17
CWB_i	+	0.45**	0.44**	0.44**	0.44*	0.50**
		0.19	0.19	0.19	0.20	0.20
CWB_i^2	−	-0.02**	-0.02**	-0.02**	-0.02*	-0.02**
		0.00	0.00	0.00	0.01	0.01
$MONETNONACC_i$	−	-2.77**	-2.84**	-2.94**	-2.72*	-3.59*
		1.27	1.22	1.27	1.39	1.67
$TRANSFERS.TO.LABOR.MARKET.OUTSIDERS_{i,t-1}$	+	1.32**	1.30**	1.32**	1.24*	1.90***
		0.53	0.52	0.50	0.75	0.64
$TAXES_{i,t-1}$	+	0.03**	0.03**	0.03**	0.03*	0.02*
		0.01	0.01	0.01	0.01	0.01
$LEFTCAB_{i,t}$			-0.00			
			0.00			
$COGRAVITY_{i,t}$				0.20		
				0.46		
$OPEN_{i,t}$	−				0.00	
					0.00	
$CAPFLOWS_{i,t}$						-0.01
						0.00
$TIMETREND$		0.35	0.35	0.34	0.35	0.40
		0.30	0.30	0.31	0.30	0.31
N		71	71	71	71	71
$Adj.R^2$		0.85	0.85	0.85	0.85	0.85

Note: ***p < 0.01; **p < 0.05; *p < 0.1. Period effects are included, but not reported.

Conclusions

Table 2.7. *Simulation results of Model 1, Table 2.6*

		Centralization of wage bargaining		
		1.5 (Norway)	7.34 (Netherlands)	13.25 (United States)
Welfare effort and tax rate	Low transfers to outsiders; low taxes	3.22	4.46	4.89
	Mean transfers to outsiders; mean taxes	4.30	5.54	5.90
	High transfers to outsiders; high taxes	7.80	9.04	9.47

in government and of the ideological composition of the government) has a significant impact on unemployment. Models 4 and 5 control for the effect of changes in the level of trade and capital flows, respectively, but find no effect of these variables that is statistically different from zero.

Using *Clarify*, I simulate the effect of an increase in the tax rates on the equilibrium level of unemployment in economies characterized by different levels of wage bargaining system centralization. The results are presented in Table 2.7. Both the variable measuring the level of transfers to labor market outsiders and the tax measure have a log-normal distribution. I report the results for the mean value and for the highest and lowest values in the sample, respectively. Holding all other variables at their mean level, an increase in the average tax rate and in the level of expenditures on labor market outsiders lead to a 3.5 percent increase in the equilibrium level of unemployment.

Conclusions

The empirical results presented in this chapter support the theoretical hypotheses of the model developed in Chapter 1. In agreement with earlier studies, we find that both labor market institutions and monetary policy have an effect on the equilibrium level of unemployment. The results also support the central explanation advanced in this book that the process of welfare state maturation constrains the effectiveness of the political exchange between unions and governments and accounts, in part, for the deterioration of the employment performance of most European economies. Both an increase in the tax rate and an increase in the policy expenditures received by labor market outsiders are positively correlated with higher levels of unemployment. This suggests that the growth in the size of the tax burden and a change in the composition of social policy commitments to outsiders exerted feedback effects and posed important constraints on the behavior of wage bargaining agents. The following three chapters will test these predictions of the model, by examining the strategies made by unions given different combinations of social policy taxes and transfers.

3

Sweden

The Swedish economy is the paradigmatic corporatist economy. There is very little disagreement in existing scholarship about this characterization and the position of the Swedish wage bargaining system vis-à-vis those of other countries. Most scholars place Sweden at the top of the corporatist scale. Two features of the wage bargaining system account for its high values on the corporatism score: First, for much of the postwar period, the wage setting process in Sweden was extremely centralized; second, Sweden has the highest levels of density for both labor and employer organizations.

Sweden shares high values for existing indicators of corporatism with other northern European countries, including Denmark, Norway, and Finland. An important difference in labor market institutions between Sweden and these economies is the lower level of state involvement in wage bargaining negotiations (Elvander 1979, 1983). Sweden has boasted a strong historical tradition of independence in the wage bargaining process that is jealously guarded by both unions and employers (Edgren, Faxen, and Odhner 1973: 29). In 1953, the Swedish trade union confederation, Landsorganisationen i Sverige (LO), argued that "there are few countries where the principle of state nonintervention in the affair of the trade unions is as deep-rooted as in Sweden" (LO 1953: 88). While recent wage bargaining rounds mark an interesting deviation from this norm, it is too early to assess whether they have brought about a permanent change in the dynamics of the wage setting process. The tradition of wage bargaining independence has precluded the imposition of income policy packages on labor market actors by the Swedish state (Elvander 1983). However, it did not preclude the emergence of wage restraint in exchange for the expansion of social policy benefits as an equilibrium strategy of the labor movement. As the model developed in Chapter 1 has demonstrated unions can choose to moderate their wage demands in response to advances in social transfers or services even without the direct involvement of the state in the wage bargaining process.

This chapter presents a succinct narrative of wage developments in Sweden during the postwar period. I test the key predictions of the theoretical model formulated in Chapter 1 by examining the wage choices made by unions given different levels of both social policy transfers and taxes. I consider when and why unions were willing to exert moderation on the wage front in exchange for social policy programs, what additional policy instruments facilitated this moderation, what social policies were most important for trade unions and most conducive to wage moderation, and in what ways the process of welfare state maturation constrained both unions' ability to pursue wage moderation and the effects of wage restraint on employment. This chapter draws on an extensive secondary literature examining the Swedish labor movement (Johnston 1962; Edgren et al. 1973; Elvander 1988, 1990; Martin 1984, 1985; Swenson 1989; Pontusson 1992). To provide clarification of the range of policy choices faced by unions during critical political moments, I have supplemented these secondary accounts with primary union publications and government documents.

Policy Developments in the Immediate Postwar Years

During the first years of the postwar period, the government led by the Social Democratic Party (Sveriges Socialdemokratiska Arbetarepartiet, or SAP) addressed numerous appeals for wage moderation to the labor movement (Johnston 1962). These exhortations were backed up by a broad array of policy instruments that included price controls, tax reform, and the expansion of social protection.

Price controls had been created during the wartime period and was an important instrument guaranteeing to unions that their moderation would not translate into higher prices and hence higher profit margins for employers (Martin 1984: 202; Johnston 1962: 279). The Price Control Board, which was established in 1942, provided this guarantee by systematically rejecting price increases from a variety of large and small firms. In implementing its policies, the Price Control Board also remained responsive to unions' concern for wage equality. Policies were not uniformly imposed on all firms but were rather implemented in a discretionary manner, and the authorities granted exemptions from the general price freeze to firms that employed low-wage workers when the LO supported their applications

(LO 1953: 52). Additional policy instruments by which the government attempted to stabilize the level of income and prices were policies that limited the payment of dividends by joint-stock companies (LO 1953). Finally, tax policy remained an important instrument by which the government tried to elicit the cooperation of unions. The tax reform enacted in 1947 reduced income taxes in low-income brackets, raised the marginal tax rate for higher incomes, and introduced an inheritance tax. All these changes responded to the egalitarian objectives pursued by the labor movement and were actively supported by the LO (Elvander 1983: 344–5, 1972).

But the most decisive inducement to trade unions to accept a policy of wage moderation came in the form of expansion of the scope of social policy transfers. The central institutional pillars of the Swedish welfare state were enacted between 1946 and 1947, a period known as the Social Democratic "Harvest Time" (Immergut 1992: 203). During this period, old means-tested policies were replaced by universalistic social policies. In 1946 and 1947, three major reforms were enacted that introduced general child allowances, sickness cash benefits, and a basic pension (Olsson 1990: 116). Additional legislation established the National Housing Board as the central authority providing subsidized loans and rent controls. The National Labor Market Board was also created to coordinate the nationalized local employment offices and supervise the union-controlled but state-subsidized unemployment insurance funds (Olsson 1990: 119). A proposal to introduce flat-rate sickness benefits – known as the Höjer reform – was defeated, however, due in large part to the strong opposition of the LO (Huber and Stephens 2001: 120; Immergut 1992: 208). This gap in social protection was closed in 1955 when medical insurance that provided earnings-related benefits was introduced.

The combination of price controls, tax policy favorable to unions, and the expansion of social policy benefits facilitated the wage moderation of the labor movement in the immediate postwar period (Johnston 1962: 276–81; Hadenius 1976: 72–75). In some cases, individual unions voluntarily agreed to forego pay increases to which they were entitled. This was the case with civil servants, who voluntarily renounced a 3 percent salary increase designed to compensate them for an increase in the cost of living (Johnston 1962: 280). In other instances, individual unions followed the recommendations for moderation made by the central leadership of the LO. The representative body of the LO recommended that "affiliated unions should exercise great restraint in their wage claims" (LO 1953; Johnston 1962: 280) and pressured affiliated unions both to accept a freeze on wage rates and to extend existing contracts for one year "on the condition that employers are forced by price controls to meet cost increases out of current profit margins" (Martin 1984: 202).

Compliance with this policy resulted in a wage freeze that was in effect between 1949 and 1950. Individual contractual increases were not permitted during this period. Local labor shortages and the desire of some employers to introduce improvements in the organization of work led to wage drift, however, which averaged around 3.5 percent during the period of the wage freeze (LO 1953: 56). In 1950, the central leadership of the Swedish Employers' Federation (Svenska Arbetsgivareföreningen, or SAF) and the LO agreed to reopen negotiations regarding adjustments for the increase in the cost of living. Individual unions decided not to make use of this option, however, and the wage freeze remained in effect for an additional year.

The wage freeze that was in effect between 1949 and 1950 was followed by an uneven and "chaotic" development in wages in 1951 (Johnston 1962: 281; LO 1953; Martin 1984; Lindbeck 1975: 70). While LO leaders reluctantly endorsed the recommendation of the government to continue the wage freeze, by this time individual trade unions were unwilling to go along with its recommendation. As an LO publication characterized the mood of individual trade unions during that period, "Nobody believed in any kind of centralization of negotiations for the 1951 agreements. It had been stated all the time that the prolongation was an exceptional measure which could not be repeated a third time and that everybody would be at liberty to make their own arrangements" (LO 1953).

Several developments account for the disintegration of the consensus behind wage moderation. In macroeconomic terms, the Korean War fueled an unexpected increase in the price level (Edgren et al. 1973: 30). The second cause was the uneven distribution of the costs of wage moderation among individual unions, which led to increased inequality among different sectors: State employees and workers in industries that faced difficulties as a result of the increase in import prices experienced a relative deterioration in their earnings during the period of the wage freeze. Employees in industries with a flexible wage system that offered piece rates, by contrast, who were able to obtain wage increases that exceeded the standard rate, had experienced an improvement in their relative wages. In 1951, both groups expressed dissatisfaction with the centrally imposed wage freeze, the former seeking compensation for their distributional setbacks and the latter out of the conviction that employers could actually afford even higher wages. As a result, individual unions were able to negotiate wage increases ranging between 10 and 25 percent, with an average of 15 percent (LO 1953). In real terms, the average wage of industrial workers rose by 7.5 percent in 1951.

The wage explosion of 1951 had far-reaching consequences for the evolution of the wage bargaining system. By demonstrating the negative consequences of interunion rivalry, this episode set the stage for the further centralization of the wage bargaining system in the following decade.

The Rehn-Meidner Model

Within the labor movement, sustained policy debates concerning the importance of unions' wage moderation in an economy committed to the principle of full employment took place at the beginning of the 1950s (Martin 1984: 204). The policy document *Trade Unions and Full Employment*, adopted at the 1951 LO Congress, summarizes these debates (LO 1953). An important issue under discussion was the question about the conditions under which unions should commit themselves to a policy of wage restraint to counteract the negative inflationary consequences that could result from an increase in aggregate demand. The LO rejected the idea that unions had an "unconditional responsibility for the preservation of national economic stability." Such an unqualified commitment to wage restraint was undesirable for two reasons: On the one hand, unions were skeptical about the extent to which a policy of wage moderation could prevent wage drift, which would inevitably result from competition for scarce labor; on the other hand, unions worried that an unreserved commitment to restraint might be detrimental to the organizational capability of the labor movement in the long run. "The acceptance of the 'permanent-restraint-line' would basically alter the duties of trade union organizations," the LO explained; "from having been organizations to defend the economic interests of a specific group, they would be changed into bodies for the purpose of adapting wages policy to the general economic policy" (LO 1953: 87). This development, the LO thought, could create an "overwhelming strain within the trade union movement" (LO 1953: 87).

In *Trade Unions and Full Employment*, the LO formulated an alternative to an unconditional commitment to wage moderation. As Gøsta Rehn, one of the architects of the plan, argued, the policy marked a "conscious break with the oversimplified form of Keynesianism" (Martin 1984: 208). In the view of unions, responsibility for the preservation of full employment rested with the state. But an important distinction had to be made between "general fiscal policy" and more targeted, selective manpower policies (LO 1953; Fulcher 1991: 191). With respect to the former, the LO recommended that the state pursue a more restrained fiscal policy than it had in the immediate postwar years. Instruments such as indirect taxes could ensure the required fiscal restrictiveness. By constraining the room for price increases available to firms, indirect taxes would also shift the burden of restraining wages back to employers (Martin 1984: 205). LO leaders realized, however, that such restrictive fiscal policies would have an uneven effect on different firms and sectors, placing a higher burden on the least profitable firms. To avoid a rise in unemployment, restrictive policies had to be complemented with "selective" compensatory measures directed at the less profitable sectors. In the words of Rudolf Meidner, "selective increases of expenditure" had to be "either directed to those points in the economy where the risk of creation [of] inflationary shortages was the most remote or where an effort to promote adaptation could improve the supply-demand relation" (Meidner 1969: 178). The mix of restrained fiscal policy and selective compensatory policies would, it was hoped, both guarantee noninflationary full employment and reduce the pressure on unions to provide an unconditional commitment to wage moderation.

Beginning with the 1922 LO Congress, the Swedish trade union movement had expressed its support for a solidaristic wage policy that would reduce income differentials between occupations (Fulcher 1991). This support for a policy reducing income differentials between occupations was reaffirmed at the 1951 LO Congress. *Trade Unions and Full Employment* placed particular emphasis on the elimination of wage differentials that were not due to differences in the degree of job difficulty or to employee performance. Wage equality meant, thus, the achievement of "equal pay for equal work" (LO 1953; Edgren et al. 1973: 41). What distinguished the policy proposals of the 1950s from earlier formulations was their concern about the complementary labor and social policies necessary to sustain the movement's solidaristic wage policy. Solidaristic wage policies had a differential impact on firms, squeezing firms with lower profitability harder. As a union publication put it, "The wage policy of solidarity put the 'worst' firms under the most severe pressure and they must choose between rapid rationalization or going to the wall" (Öhman 1974: 34). To avoid an increase in unemployment and other economic imbalances, additional policy interventions were necessary. For unions, the most important complement to solidaristic wage policies was active labor market policies.

As Gøsta Rehn referred to this complementarity, "Labor market policy was the next great social policy reform" (Öhman 1974: 34). Active labor market policies would aim to "stimulate labor market mobility" and facilitate the movement of labor from declining to expanding industries (Öhman 1974: 48).

Deliberations at the 1951 LO Congress also underscored the importance of housing policies to the Swedish labor movement. The demand for increased investment in the construction of housing and for higher public subsidies devoted to this goal, expressed in a number of motions, was motivated in part by housing shortages (LO 1951). But an additional motivation for these demands was the concern that the absence of a satisfactory supply of houses hampered the process of economic modernization and labor market adjustment. Workers might be unwilling to move from declining to prosperous economic areas if housing arrangements in the latter were inadequate. Thus, unions regarded housing policies as complementary to active labor market policies and solidaristic wage policies. Their goal was to "facilitate and speed up structural change" and "to encourage the concentration of industry in the expanding areas of the country" (Öhman 1974: 39).

In institutional terms, the Swedish wage bargaining system remained relatively decentralized at the beginning of the 1950s. Wages were determined at the industry level in negotiations between individual unions and employers' associations. Some informal coordination was also in place: Agreements reached in the metalworking industry became the norm for other industries. What distinguished Sweden from other economies with industry-level wage setting institutions was the "regularity and simultaneity of the agreement periods and the sequence of negotiations" (Edgren et al. 1973: 52). In the 1950s, movements toward greater centralization and coordination were followed by reversals toward industry-level wage setting as individual unions resisted the delegation of authority to the LO executive. Centralization was greatest during the 1952 and 1956 wage bargaining rounds. In 1952, the LO executive attempted to "ensure wage restraint [and] economic stabilization" in the wake of the 1951 disaster (Swenson 1989: 132; Johnston 1962). During that year, the LO and the SAF carried out the first coordinated negotiations of the postwar period. In 1956, the centralization was brought about by Swedish employers' decision to initiate joint simultaneous negotiations with all labor market organizations "to avoid a race between them" (Edgren et al. 1973: 53). The 1953 wage bargaining round, by contrast, was much more decentralized, with wages determined by individual unions.

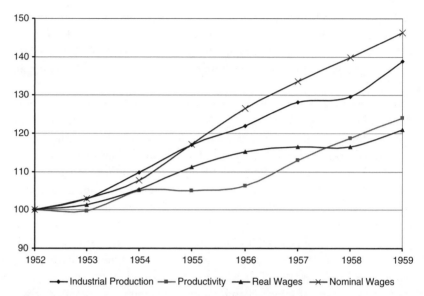

Figure 3.1. Sweden: Wages, output, and productivity, 1952–1959. (*Sources:* Sweden. Statistical Office, *Statistical Yearbook of Sweden*, various years; Martin 1984; and U.S. Bureau of Labor Statistics, *Handbook of Labor Statistics*, various years.)

The absence of a centralized arena for the resolution of wage settlements created important obstacles to the ability of unions to pursue a solidaristic wage policy. Though the LO had officially adopted the Rehn-Meidner model as a template for the wage demands of the labor movement at the 1951 Congress, this adoption was "by no means a clear policy mandate with respect to solidaristic wage policy or with regard to economic policy," as Swenson (1989: 132) has pointed out. In the first years following the adoption of the Rehn-Meidner model, strong opposition from high-paid unions such as Metall, the metalworkers' union, further prevented the implementation of a solidaristic wage policy (Swenson 1989: 132). As a result, the wage agreements of the period contained only a few sporadic provisions aimed at the equalization of wages. Even the two highly centralized agreements of 1952 and 1956 contained almost no policies for low-wage groups (Edgren et al. 1973: 42).

The descriptive statistics of the evolution of wages, productivity, and output for the 1952–1960 period presented in Figure 3.1 suggest several interesting conclusions. If we take the gap between the growth in real wages and the growth in productivity as a measure of wage moderation, we observe several turning points in the wage behavior of the Swedish labor movement in this period. The 1952 wage bargaining round, which was characterized by a high level of wage bargaining centralization, yielded rather moderate wage increases. By contrast, in the period between 1954 and 1957, real wage growth exceeded productivity growth. The absence of moderation was particularly pronounced during 1955 and 1956, years characterized by intense political conflict between trade unions and the Social Democratic Party. This pattern was reversed during the second half of the decade, which saw significant wage restraint. One factor that contributed to the higher level of wage moderation in the second half of the decade was the increase in wage bargaining centralization; another was the stronger political commitment of the Social Democratic Party to the Rehn-Meidner model. As a consequence of the SAP policy shift, policies and programs that were critical preconditions for the success of the Rehn-Meidner model, such as labor market policies and housing policies, experienced a strong expansion.

The 1955 wage bargaining round was notable for the significant militancy of the labor movement (Johnston 1962; Martin 1984). Unions obtained contractual wage increases that averaged 5.1 percent, which exceeded the average productivity growth of the Swedish economy. At the root of the wage explosion was a political disagreement between unions and the Social Democratic Party. This conflict erupted as the central leadership of the LO refused to accommodate the finance minister's call for wage moderation. In a speech to the parliament, LO chairman Axel Strand argued that the government was trying to shift too much of the burden of adjustment of its expansive economic policy onto unions (Martin 1984: 208; Hadenius 1976: 85). The argument echoed the position expressed by the LO in *Trade Unions and Full Employment*. Social Democratic Party leaders retracted and convened a conference to bring about a closer alignment in the policy positions of unions and the party. During this conference, Tage Erlander, the SAP leader and prime minister, "took the occasion to declare his own conversion to the LO position, particularly the selective manpower policy which he understood as the heart of it" (Martin 1984: 212).

The SAP's acceptance of the basic premises of the Rehn-Meidner model in the mid-1950s led to an expansion of policy instruments that complemented unions' solidaristic wage policy. One of these instruments was housing policy. During the early 1950s, the government had been unable to meet the annual target of 60,000–75,000 new apartments per year outlined by the Social Housing Commission. Until 1955, production of new housing

Figure 3.2. Expenditures on active labor market policies, 1947–1960. (*Source:* Öhman 1974: 80.)

stood at about 40,000 new apartments per year, a figure that was lower than the prewar high (Davidson 1994: 105). The rate of development of new houses accelerated significantly toward the end of the decade, however, fueled in part by an infusion of money from the rapidly growing general pension fund. During the late 1950s, the development of new houses stood at 75,000 per year (Davidson 1994).

Active labor market policies also expanded significantly in the second half of the decade. Figure 3.2 presents the evolution of expenditures on active labor market policies between 1947 and 1960. During the early 1950s, these expenditures grew at a relatively slow rate due both to the opposition of the Agrarian Party (the junior coalition party of the SAP) to these programs and to considerable skepticism among key Social Democratic Party policy makers about the Rehn-Meidner model (Pontusson 1992: 64–5; Martin 1984: 211–13). Dramatic expansion of active labor market policies took place only during the second half of the decade, following the acceptance of the Rehn-Meidner model by the SAP. In current prices, total expenditures on active labor market policies stood in 1957 at 196.5 million kroner, or 1.6 percent of total government expenditures; in 1959, they reached 504 million kroner, or 3.6 percent of government expenditures, an increase in excess of 150 percent (Johannesson 1981: 76).

After a long political struggle, the Swedish Social Democratic Party enacted the supplementary pension system, or the ATP system, in 1959. The reform fulfilled two important, long-standing desiderata of the trade union movement. First, it corrected some of the inadequacies of the universalistic policy that had been introduced in 1946. While the 1946 policy had provided benefits to all citizens, benefit levels remained quite meager and failed to address the risk of poverty during old age. At the time the ATP reform was introduced, the basic pension level for a single person stood at 4,200 kroner a year, which represented about 20 percent of the average wage of an industrial worker (Olsson 1990: 157). The introduction of a mandatory second-tier pension dramatically improved old-age benefits. In combination, the two pension systems provided an average retirement income equivalent to two-thirds of the highest 15-year average income from earnings.

The second-tier pension system also served as a "mechanism for collective savings" – in other words, as an instrument that could supply capital to those policies that were important priorities for the labor movement. As Pontusson has shown, "the idea of using the ATP system as a mechanism for collective saving thus fits very well within the logic of the Rehn-Meidner model, which advocated squeezing corporate profits through a combination of tight fiscal policy and wage solidarity" (Pontusson 1992: 79–80). During the first decades of its existence, the ATP system accumulated a large surplus, which was supplied as credit to the central and local government, to the development of housing, and to other private sectors. Housing policies were the largest beneficiary of this influx of capital, receiving around 45 percent of the total funds lent during the following decade (Pontusson 1992: 79–80).

Analysis of the wage and social policy developments of the 1950s provides support for several hypotheses advanced in this study. Unions' wage moderation was significantly higher in the period after 1957 than in the first half of the decade. An important causal variable accounting for this development was a change in the institutional structure of the wage bargaining system that led to an increase in the level of coordination among different unions over the decade. A second factor was the massive expansion of policies and programs regarded by the LO as vital complements to the Rehn-Meidner model. Active labor market policies, housing policies, and

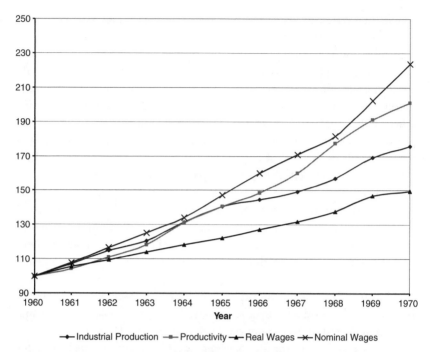

Figure 3.3. Sweden: Wages, output, and productivity, 1960–1970. (*Sources:* Statistical Office, *Statistical Yearbook of Sweden*, various years; Martin 1984; and U.S. Bureau of Labor Statistics, *Handbook of Labor Statistics*, various years.)

the ATP reform provided support for the labor movement's pursuit of a solidaristic wage policy.

Wage and Social Policy Developments of the 1960s

During the 1960s, wage bargaining negotiations in Sweden yielded very moderate wage settlements. Figure 3.3 presents these developments. Negotiated wage increases lagged significantly behind growth in productivity. Given unions' pursuit of a solidaristic wage policy, these aggregate figures underestimate wage moderation in the dynamic export sectors (and overestimate the gap between wage and productivity growth in the sheltered domestic sectors). An additional indicator of wage moderation is the persistence of a very high number of unfilled jobs in relation to the unemployment level, which demonstrates that unions did not take advantage of persistent labor market shortages to raise the wages of workers in short supply (Flanagan, Soskice, and Ulman 1983: 302). Unit labor costs also rose only very slowly in this period, a development that stands in sharp contrast to subsequent decades. While the index of productivity increased by 100 percent, unit labor costs increased by only 37 percent. Thus, in retrospect, the Swedish economy experienced its best economic performance during the 1960s. As Pontusson argues, "if we take into account the rate of productivity growth, the development of labor costs was considerably more favorable to business in Sweden than in any other Nordic country from 1960 to 1973" (Pontusson 1992: 102).

The model formulated in Chapter 1 hypothesizes that two factors facilitate a sustained policy of wage moderation: centralization of the wage bargaining system and growth in transfers and services to union members. A change of both variables in the predicted direction contributed to Sweden's extraordinary wage restraint in the 1960s. First, a number of institutional reforms introduced at the beginning of the decade facilitated the increased centralization of the Swedish wage bargaining system. A constitutional change enacted in 1961 empowered the LO executive to carry out central wage negotiations (Fulcher 1991: 189; Victorin 1975: 74). It is important to point out that centralization in the hands of the LO executive was not absolute, as individual unions retained the rights to reject the recommendations of the LO executive and to formulate alternative wage proposals. Reflecting on the impact of wage bargaining system centralization on the wage demands of Swedish unions, a report of leading economists from all labor market organizations (including employers) commended unions for their ability to "internalize" the adverse consequences of wage militancy:

The primary task of the unions is to negotiate as large a share of the production result as possible for their members. But with the strength that these organizations have nowadays in Sweden, they must sense a responsibility for the economy which goes far beyond this primary task. It is true that they have often been accused of demanding too much in wage negotiations and, consequently, of having caused price increases....But in negotiations the unions have been aware of the risk of making such heavy inroads into profitability that the basis for future development in business enterprises deteriorates. The negotiators have long ago become aware of the existence of a point beyond which no claim should be pushed lest it impairs the prospects for future wage increases. (Edgren et al. 1973: 222–3)

Massive expansion in the size of the welfare state served as a second source of wage moderation. Total government expenditures as a percentage of the GDP increased from 30 percent in 1960 to 44.3 percent in 1970, while total social policy expenditures rose from 15.8 percent of the GDP in 1960 to 24.9 percent in 1970 (Flora and Alber 1983: 428). Both the consolidation of existing policies and the development of new programs spurred the growth of expenditures. Developments in health services serve as an example of how existing policies were broadened and deepened: The construction of new hospitals, greater investment in the health care sector, and an increase in the number of medical personnel led to a particularly sharp increase in expenditures on health services in the 1960s (Sweden Ministry of Finance 1966: 188). New programs were introduced in such areas as family and labor market policy: In 1962, Sweden introduced a maternity allowance that provided a 6-month period of paid leave to new mothers (Burtless 1987: 200); meanwhile, the National Labor Market Board added new labor market programs, including training services, mobility allowances, educational allowances for retraining, and employment creation schemes (Olsson 1990: 133).

An examination of changes in the eligibility conditions for and the generosity level of existing benefits also demonstrates significant increases in the social wage during the 1960s. Policies providing benefits in case of sickness were significantly improved. The number of waiting days was lowered, and the average replacement rate was raised to 80 percent of lost earnings (Burtless 1987: 200). Unemployment benefits were also progressively raised, and, as a result of a reform enacted in 1968, the maximum duration of unemployment benefits was increased from 30 to 60 weeks (Burtless 1987: 197). Such improved transfers and services were financed by higher levels of taxes. While in 1960 the marginal payroll tax was 3.4 percent of wages, it increased to 11.7 percent in 1969. Another important source of taxation for many policies was the value-added tax, which increased from 4.3 percent in 1960 to 11.1 percent in 1969 (Aronsson and Walker 1995: 256–7).

Throughout the 1960s, trade unions struggled to find the optimal wage response to these higher levels of taxation, which presented a distributionally divisive problem for the labor movement. The LO proposed that unions should not seek wage increases to compensate for income lost to taxes. It justified this call for wage moderation by arguing that "the social services paid by the taxes were part of the increase in living standards enjoyed by workers" (Martin 1984: 240). Econometric evidence presented by Bertil Holmlund shows that some of the tax increases of the period were shifted back to labor in the form of lower wages (Holmlund 1983). The Swedish Confederation of Professional Employees (Tjänstemännens Centralorganisation, or TCO) joined the LO in rejecting the requests of more militant members for wage increases proportional to the income lost to taxes. The two unions differed, however, in their position regarding the optimal level of taxes, with the TCO advocating a reduction of marginal tax rates (Martin 1984: 240). During the second half of the 1960s, the position of the LO and the TCO came under intense challenge from other unions. The Swedish Confederation of Professional Associations (Sveriges Akademikers Centralorganisation, or SACO) defended the alternative position on this policy trade-off, arguing that unions should respond to the increase in the tax burden with a more aggressive wage policy. The white-collar workers who were represented by SACO faced a much higher sensitivity to higher tax rates than blue-collar workers and were consequently less willing to adopt the policy of wage restraint advocated by the LO.

This policy disagreement turned into an open political conflict during the 1966 bargaining round. At the time, negotiations between the LO and the SAF were especially divisive and were concluded only after the intervention of the mediation commission. These negotiations culminated in a 3-year agreement that yielded wage increases of 4.3, 3.5, and 2.9 percent, respectively (Martin 1984: 239). Policy developments were complicated by the decision of unions representing white-collar workers to break with the tradition of coordinated bargaining established by the LO and the SAF and to negotiate independent wage settlements. An important policy demand of these white-collar unions was for compensation for the income lost to higher taxes, precisely the issue that had been opposed by the LO (Flanagan et al. 1983: 339). As Martin argues, "SACO took the position that its members were entitled to compensation for earnings foregone while they acquired their higher education, using 'lifetime earnings' as a basis for comparison, and also for the effects of income taxation" (Martin 1984: 240). "These effects were greater for its members, it argued, because their higher nominal incomes were subjected to higher marginal tax rates, further diminishing the real effects of nominal increases already eroded by inflation" (Martin 1984: 240). After a long and bitter strike, the white-collar unions succeeded in obtaining wage increases that exceeded the settlements negotiated by the LO by 20 percent. This was a stunning, unprecedented defeat for the LO.

The LO considered two alternative strategies as potential responses to this major political crisis. The first was to turn to the state and involve the government in the interunion conflict about appropriate wage policy. Proponents of this strategy argued that unions' choices were inextricably linked to policies pursued by the state regarding taxation, social transfers, and public employment (Martin 1984: 240). Arne Geijer, the chairman of the LO, was one advocate of the turn to a state-led incomes policy. At the 1967 SAP Congress, Geijer argued that "the achievement of greater equality in Sweden might not be possible without sacrificing the tradition of collective bargaining without state intervention, implying that it would require a state-led incomes policy" (Martin 1984: 241). The alternative was to maintain the independence of the wage setting process but to increase coordination among the various unions. Proponents of this strategy prevailed. An investigative commission that included representatives of all major trade union organizations as well as employers was established to provide recommendations about the criteria that should guide the determination of wages. This commission was known as the EFO group, based on the initials of the top researchers in the major organizations: Gøsta Edgren (TCO), Karl-Olof Faxen (SAF), and Clas-Erik Odhner (LO). The commission argued that the competitive position of Sweden's economy could be maintained only if the export sector assumed the role of wage leader. Thus, the constraints facing this sector, which resulted from both productivity developments and changes in the international price level, set an upper bound to wage increases for all unions, not just unions in the export sector (Edgren et al. 1973: 113). While the report identified a limit to wage increases that could be observed by all wage bargaining partners, it established no guidelines regarding how gains resulting from productivity increases should be divided between unions and firms (Scharpf 1991: 96).

During the ensuing bargaining round, the LO attempted to implement the recommendations of the EFO report. To solve the outstanding disagreements between white- and blue-collar unions concerning the appropriate wage differentiation between these sectors, the LO's chief negotiators decided to delay the conclusion of the wage settlements and push the decision to the mediation commission (Martin 1984: 246). This strategy was only partially successful. Several unions representing private-sector white-collar workers – such as SIF (the Union of Clerical Employees in private industry), SALF (the Union of Foremen and Supervisors), and CF (the union of civil engineers) – successfully concluded individual agreements with employers at the outset of the bargaining round (Flanagan et al. 1983: 339; Fulcher 1991: 207). The LO succeeded, however, in achieving co-ordination between the wage settlements of the remaining public- and private-sector unions. The three-year wage agreements concluded in 1969 yielded relatively low levels of wage increases while guaranteeing very similar levels of wage growth in the public and private sectors. During these years, negotiated wage growth lagged behind growth in productivity.

Individual workers perceived the level of restraint as excessive, however, and in the wake of the 1969 agreements the Swedish economy was swept by an unprecedented number of wildcat strikes (Korpi 1981; Fulcher 1991). In 1970, Sweden lost over 150,000 working days to strikes, a figure that represented a 330 percent increase over 1968. The strikes began in firms in the metalworking industry, such as ship-building, but quickly spread to other sectors. To many observers, this strike wave seemed to challenge the core practices underpinning centralized wage bargaining and to signal an end to the harmonious "Saltsjøbaden spirit" in industrial relations (Fulcher 1991: 204). Several factors account for the explosion of militancy. As suggested, the most significant factor was frustration with the wage settlements (Pontusson 1992: 196). In a survey of strikers conducted by Metall, 74 percent of the respondents listed concerns about wages and earnings as their primary reason for striking (Korpi 1981: 364). High levels of wage drift demonstrated to many workers that unions had failed to capture an adequate share of firms' profits. An additional source of discontent was frustration with the fiscal policy of the government, perceived by unions as excessively austere and poorly timed (Martin 1984: 249; Erixon 2001: 27).

Thus, at the end of the decade, the wage policies pursued by the LO were coming under increasing attack. As the 1953 publication *Trade Unions and Full Employment* had intimated, the pursuit of wage moderation over a long period of time – even when compensated by the expansion of social policy transfers and benefits – had severely undermined the internal cohesion of the labor movement. The strike wave at the end of the decade demonstrated the discontent of individual workers with the moderation shown by the LO leadership in its bargaining. The decision of LO leaders to refrain from pushing for wage increases as compensation for income lost to tax increases was increasingly challenged. The strikes also reflected dissatisfaction with the consequences of the solidaristic wage policy. Finally, the efforts of the LO to coordinate wage settlements across the entire economy were challenged by a number of unaffiliated white-collar unions (Swenson 1989; Pontusson 1992: 196). In the coming decade, the ability of the LO to successfully accommodate these competing goals in the formulation of wage policy would be further strained by exogenous macroeconomic developments and by the growth of the tax burden.

Strains on the System: Interunion Rivalry, 1970–1976

Reflecting on social policy developments enacted during the early 1970s, the 1976 LO report concluded that "the major social policy demands, formulated by the labor movement at its previous congress, have been fulfilled" (LO 1976: 631–2). During the first half of the 1970s, the level of benefits provided by every subsystem of the welfare state improved significantly. Policy changes raised the replacement rate for the basic old-age pension from 42 percent of the average wage in 1969 to 57 percent in 1975 (Aldrich 1982: 5). A 1974 reform of the health-care system integrated all health services and raised the minimum replacement rate from 64 to 90 percent of earnings (Burtless 1987: 198; Aronsson and Walker 1997: 219). The introduction of universalistic dental insurance contributed to a further expansion of medical benefits (Olsson 1990: 151). Finally, in the area of unemployment insurance, a number of reforms raised replacement rates and enlarged access to benefits (Björklund and Holmlund 1989). Prior to these policy changes, eligibility conditions for the existing union-administered unemployment insurance were rather stringent, requiring jobless workers a minimum of five months of employment preceding the onset of unemployment; this requirement prevented many from qualifying for unemployment benefits. A 1974 reform created supplementary unemployment assistance, which provided benefits to workers who were ineligible for existing benefits (Burtless 1987: 198).

As a result of the significant expansion of welfare programs, the difference in the size of the public economy between Sweden and other countries rose sharply during this period. A few indicators can illustrate these developments. Total central, state, and local government receipts increased from 32 percent of the GDP in 1960 to 46 percent in 1970 and 55 percent in 1976. Government expenditures grew at a similar rate, from 31 percent of the GDP in 1960 to 52 percent in 1976 (Huber, Ragin, and Stephens 1997). Public sector employment expanded dramatically, from 15.1 percent of total employment in 1970 to 23.5 percent in 1979. By 1976, Sweden had the largest welfare state of any advanced industrialized economy.

To maintain the competitiveness of Sweden's exports and to prevent additional economic imbalances, strong moderation on the wage front was necessary. However, all wage bargaining rounds between 1971 and 1976 were characterized by unexpected tensions and conflict. Two changes in the policy environment within which wage bargaining took place affected the strategies pursued by unions during these negotiations. The first of these developments was the decentralization of the wage bargaining system. Wage bargaining decentralization can be attributed in part to the weakening of the coordinating capacity of employers, which led to "a rupture of institutional linkages between the determination of pay in the public and the private sector" (Flanagan et al. 1983: 328). The second factor that exerted a significant impact on the wage policies unions pursued was the growth in the tax burden. Taxes grew from 15 percent of the total wage bill in 1960 to 33 percent by 1976 (SAF 1978). One consequence of this growth was that wage earners in the median income tax brackets experienced no improvements in their real after-tax income (Elvander 1979: 430, 1983). In response to the dissatisfaction expressed by its members, the LO changed its position on the question of taxes and began to demand reductions in tax rates as a precondition for wage moderation. Social Democratic governments accommodated these requests during the 1974 wage bargaining round.

Developments in the 1971 wage bargaining round illustrate the negative consequences of interunion rivalry for the evolution of nominal wages. The intensity of the conflict between public- and private-sector unions was at an all-time high in 1971. Both public- and private-sector workers could identify areas in which their relative position had either deteriorated or failed to come close to the egalitarian ideal espoused by the labor movement. For the LO, the continuing existence of asymmetries in social policy benefits between white- and blue-collar workers was of special concern. Among the objectives pursued by the LO during the 1971 negotiations were the introduction of parity in supplementary pension and sick-pay benefits and the elimination of differences in retirement age between blue- and white-collar workers (Martin 1984: 265). By contrast, unions in the state sector were frustrated with the persistence of wage differentials between the public and private sectors. This inequality could be attributed to a greater shortage of blue-collar employees and to a higher incidence of incentive pay systems in manufacturing than in the public sector. Wage drift – a development that benefited private-sector workers – counteracted some of the effects of the egalitarian wage policy. According to the estimate of Flanagan, Soskice, and Ulman, the average annual wage drift was three times higher than the annual salary drift (Flanagan et al. 1983: 337). To address this issue, the Union of State Employees (Statsanställdas Förbund, or the SF) demanded much higher relative improvements in the wages of lowerpaid employees (Martin 1984: 265).

A number of public-sector unions challenged the effort of the LO to assume the role of pace-setter in wage negotiations. The SF and the cartel of TCO unions in the state sector sought to negotiate a settlement before the LO, thus violating the recommendations of the EFO model. They were followed by other unions that represented white-collar employees, such as SACO and SR. The level of industrial conflict intensified when public-sector employers, who were organized within the state negotiating agency (SAV) resorted to a lockout. Government intervention brought this intense confrontation to a temporary halt. Special emergency legislation mandated labor peace for a period of 6 weeks, creating a window of opportunity that allowed bargaining actors to hammer out a wage agreement. As they had obtained the "first-mover advantage," public-sector unions called for unusually high wage increases, leaving LO negotiators no choice but to follow (Martin 1984: 268). The 1971 negotiations led to the conclusion of a 3-year agreement guaranteeing contractual wage increases of 6.5 percent, 7.4 percent, and 4.3 percent, respectively. Due to wage drift, nominal wages rose by 30 percent during the same period. The government responded to the unusual increase in wages with a restrictive fiscal policy. The presence of active labor market policies and the availability of public-sector jobs acted as a cushion, preventing unemployment from rising.

Faced with these developments, the LO continued to advocate for moderation in wage demands, but its response to growth in the tax burden underwent a significant change. In the previous decade, the only unions to draw public attention to the "oppressive" impact of tax developments on the real income growth of their members had been those that represented higher earning white-collar employees, such as SACO (Elvander 1979: 430). At the beginning of the 1970s, however, the position of blue-collar employees' unions changed. The important variable accounting for this change in strategy was the increase in inflation, which pushed more wage earners into brackets with higher marginal tax rates. For such workers, negotiated wage increases often brought no increases in earnings. In 1973, policy experts for Metall issued a number of statements calling for a reduction in taxes as a precondition of wage moderation (Elvander 1979: 340). The LO incorporated these recommendations as part of its demands during the 1974 wage bargaining round. In discussions with the government, the LO offered to moderate its wage demands in exchange for a reduction in the level of income taxes (Martin 1984: 290). Unions and the government agreed on a policy solution that involved a reduction in employees' contributions to the basic pension. To offset these measures, the government decided to increase the payroll taxes of employers. These tax measures, which led to an estimated 6 percent increase in the real disposable wage income of workers, facilitated moderate wage increases during the 1974 wage bargaining round (Flanagan et al. 1983: 350).

Emboldened by this policy success, the government and unions began negotiations toward a similar *quid pro quo* involving tax reduction in exchange for wage moderation. These discussions culminated with an informal agreement known as the "Haga Accord." Its central provisions were two reductions in the marginal tax rate for middle brackets, which were scheduled to come into effect in 1975 and 1976. In addition, the government committed itself to expand social security benefits (Flanagan et al. 1983: 350; OECD Economic Surveys Sweden 1975: 37–8). In exchange, the LO pledged to "take into account" these favorable policy changes in the formulation of its wage demands (Martin 1984: 292). But in stark contrast to 1974, the executive of the LO remained unable to convince individual trade unions to comply with its recommendations. Public-sector unions broke again from the central negotiations and succeeded in reaching an agreement prior to the private sector. This in turn led to wage settlements that exceeded the moderate goals formulated by LO leaders (OECD Economic Surveys Sweden 1975: 37–8). The two-year agreement signed in 1975 contained contractual wage increases of 11 and 7.8 percent. The added wage drift led to a total increase in the average hourly earnings of industrial workers of 31 percent over a two-year period, the largest two-year increase since the Korean War (Martin 1984: 294). As Flanagan, Soskice, and Ulman argue, "By Swedish standards, this must be considered a case of bargaining failure.... A situation that called for greater bargaining restraint, flexibility or both failed to elicit either" (Flanagan et al. 1983: 327). The growing radicalization of labor unions contributed to the electoral loss of the Social Democratic Party in 1976.

The policy developments of the early 1970s allow us to test an additional observable implication of the model developed in Chapter 1. The political exchange between unions and governments can sometimes involve reductions in the tax rate in exchange for wage restraint. This particular type of exchange was at the center of the negotiations between unions and the government in the early 1970s. During the 1974 wage bargaining round, the LO was persuaded to accept lower wage settlements in exchange for reductions in the contributions of employees to old-age insurance. The erosion of control exerted by the LO leadership in the wage setting process and the intensification of interunion rivalry, however, prevented the achievement of similar results in subsequent bargaining rounds. Thus, what Flanagan, Soskice, and Ulman call the "bargaining failure" of 1975 and 1976 can be attributed to the partial decentralization of the wage bargaining system.

Policy Developments Under Conservative Governments, 1976–1982

In 1976, Thorbjörn Fälldin, a Center Party politician, formed Sweden's first non–Social Democratic government in over half a century. At the time of this historic change in power, the Swedish economy was confronting a severe economic crisis. The economic recession that affected all major industrialized economies during 1973 and 1974 hit Sweden with a lag beginning in 1975 (Sweden Ministry of Economic Affairs 1981). The increase in unit labor costs (which had its roots in domestic political developments), coupled with a worldwide decline in demand for manufactured goods, affected Swedish exports unfavorably. Important sectors of the Swedish economy such as ship-building were particularly hard hit by the decline. As a result, the restoration of export growth became an important economic priority for the incoming center-right government.

To this end, one of the first policies adopted by the government was a massive devaluation of the kroner. The goal of this policy was to lower relative export prices and counteract the effect of nominal wage increases on Sweden's relative labor costs (Sweden Ministry of Economic Affairs 1981: 47; Martin 1984: 294). The devaluation was introduced in three steps: A first devaluation in October 1976 was followed by two others in April and August 1977 that were linked to Sweden's withdrawal from the Snake (Martin 1985: 454). As a consequence of the devaluations, the price of the kroner declined by 15 percent relative to other currencies. To counteract the adverse impact of this policy on the domestic price level, the devaluation was linked to an array of fiscal policy measures that attempted to limit domestic price increases. These included the introduction of a price freeze and an increase in the value-added tax from 18 to 23 percent (Sweden Ministry of Economic Affairs 1981).

Fiscal tightness on the revenue side was not matched by a similar level of austerity on the expenditure side. In Fritz Scharpf's words, the policy mix of the government consisted, in fact, of a combination of "socialist spending policy and conservative taxing policy" (Scharpf 1991: 100). The increase in government expenditure was financed primarily through deficit spending: Public deficit increased dramatically during the 6-year period in which various center-right coalitions governed, from 2 percent of the GNP in 1976 to 8.4 percent in 1978 and 12.3 percent in 1982 (Scharpf

1991: 108). Several factors account for the reluctance of the centrist parties to pursue policies of fiscal austerity and retrenchment. First, they had only a narrow parliamentary majority: In 1976, it consisted of 11 seats; this fell to 1 seat following the 1979 election. Strong and credible opposition from the Social Democratic Party constrained these governments from introducing policies that departed significantly from the postwar status quo (Gould 1996; Stephens 1996; Swank 2002). Second, public opinion data suggested the existence of strong public support for the existing policies. In a survey conducted in 1980, 57 percent of the respondents agreed with the statement that "considering the public benefits provided by the government, taxes are not too high" (Edlund 2000: 45). Finally, the political support of trade unions – and labor's moderation on the wage front – was critical to the success of the economic policies designed to bring inflation under control. Arousing the hostility of the labor movement through intensive cutbacks in existing social programs, then, was a risky and undesirable political option.

While the conservative government needed wage moderation from the labor movement, it attempted to influence the political terms of this exchange rather than acquiesce to the terms demanded by the trade unions. The government rejected an initial LO proposal to introduce union-administered codetermination funds in exchange for wage moderation (Flanagan et al. 1983: 358). Instead, during the 1977 wage bargaining round, the government offered two types of policy inducements to the labor movement: an increase in expenditures on programs that minimized the visibility and costs of open unemployment and changes in the tax structure.

Conservative governments presided over an expansion of active labor market programs that cushioned the employment consequences of the economic recession. Expenditures on active labor market policies rose from 1.8 percent of the GNP in 1975 to 3.2 percent in 1978, receding slightly to 3.0 percent in 1982 (Johannesson and Persson-Tanimura 1984). This steady increase in outlays suggests that active labor market policies were as important for conservatives as for their Social Democratic predecessors. Figure 3.4 presents time series data of the evolution of various programs financed by the National Labor Market Board. Training programs and employment creation measures still occupied the largest share of expenditures, but the funds allocated to these programs experienced a significant decline over the period. By contrast, expenditures on programs designed to minimize economic dislocation by creating wage-subsidized employment or sheltered workshops increased. Finally, subsidies to unemployment

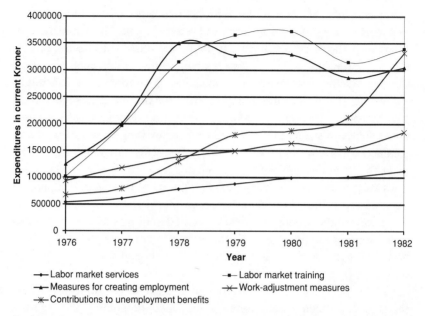

Figure 3.4. The evolution of labor market programs, 1976–1982. (*Source:* Johannesson and Persson-Tanimura 1984: 43–44.)

benefits rose dramatically. The consequence of this change in emphasis was a decline in the ratio of active to passive labor market expenditures.

The first bargaining agreements of this period produced remarkable levels of wage moderation. At the expiration of the 2-year 1975 contract, labor market actors concluded an agreement that provided for a contractual increase of 5.4 percent in the average wage of industrial workers (Martin 1984: 300). This wage increase was significantly lower than the rise in the consumer price index, which rose by 12.8 percent, leading to a sizeable drop in the real incomes of workers. An important factor that explains the trade unions' return to a "responsive" and "restrained" approach to wage negotiations is the ability of the LO executive to restrain the rivalry between public- and private-sector unions that had caused the leapfrogging of the previous bargaining round.

The 1978 wage bargaining round took place in extremely difficult economic circumstances. In 1977, industrial investment fell by 17 percent, which was the largest decline experienced by the Swedish economy in the postwar period. Inflation stood at around 7 percent, a level that was significantly higher than in neighboring countries. The number of persons participating in various labor market programs – a measure of the hidden unemployment – was also at a record level. In an effort to stimulate economic growth, the government announced the elimination of the general payroll tax, which stood at 4 percent, prior to the onset of wage negotiations. Negotiations culminated with an agreement that mandated a 2.7 percent increase in wages for 1978 and a 3.9 increase percent for 1979. Due to rising consumer prices, workers' real wages fell by 1.8 percent in 1978 and 2.3 percent in 1979 (Martin 1984: 344). By all accounts, this was a remarkable level of wage moderation. The conservative budget minister hailed the "responsible agreement reached in the labor market" (Martin 1984: 302).

In anticipation of the 1980 wage bargaining round, several public-sector unions, such as PTK and SACO-SR, called for the formulation of a social contract between unions, employers, and the government that would link wage negotiations to changes in tax policies (Martin 1984: 314). While all labor market actors agreed on the importance of reforming the tax structure, they disagreed profoundly about the desired magnitude and distribution of the costs of these changes. Lamenting the massive increase in the size of the public sector, employers called for an across-the-board reduction in taxes and for changes in the structure of the taxation of profits that would exempt dividends from income taxation. By contrast, the LO demanded policy changes that followed up on the Haga model by concentrating tax cuts on low-income earners. Simultaneously, the LO called for the reintroduction of the payroll tax and asked for changes in the policy that indexed incomes to rising prices (Hadenius 1981; Martin 1984: 312).

For many months, the disagreements among the various labor market actors remained insurmountable. The 1980 wage negotiation process was extremely disruptive, involving a large number of strikes and lockouts, unofficial protests, and other forms of confrontation (Flanagan et al. 1983). Invoking the economic difficulties experienced by the Swedish economy, employers staunchly resisted any increases in the real wages of workers, while union negotiators faced intense pressures from their members to stop the fall in real wages. The intense confrontation of 1980 was fueled by rivalry among the various unions. As in 1971, public-sector unions defected from coordinated agreements and claimed wage increases that exceeded the more moderate wage demands formulated by the LO. An agreement on wages was reached only in conjunction with a stabilization package put together by the government. The package included price and rent freezes, food subsidies, and a reduction of the income tax for low- and medium-income brackets (Flanagan et al. 1983: 354). While the wage settlement of

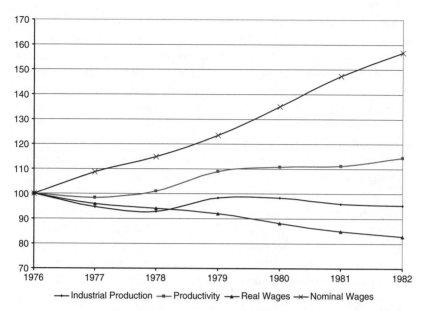

Figure 3.5. Sweden: Wages, output, and productivity, 1976–1982. (*Sources:* Statistical Office, *Statistical Yearbook of Sweden*, various years; Martin 1984; and U.S. Bureau of Labor Statistics, *Handbook of Labor Statistics*, various years.)

the period thus came closer to meeting employers' demands, the progressivity of the tax changes accommodated the desires of the LO.

This narrative of policy developments in the late 1970s and early 1980s suggests that center-right governments did not abandon the notion of a political exchange with unions. Quite the contrary: In an effort to elicit moderation on the wage front, conservatives presided over a significant expansion of social programs and enacted tax changes that attempted to increase the take-home pay of individual workers. Unions responded to these policy inducements by displaying remarkable wage moderation. Figure 3.5 summarizes the evolution of wage developments in the period between 1976 and 1982, during which real wages consistently lagged behind productivity developments by a significant margin. Even the confrontational wage bargaining round of 1980 resulted in relatively moderate wage settlements.

The Return of the Social Democrats, 1982–1990

The Social Democratic Party returned to power in September 1982. The party's electoral program advocated a "third road" in economic policy situated between neoliberalism and reflationary Keynesianism (Misgeld, Molin, and Åmark 1992; Bergström 1992: 288; SAP 1981; Benner and Vad 2000: 422). But the policy constraints of the early 1980s differed in important respects from those of earlier periods. Some of these constraints were conjunctural in nature: The global economy had not yet recovered from the post-OPEC recession; consequently, demand for Swedish exports remained low, and economic forecasts projected zero growth. Other constraints were structural: In the previous decade, the public economy in Sweden had grown at a much higher rate than in neighboring economies; in 1970, total taxation as a percentage of the GDP was at 39.8 percent, a figure that exceeded the OECD average by 5 percent, and by 1981 taxation as a percentage of the GDP had risen to 50.1 percent, the highest in the world (OECD 2000b). Public economy growth had also been partially financed through deficit spending, which had experienced particularly high levels of growth during the center-right government, reaching a record level of 83 billion kroner in 1982 (OECD Economic Surveys Sweden 1985: 8). Given the high levels of taxes and deficits, any recovery strategy premised on public-sector expansion alone was economically unsustainable. Instead, the government had to reduce the deficit, slow down the rate of public economy growth, and revitalize growth in the private economy. In pursuit of these objectives, the Social Democratic Party's economic policy package had three components: economic devaluation, fiscal moderation, and sustained pressure on labor market actors to deliver moderate wage settlements.

Immediately after taking office, the government devalued the kroner by 16 percent (OECD Economic Surveys Sweden 1984: 21). The primary goal of this policy was to improve the competitive advantage of Swedish exports and achieve an export-led recovery. The effect of the devaluation was intensified by a rise in the exchange rate of the dollar, which provided a significant boost to Swedish exports (Scharpf 1991: 109). The devaluation was strongly supported by all major labor organizations. In a statement issued immediately after the decision to devaluate the kroner was announced, the LO promised not to demand compensation in the form of higher wages for any increase in the price level the devaluation might cause. In its meetings with the government, the TCO took a similar position (Elvander 1988: Chap. 2).

A second element of the economic strategy of the social democratic government was a policy of fiscal consolidation (OECD Economic Surveys Sweden 1984, 1985). Between 1982 and 1985, it succeeded in reducing the deficit level from 12.2 percent to 6.3 percent of the GNP, a trend that was slightly reversed after 1987 (OECD Economic Surveys Sweden 1994:

Table D). The fiscal policies pursued by Social Democratic policy makers differed in their distributional implications from the policies of previous center-right governments. The government introduced new taxes or raised existing taxes that primarily affected higher income groups. Thus, for example, capital gains and wealth taxes were raised in 1984, and new property taxes and taxes on dwellings were introduced (OECD Economic Surveys Sweden 1985: 70–1). It also presided over changes in taxation, reducing taxes that affected employment, compensating for the loss in revenue through an increase in indirect taxes, and imposing strict growth targets on public services (OECD Economic Surveys Sweden 1985: 70–1). Second, the government rejected the economic policy premised on a transfer of resources to declining industries practiced by their predecessors. Thus, the long-term budget of April 1983 reduced subsidies to ailing industries by nearly 70 percent (Elvander 1988; OECD Economic Surveys Sweden 1985: 70–1, 1984: 24).

Despite the efforts at fiscal consolidation, the SAP did not enact major cutbacks in social policy programs. On numerous occasions, in fact, the government increased social transfers. Thus, for example, the 1984 budget increased child allowances to cushion the negative impact of devaluation on low-income groups (OECD Economic Surveys Sweden 1984b: 22). Similar polices, together with an increase in the minimal parental benefit, were introduced in 1987. As part of the 1987 budget, unemployment insurance benefits and cash unemployment support were increased, and pensioners obtained compensation for income lost due to the 1982 devaluation (OECD Economic Surveys Sweden 1989: 97).

Social Democratic policy makers also presided over an important change in the function of labor market policies. This consisted of a reorientation of the character of these policies to the initial functions ascribed to them by the Rehn-Meidner model (Scharpf 1991). As discussed previously, the centrist coalition had increased the share of passive expenditures of the labor market policy expenditures. As a result, the number of labor market outsiders increased while the center-right governments were in office. This category included early retirees, persons in various "rehabilitation" programs, and "discouraged workers" – persons who had given up searching for a job. The economic growth of the mid-1980s led, however, to the mobilization of these "hidden reserves." According to OECD estimates, the ratio of discouraged workers to unemployed workers declined from 40 percent to around 20 percent during this period (OECD Economic Surveys 1989: 61).

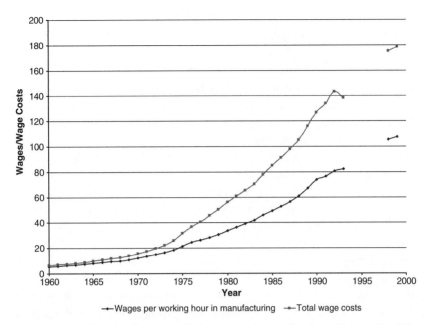

Figure 3.6. The development of the tax wedge in Sweden. (*Source:* Swedish Employers' Confederation, various years.)

Finally, the third element of the government's economic strategy was sustained pressure on labor market actors to moderate wage settlements (Elvander 1988, 1990; Scharpf 1991; Benner 1997). The policy environment within which wage bargaining actors operated differed in important respects from the environments of previous decades. By 1982, it had become clear that the process of welfare state maturation exercised strong constraints on the wage bargaining process. Figure 3.6 illustrates these developments. While in 1960 wages constituted 84 percent of the total wage bill, this ratio had declined to 60 percent by 1982. Higher tax rates necessitated higher levels of wage moderation to reduce unit labor costs. But at the same time, high levels of payroll and income taxes lowered the take-home pay of workers, reducing their ability to accept the strong moderation demanded by union leaders and elected politicians. While this constraint had been present in earlier periods, the continuing growth of the fiscal burden amplified its severity. In 1970, the payroll tax (which financed the ATP pension and health insurance) stood at 10.5 percent. By 1982, it had risen to 19.9 percent. An additional payroll tax also rose from 1.4 percent in 1970

111

to 13.16 percent in 1982, while the average local tax rate rose from 21 percent in 1970 to 29.74 percent in 1982 (Aronsson and Walker 1997: 257–8).

We can identify two distinct strategies by which the government tried to influence the outcome of the wage bargaining process in a direction of greater moderation. First, it relied on its role as a public-sector employer to limit wage increases in that sector and influence agreements in the entire economy. Second, it made significant efforts to link reduction in taxes to unions' agreements to moderate their wage settlements. The Social Democratic minority government of 1973–1976 and the center-right governments of 1976–1982 had both also used reductions in the marginal tax rates to "smooth the way for the wage negotiations" (Elvander 1990: 13). Developments during the 1984–1985 wage bargaining round, known as the Rosenbad negotiations, illustrate both strategies. At the onset of the wage bargaining process, the government attempted to steer the negotiations in the direction of greater moderation by setting a low-level agreement for public employees that would provide a model for the entire labor market. It thereby gave a green light to public-sector employers to initiate discussions concerning future wage developments ahead of negotiations in the private sector. The government proposal to limit wage growth to 5.5 percent over a 2-year period met with opposition, however, from some public-sector unions such as TCO-S and SF. Contrary to the wishes of the government, negotiations resulted in a settlement that gave public-sector workers nominal wage increases of 5.2 percent for 1984 and 5.5 percent for 1985. The announcement of the public-sector agreement set in motion an escalation of wage settlements in the private sector. Metall, the largest private-sector union, announced that a wage settlement lower than the public-sector settlement would be unacceptable, thus turning the public-sector wage agreement – intended by the government to be a wage ceiling – into a wage floor for private-sector wage bargaining (Elvander 1988: Chap. 3).

Faced with the imminent danger of inflationary wage settlements, the government convened all labor market actors for a number of meetings in Rosenbad in April 1984. During these meetings, policy makers expressed their recommendation that wage increases (including wage drift) stay below 5 percent (Elvander 1988: Chap. 3). This demand was premised on the assumption that the increase in the price level during the following year could be limited to 3 percent. In exchange for this moderation, Finance Minister Kjell-Olof Feldt promised unions a reduction of the marginal tax rate, which was predicted to increase the take-home pay of all full-time wage earners by 600 kroner (Elvander 1990: 14). In response to the LO's demand that the progressivity of the tax system be adjusted, the policy package also raised the tax rate for high-income earners. LO officials supported the government proposal, seizing the opportunity to reestablish their organization's coordinating role in the bargaining process. While accepting the broad parameters proposed by government officials, LO negotiators demanded additional changes in social policy benefits and labor market conditions as compensation for wage moderation. These included the equalization of sickness benefits between blue- and white-collar workers, additional holidays, and a reduction in working time. The framework agreement, which was signed by the LO and the SAF in February 1985, accommodated these additional demands. In their announcement of tax policy changes following the completion of wage negotiations, government officials stated explicitly that wage moderation was a precondition of tax compensation: "The government will propose to the Parliament a reduction of taxes for all wage-earners on the condition that these wage agreements stay within the limit of 5 percent" (Elvander 1988: Chap. 3). This announcement was extremely effective in bringing outstanding sectoral negotiations to a speedy resolution. At the same time, the government's effort to impose the 5 percent ceiling strengthened the ability of employers to control wage drift.

Compared to other wage negotiations of the period, the 1984 wage bargaining round was characterized by the highest level of wage setting coordination; by contrast, the 1982, 1986, and 1988 wage bargaining rounds were characterized by significant decentralization of wage settlements. The most important factor accounting for the hollowing out of the internal authority of peak associations was the dissatisfaction of export-sector employers with centralized wage setting and their ability to forge a coalition with export employees against the central agreements (Pontusson and Swenson 1996; Elvander 1988). Beginning in the 1970s, the association representing employers in the engineering sector (Verkstads Förening, or VF) began to voice its opposition to the presence of provisions for low-wage employees in wage setting agreements and its dissatisfaction with the "rigidity" of centralized frameworks. In 1982, the VF was able to push through a significant institutional change of the internal rules of the SAF, giving sectoral organizations the right to sign independent agreements and to impose lockouts. In the same year, the VF used this rule for the first time, informing the SAF of its decision not to participate in the central negotiations (Elvander 1988: Chap. 2). Instead, it invited its counterpart, Metall, to negotiations outside the LO-SAF framework. The core elements of the VF-Metall agreement differed in important ways from the LO-SAF agreements of the period. Employers won the elimination both of the low-income guarantee and the increase in the number of salary groups, which responded to the demands of many engineering firms for a more differentiated wage structure. Metall, on the other hand, obtained a reduction in working hours that affected workers with two shifts and concessions on issues affecting workers' rights during workplace reorganization and temporary dismissal (Elvander 1988).

The defection of the export-sector coalition of unions and employers from centralized wage negotiations accentuated other distributional conflicts. As discussed previously, the issue of the compensation of public-sector workers for the higher level of wage drift in the private sector was at the center of the conflict between public- and private-sector unions. The political solution to this problem was the earnings-trend guarantee (*förtsjänsutvecklingsgaranti*), which promised that workers in sectors that were losers from wage drift would be compensated during the ensuing bargaining round. Beginning in 1975, every wage bargaining agreement included an automatic earnings-related guarantee. Metall's decision to accept an agreement that did not include compensation for low-income workers reopened the political debate about the provisions that were necessary in centralized wage agreements to ensure the equalization of income between the different sectors. Employers in the public sector seized on this issue during the 1986 wage bargaining round and refused to give in to unions' demands for automatic compensation for wage drift. While unions initially resisted this move (which led to intense confrontation and a public-sector lockout), their unity ultimately disintegrated over the question of appropriate strategy. As a result, the 1986 agreement marks an important change in wage setting practices. The automatic earnings-trend guarantee was eliminated, and unions agreed instead to a deduction of excessive wage drift from wage increases in the following year (Elvander 1988: Chap. 4).

As Figure 3.7 illustrates, the political strategy pursued by the Social Democratic government enjoyed a mixed degree of success. The various income policies negotiated with unions guaranteed very modest increases in real wages. Real wage moderation continued to sustain the expansion of social programs and services throughout the late 1980s. But nominal wages grew at a dramatic rate, fueling much higher levels of inflation than in neighboring economies. By the end of the decade, the inflationary gap had become unsustainable, leading to a change in macroeconomic policy.

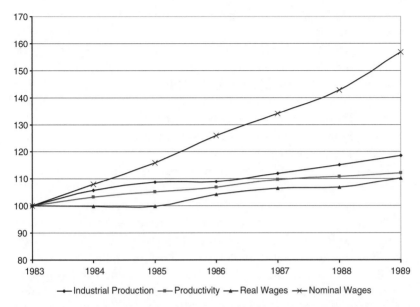

Figure 3.7. Sweden: Wages, output, and productivity, 1983–1989. (*Sources:* Statistical Office, *Statistical Yearbook of Sweden*, various years; Martin 1984; and U.S. Bureau of Labor Statistics, *Handbook of Labor Statistics*, various years.)

The Double Sacrifice: Wage and Social Policy Developments of the 1990s

At the beginning of the 1990s, Sweden experienced its deepest economic decline since the Great Depression. Between 1990 and 1992, the Swedish economy contracted by over 6 percent. This deep recession resulted from a combination of underlying structural factors and short-term policy mistakes and miscalculations (Benner and Vad 2001: 455; Tranøy 2000). The rise in nonwage labor costs of the 1980s led to a substantial decline in Swedish manufacturing exports, which lost about 17 percent of the market share between 1988 and 1991 (National Institute of Economic Research 1992). But the policy mistakes of the Social Democratic government – and the ill timing of its policy interventions – aggravated the magnitude of the downturn (Benner and Vad 2001: 455). The economic decline had far-reaching consequences for Sweden's labor market performance. Between 1990 and 1999, total employment declined by 11.4 percent. This decline was unevenly distributed across the public and private sectors. While employment in the private sector shrank by 5.8 percent, public-sector employment experienced a 21 percent decline (Kautto 2000: 28). Unemployment rose from 1.8 percent in 1991 to 5.6 percent in 1992 and then to 9.8 percent in 1994 (U.S. Bureau of Labor Statistics, various years). Over one-third of the persons out of work were unemployed for a period longer than 2 years (Palme, Bergmark, Bäckman, Estrada, et al. 2002). In addition to rising unemployment, those excluded from the labor force – a category that includes the "chronically ill, early retirees and latent job seekers" – increased from 800,000 to 1,300,000 (Sweden Ministry of Finance 2000: 161; compare Trehörning 1993).

There was remarkable consensus among the various political parties that governed in this period – a center-right government from 1991 to 1994 and a Social Democratic government after 1994 – regarding the policies needed to overcome the crisis. The economic strategy had three major components: Its first element was a firm commitment to a noninflationary policy; its second pillar was a policy of fiscal consolidation that attempted to balance the budget; and its third element was an effort to recentralize the wage bargaining system. To achieve the third goal, the government resorted to exercising an unprecedented level of political influence in the wage bargaining process.

The commitment to a noninflationary policy was regarded as necessary to stem international currency speculation and outflows. In the early 1990s, the Productivity Commission formulated an initial call for this policy shift (Sweden Productivity Commission 1991). In its economic program, the Social Democratic Party distanced itself from the "third-road" strategy, which had led to unsustainable inflation and a loss of export competitiveness (SAP 1989; Benner and Vad 2001). "The inflationary route for the Swedish economy is blocked," the SAP explained. "Historically it has resulted in devaluations that interfere with the necessary structural adjustments of the economy. Price stability is the precondition for a sustained reduction in unemployment" (Iversen 1999: 146).

The first steps toward fulfilling the new policy objective were taken in the 1990 budget, which ranked price stability ahead of full employment as the overarching policy target. A number of additional institutional changes reinforced the commitment to a noninflationary policy. In late 1990, the Social Democratic government decided to peg the value of the kroner to the European currency unit (ECU). Simultaneously, Sweden applied for membership in the European Commission and participation in the European Monetary System. The center-right government that came to power in 1991 continued this policy. Yet, in the fall of 1992, the currency peg came under increasing speculative attack and was eventually abandoned. Instead, the board of the central bank (Sveriges Riksbank) replaced the fixed exchange rate as the primary target of central bank policy with a target of price stability (Benner and Vad 2001: 427). An inflation rate of 2 percent became the new monetary policy goal.

The change in policy orientation triggered intense deliberations among trade unions. At its 1991 congress, the LO appointed a number of commissions to examine the implications of the new macroeconomic constraints on unions' wage policy (LO 1991). The responsibilities of these commissions were to define "the room for wage cost increases that was compatible with economic balance" (Elvander and Holmlund 1997). The most influential commission was the "Edin group," which was formed in the fall of 1994 and included economists from ten leading labor market organizations. The commission formulated a number of informal guidelines, setting an upper target for growth in wages, wage drift, and payroll taxes. These guidelines, which supported the 2 percent inflation target set by the central bank, were highly influential in preparations for the 1995 wage bargaining round.

The second element of the strategy of the government was a policy of fiscal stabilization. Successive Swedish governments remained committed to very restrictive fiscal policies that attempted to balance the budget and the current account and reduce the interest rate premium. Three major programs of fiscal stabilization were negotiated during this period. The first fiscal package was enacted by the conservative government as part of the 1992–1993 budget (OECD Economic Surveys Sweden 1994a: 29). Its main elements of fiscal tightening included a reduction in the level of benefits for old-age, sickness, and disability insurance; a diminution of the government contribution to health insurance; and cutbacks in housing subsidies. Together, these measures generated fiscal savings of about 26.9 billion kroner (OECD Economic Surveys Sweden 1994a: 56). The second reform package, introduced in September 1992, mandated a further reduction of employers' contributions to social insurance by 4.3 percent and the abolition of two days of annual leave. Upon its return to power in 1994, the SAP continued the policy of fiscal stabilization initiated by its predecessors. A fiscal package adopted in November 1994 introduced expenditure cuts totaling 24.5 billion kroner (OECD Economic Surveys Sweden 1995: 32). Child care support and early retirement pensions were most affected, with cuts of 6.9 and 4.3 billion kroner, respectively (OECD Economic Surveys Sweden 1996: 32). The 1995 budget adopted additional spending reductions distributed among all subsystems of the welfare

Table 3.1. *Sweden: Replacement rates for sickness insurance, work injury insurance, unemployment insurance, and parental leave, 1990 and 1997*

	1990	1997
Sickness insurance	100	75
Work injury insurance	100	75
Unemployment insurance	90	75
Parental leave	90	80

Sources: Anderson 1998: 182–3, 319; Palme et al. 2002: 342.

state, including sickness insurance, old-age insurance, and education. Labor market programs such as training subsidies for active labor market policies and enterprise-based training programs also experienced significant cutbacks.

What was the net effect of these policies of fiscal consolidation on the various subsystems of the welfare state? Table 3.1 addresses this question by comparing the evolution of replacement rates in four major programs. As the summary statistics illustrate, the replacement rates of all major subsystems of the welfare state fell during the 1990s. Additional austerity measures increased the stringency of eligibility criteria for the receipt of social policy benefits. In the case of sickness and work-injury insurance, policy makers introduced one additional waiting day and changed the formula for calculating qualifying income (Anderson 1998). In the case of unemployment insurance, they attempted to end an ongoing practice of rotating between cash benefits and participating in labor market programs. To this end, the receipt of unemployment benefits after 200 days was made conditional upon participation in labor market programs such as retraining or public relief work (Anderson 1998: 310).

Pension benefits were also reduced significantly in the 1990s. In this case, social policy retrenchment came about primarily through several changes in the indexing rule. As Pierson (1993, 1994) has argued, these changes were politically expedient because they were less transparent and involved a longer causal chain between the policy instrument and the unpopular outcome. Beginning in 1991, policy makers decoupled the "base amount" used to calculate benefits for basic, ATP, disability, and part-time pensions from changes in the consumer price index (Anderson 1998: 215). A further reduction in benefits was enacted during the November 1992 crisis, when the Bildt government enacted legislation that reduced pension benefits to

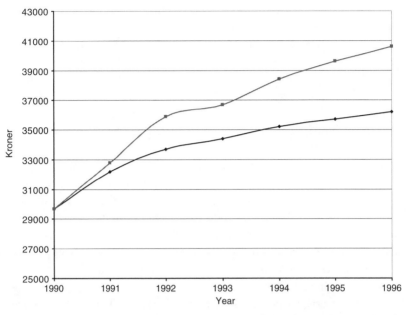

Figure 3.8. Pension retrenchment, 1990–1996. (*Source:* Anderson 1998: 217.)

98 percent of the already reduced base amount. In 1995, Social Democratic policy makers modified the indexing rule yet again, linking pension increases to the size of deficits and the level of government finances. According to the new rule, the base amount was adjusted by only 60 percent of the consumer price index as long as the budget deficit exceeded 100 billion kroner (Anderson 1998: 216). Figure 3.8 examines the impact of these changes by comparing the evolution of the base pension and a simulated amount that reflects the pension prior to the changes. Between 1990 and 1996, the various changes to the indexing formula brought about a reduction in the pension base amount of 11 percent.

What is remarkable about the changes to social protection of this period is that there were almost no cutbacks in social services (Palme et al. 2002). Developments in two policy areas – public provision of child care and public care for the elderly – are illustrative. A Welfare Commission report commented on the changes in the area of child care: "In terms of legislation, it is reasonable to speak of an expansion . . . in terms of accessibility there was a clear trend towards increased universalism" (Palme et al. 2002: 345). Beginning in 1995, municipalities were assigned greater obligations for child care, and the number of children enrolled in child care programs expanded during this period. In the case of old-age care, expenditures also increased between 1993 and 1997 (Kautto 2000: 61). In this case, however, rather than increase universalism, resources were concentrated on those with the greatest need (Palme et al. 2000: 341). As a result of these trends, the service intensity of the Swedish welfare state increased in the 1990s.

In addition to social policy cutbacks, successive Swedish governments relied on tax increases to achieve fiscal consolidation. In 1990, Sweden enacted what was hailed as the "tax reform of the century" (Agell, Englund, and Södersten 1996: 643). It reduced the top rate of the income tax, eliminated various tax shelters, and widened the tax base of the value-added tax (Birch Sørensen 1998; Kautto 2000: 36). Because the tax reform enjoyed the support of all political parties and of the LO, any additional tinkering with its provisions was politically undesirable. As a result, policy makers resorted to making tax changes only hesitatingly. But tax increases could not be altogether avoided.

While conservative governments lowered the contributions of employers to social insurance, they attempted to offset the budgetary impact of these cuts by raising the consumption tax from 18 to 21 percent and by canceling other previous cuts in sales taxes (OECD Economic Surveys Sweden 1994: 59). An additional notable change was the introduction of an individual social insurance contribution (*allmän egenavgift*) in 1993. At first, this contribution was only at 0.95 percent of income, but within five years it had reached 6.95 percent (Kautto 2000: 83). The consolidation package adopted by the Social Democratic government in November 1994 also increased individuals' contributions to sickness insurance in an effort to generate additional revenues of 14 billion kroner (OECD Economic Surveys Sweden 1995: 32; Andersen 1998: 168). Finally, the Social Democrats raised the national income tax for higher earning employees from 20 to 25 percent (Kautto 2000: 83). Table 3.2 summarizes the most important changes in taxation enacted during this period.

The combination of spending cuts and tax increases had two significant consequences. The share of total government expenditures decreased from its peak of 69.8 percent in 1993. Moreover, the policies of fiscal consolidation were successful in lowering the public debt. While the gap between government outlays and receipts stood at 14 percent of the GDP in 1993, it was virtually eliminated in 1999 (OECD 2000c: 68; Kautto 2000).

120

The Double Sacrifice

Table 3.2. *Sweden: Changes in tax rates, 1991–1999*

	1991	1999
Personal income tax		
Top marginal rate	20	25
Lowest marginal rate	0	0
Average local income rate	31.15	31.15
Social security contributions of employers	38.77	33.06
Employees	0	6.95
Self-employed	35.49	31.25
Value-added tax, standard rate	25	25
Taxation of assets in pension funds	10	15

Source: OECD 1999a: Appendix iv.

The third component of the government's political strategy in the 1990s aimed to increase the coordinating capacity of the wage setting process. The efforts of Swedish policy makers in this direction departed strongly from the tradition of government noninvolvement in wage bargaining. The strategy pursued by the government had two components. Its first element was the strengthening of the role of the mediation commission in the wage determination process. In 1991, the Larsson government established a mediation commission known as the Rehnberg Group. Its purpose was to closely monitor the wage setting process and steer labor market actors toward agreements that were aligned with the inflationary targets laid out by the central bank. On numerous occasions, the wage bargaining partners were urged to "accept wage restraint" and to "include considerations of a wider economic and social nature than the usual partisan politics as part of the agreements" (Elvander and Holmlund 1997: 26). As Elvander and Holmlund characterized the activities of the commission, "The Rehnberg Group was a kind of reinforced mediation institute which also carried out some elements of an 'indirect' incomes policy (the consumer price action and adjustments with reference to the recent reductions of marginal tax rates). The formal rule system for conflict resolution was not changed in the period 1990–1996, but the mediation institute has been strengthened in an informal way, starting with the stabilization drive and followed up by the former members of the negotiation commission, Lars-Gunnar Albåge and Rune Larson" (Elvander and Holmlund 1997: 76). The government also threatened to intervene in the wage setting process if labor market actors failed to agree on "reasonable" and "economically sound" wage settlements. To make this threat credible, it prepared a draft bill that specified a ceiling for "accept-able" wage increases. The bill enjoyed the political support of a sizeable parliamentary majority. Thus, the possibility of government involvement in the wage setting process – an outcome denounced by unions as "wage bargaining through coercive legislation" – was stronger in the 1990s than at any other point during the postwar period (Elvander and Holmlund 1997: 81).

These changes in the policy environment confronted unions with much more difficult choices than at any moment of the postwar period. They were asked to accept a "double sacrifice": a reduction in social policy trans-fers to their members as well as a reduction in their take-home pay. What distinguishes Sweden from other economies that experienced a similar level of fiscal austerity is the fact that the provision of social services experienced no decline. Overall, LO leaders advocated high levels of restraint. The LO expressed support for the various stabilization plans while formulating moderate wage demands. The ability of union leaders to appease the dis-content of workers was especially strong during the 1991 and 1994 wage bargaining rounds. But the willingness of rank-and-file members to comply with the moderation advocated by LO leaders reached its limits during the 1995 round. The discontent of particular sectors led to the conclusion of higher wage settlements as well as to the renewed decentralization of the wage bargaining system.

Both the 1991 and the 1993 wage bargaining rounds were characterized by significant wage setting centralization. In 1991, wage negotiations took place under the strong threat of government intervention. All discussions took place under the supervision of the mediation committee. Govern-ment representatives pressured union leaders to conclude moderate settle-ments and to develop sanctions against local negotiators that offered wage increases in excess of the negotiated settlements, thus lowering the wage drift. Wage negotiations were successful in meeting both objectives. Unions accepted negotiated wage increases of 3 percent for 1991 and 1992 (OECD Economic Surveys Sweden 1992: 30–1). Due to the high inflation rate of the early 1990s, these wage agreements brought about a 4 percent reduc-tion in real wages in 1991. In 1992, real wages rose by a modest 1 percent. In an effort to reduce wage drift and break the wage-price spiral, unions accepted a policy whereby "the 'illegitimate' wage drift of the first year could be deducted from wage increases during the second year" (Elvander and Holmlund 1997: 20). As a result, wage drift declined from 2.9 percent in 1991 to 1.1 percent in 1992 (National Institute of Economic Research 1997).

The stabilization policies introduced beginning in 1992 established the policy parameters for the 1993 wage bargaining round. At a time of intense national crisis, the LO expressed support for the stabilization package and for the efforts of the government to restore the confidence of international investors in the kroner. In January 1993, LO leaders initiated wage negotiations and advocated the need for economic sacrifices as an important contribution to the success of the stabilization policy. The LO's initial wage demands recommended a 2 percent increase, allowing an additional raise of 1 to 2 percent for low-wage employees (Elvander and Holmlund 1997). At the same time, LO leaders advocated a return to "coordinated national union bargaining" and an increase in the importance of the national agreement to regulating wages and working conditions for all sectors. Improved centralization was regarded as an institutional precondition for wage moderation.

The negotiations produced quite moderate settlements. At the basis of all of the wage agreements was a contract between the Union of Commercial Employees (HAO) and employers in the commercial sector that was signed under intense pressure from the mediation commission. Contractual wage increases averaged 1 percent for the first year and 2 percent for the second year. Following the precedent set in the 1991 wage bargaining round, any wage drift in the first year was deducted from the wage increases of the second year. This resulted in a decline in the real wage of 1 percent, followed by a modest 1 percent increase the following year. An additional important setback experienced by unions during this wage bargaining round was the elimination of compensation mechanisms for low-wage employees, such as wage drift compensation clauses or other forms of wage indexation.

Following Sweden's accession to the European Community in 1994, a number of LO committees began to advocate a wage policy that followed the evolution of labor costs in other European countries more closely. This recommendation, known as the "Europe Norm," was regarded by LO leaders as "a necessary, although not sufficient condition for low inflation, real wage increases and a long-term improvement in the economic situation" (Elvander and Holmlund 1997). In 1995, labor costs in European economies were expected to rise by 3.5 percent. To LO leaders, this figure represented an informal "ceiling" for the evolution of hourly labor costs (including wage drift) and taxes in Sweden.

By 1995, the willingness of individual workers to go along with the policy of wage moderation advocated by LO leaders had reached its limit (Benner and Vad 2001: 428). Dissatisfaction was particularly high among public-sector employees. As a consequence of the policy of fiscal austerity, these workers had experienced the greatest decline in their real wages during the previous wage bargaining rounds. Public-sector strikes, which began with strikes by nurses, extended across Sweden. The 1995 strikes were the largest industrial conflict since the 1980 strike, and they resulted in 627,000 lost working days. The LO's effort to coordinate wage agreements around the Europe norm remained unsuccessful (Elvander and Holmlund 1997: 42). Wage agreements signed during this period led to extremely uneven wage developments. Sweden's export sectors negotiated increases that were quite close to the Europe norm, with a 3.5 percent increase in engineering and a 3.8 percent increase in the forest industry. The construction industry, which had been hit hard by the economic recession, negotiated wage increases of 2.4 percent a year. By contrast, the transportation and commerce sectors negotiated wage agreements that were significantly higher than the Europe norm (Elvander and Holmlund 1997: 56, 89). Wage increases for employees in central and local governments also exceeded the Europe norm by 1.5 percent (National Institute of Economic Research 1992).

One consequence of the conflictual character of the 1995 wage bargaining process was the uneven length of the wage agreements signed by the different sectors. Their duration varied from a one-year agreement in the forest industry to three-year agreements in the engineering, commerce, and government sectors (Elvander and Holmlund 1997: 89). This temporal unevenness remained an important obstacle to a return to economy-level wage bargaining coordination. The 1997 wage bargaining round was characterized by sectoral-level negotiations. LO leaders explicitly warned against the potential dangers associated with the return to sectoral bargaining, such as inflationary wage increases and labor market segmentation (Benner and Vad 2001: 429). The negotiations led to average negotiated wage increases of 4.4 percent in 1996 and 3.8 percent in 1997. These increases were slightly higher than the wage outcomes of the centralized bargaining rounds of 1991 and 1993, though wage drift continued to remain very low (1.7 percent in 1996 and 0.6 percent in 1997).

Figure 3.9 summarizes data on the evolution of wages, productivity, and output during the period between 1990 and 1997. A few developments should be noted. First, the macroeconomic shift to a nonaccommodating policy is associated with a reduction of both nominal and real wage

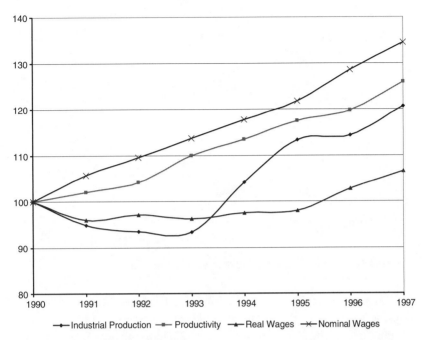

Figure 3.9. Sweden: Wages, output, and productivity, 1990–1997. (*Sources:* Statistical Office, *Statistical Yearbook of Sweden*, various years; and National Institute of Economic Research, *The Swedish Economy*, various years.)

increases. After half a decade of decline in the compensation of workers, real wages returned to their 1990 level only in 1996. Given that unions also accepted significant cuts in various programs during this period, these data underestimate the actual level of moderation exercised by the Swedish labor movement. The high level of restraint can be attributed in part to the increase in wage bargaining system centralization during the 1990s. As hypothesized by the model developed in Chapter 1, an additional factor facilitating wage moderation was the continuous commitment of the government to the provision of social services – such as public provision of child care – which were not affected by the austerity policies.

In response to the most severe economic crisis since the Great Depression, Swedish policy makers turned to labor market actors and attempted to persuade unions to accept dramatic cuts in their real wages. In conjunction with the change in macroeconomic policy, wage moderation contributed to a reduction in unemployment. Unemployment declined from 10 percent

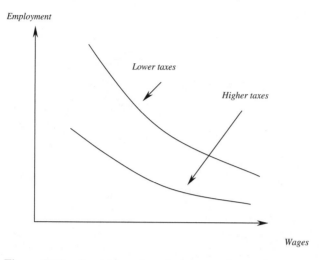

Figure 3.10. Sensitivity of employment to changes in wages.

in 1991 or 1992 to 7 percent in 1997. High levels of payroll and income taxes, however, constrained the effectiveness of wage restraint in lowering unemployment. Recall from equation (22) in the appendix to Chapter 1 that, under conditions of high taxes, the sensitivity of employment to wages declines. In Figure 3.10, I present this result graphically.

This result allows us to address the counterfactual question: Would a similar level of wage restraint have caused a sharper decline in unemployment if the fiscal burden had been lower? The answer is affirmative. Under current conditions, when wages constitute only 40 percent of the total non-wage labor costs of firms, even large cuts in the take-home pay of union members are likely to have only a modest effect in lowering unemployment (Svenskt Näringsliv 2002). As a result of the relative decline in the effectiveness of this policy, unions and their members are confronted with much tougher choices than during the policy environment of the early postwar period.

Conclusion

This chapter has tested the theoretical predictions of the model developed in Chapter 1 using a longitudinal research design. I have examined the wage strategies pursued by Swedish trade unions from 1945 to 1998 in response to changes in macroeconomic policy on the one hand and changes

Conclusion

in social policy benefits and transfers on the other. The narrative supports several hypotheses advanced in this study. First, Swedish unions responded to the expansion of social policy benefits and services by pursuing strong moderation on the wage front. As a publication of the LO reflected on this strategy of the labor movement, "By refraining from wage increases to the advantages of social insurances, the labor movement has contributed to social security" (LO 1976: 650). In addition to the growth of the major social insurance programs, such as old-age or sickness insurance, social policies that provided complementary institutional support for the solidaristic wage policy were of particular importance to Swedish unions. These included active labor market policies and housing policies. Second, increases in wage bargaining system centralization in 1952, 1956, 1982, and 1991 contributed to greater moderation in the wage demands of trade unions. This policy of wage moderation that was pursued by union leaders was not always uncontroversial, however, and it led on several occasions to labor market unrest and severe industrial conflict.

Over time, the growth of the tax burden placed constraints on the political exchange. The growth of the tax burden had two important consequences. Higher taxes reduced the take-home pay of individual workers, undermining their willingness to accept the moderation advocated by union leaders. In response, successive governments began to offer reductions in taxes in exchange for promises of wage moderation. These exchanges were critical elements of the 1974 wage bargaining agreement and of the 1984 Rosenbad negotiations. At the same time, the growth in the tax burden reduced the effectiveness of the wage restraint policy in lowering unemployment. While trade unions have accepted remarkably low wage increases in recent years, income policies have experienced great difficulties in restoring the virtuous cycle of full employment and high levels of social protection.

4

Germany

focus on wage strategies [handwritten annotation]

This chapter tests the theoretical predictions of the model developed in Chapter 1 by examining the impact of social policy developments on the wage strategies pursued by the German labor movement in the postwar period. Were German unions willing to moderate their wage demands in exchange for the expansion of social policy transfers and services? What were the consequences of the growth in taxes and social policy commitments for the wage demands of German trade unions? How did the growth in the number of labor market outsiders affect the strategies of German unions? In this chapter I test the micro-level implications of the model using a combination of union documents, economic data, and secondary sources.

The chapter proceeds chronologically. The first section examines the strategies pursued by the Federation of German Trade Unions (Deutscher Gewerkschaftsbund, or DGB) under the Christian Democratic governments of Konrad Adenauer and Ludwig Erhard. In this period, German policy makers decided to reconstruct the welfare state along Bismarckian lines and rejected alternative proposals advanced by the Social Democratic Party to introduce universalistic social policies. Next I explore the evolution of the wage–social policy nexus under the Grand Coalition of Georg Kiesinger and the Social-Liberal Coalition government led by Willi Brandt. These administrations shared a commitment to continuous welfare state expansion and to the involvement of trade unions in the macroeconomic management of the German economy. The remaining two sections examine wage and policy developments during the 1980s and 1990s. They consider the new constraints imposed by a high fiscal burden on the wage demands of German unions and on the effectiveness of wage policy in improving Germany's employment performance.

summary of chpt [handwritten annotation in left margin]

128

The Wage–Social Policy Nexus During the Adenauer-Erhard Period, 1950–1966

The reconstruction of the German labor movement in the postwar period proceeded at a brisk pace. Many scholars of the German labor movement speak of an "organizational miracle" of trade unions (Markovits 1986: 63; Schönhoven 1987). In October 1949, the unions of the British, American, and French zones merged and established the Federation of German Trade Unions (DGB). Legislation introduced the same year created the principle of *Tarifautonomie*, which gave trade unions and employers the right to establish wages without government involvement during this process (Herschel 1973; Nautz 1998, 1999). In contrast to the Weimar period, when the German labor movement was divided along denominational lines, the DGB – an umbrella association of 16 industrial unions – was established as a unitary labor movement (*Einheitsgewerkschaft*) comprising both Christian Democratic and socialist unions. In the first decade of the Federal Republic, the policy responsibilities of the federation vis-à-vis individual unions were not clearly defined and were contested on several occasions. Individual unions successfully resisted the efforts of central federation officials to centralize authority and control over the determination of wages. The metalworking union, IG Metall, which was the largest of the individual unions, gradually established a central "pattern-setting" role in determining the level of wage growth in the late 1950s (Noe 1970; Pirker 1960; Kalbitz 1979; Manow 2000).[1]

Labor market developments of the 1950s were characterized by significant wage moderation but also by an unusually high level of strikes compared to subsequent policy periods in Germany. Figure 4.1 contrasts the evolution of both nominal and real wages to two additional indicators: output and productivity. Between 1950 and 1959, both nominal and real wages tracked growth in productivity closely, with real wages growing more slowly than productivity. An important observation about Figure 4.1 is that wage moderation (measured as the gap between the growth in real wages and the growth in productivity) was especially pronounced after 1957, the year in which comprehensive old-age insurance was introduced. The wage moderation of the German labor movement had far-reaching economic implications, contributing to the "supply-side miracle" of the 1950s. "Through this

---

[1] Several authors point to the 1956–1957 Schleswig-Holstein strike and to the Baden-Württemberg strike of 1962 as the decisive events that established the current system of "pattern bargaining" dominated by IG Metall (Pirker 1970; Noe 1970; Kalbitz 1979).

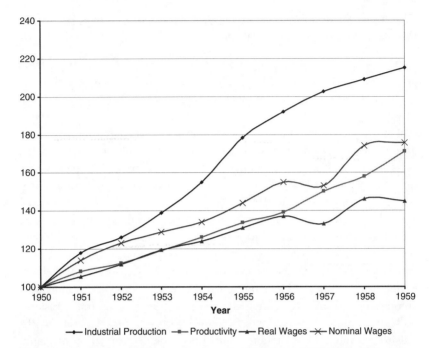

Figure 4.1. Germany: Wages, output, and productivity, 1950–1959. (*Source:* Germany. Statistisches Bundesamt, *Statistisches Jahrbuch für die Bundesrepublik Deutschland*, various years.)

particular wage moderation in the form of disregard for the terms of trade gains in times of business cycles upswings," Giersch, Paqué, and Schmieding argue, "the profitability of investment was kept high" (Giersch et al. 1992: 72).

Existing studies have formulated several competing explanations for the wage moderation of the immediate postwar period.[2] (For a summary, see Giersch et al. 1992: 75–9). The first of these explanations, advanced by Mancur Olson, suggests that wage moderation was the result of union weakness: "The postwar economic miracles in countries such as Japan and Germany can be explained because their distributional coalitions have been emasculated or abolished by totalitarian governments or foreign occupation" (Olson 1982: 75). But this characterization of unions is misleading. Though

---

[2] These competing explanations are discussed in Giersch et al. (1992). I follow their exposition but disagree with their conclusions.

130

the 1948 currency reform dealt a blow to the power of unions, destroying much of their resources and weakening their ability to wage massive strikes, the decline was only temporary. By 1952, unions' finances had recovered. In that year, the DGB had about 36 million DM that could be deployed in the case of a strike, and the combined income of individual unions was estimated to be about 400 million DM (Pirker 1960: 286–7). Other labor market indicators also suggest that this characterization of unions' weakness is misleading. In 1950, unions' density stood at 40.8 percent of the workforce, and it reached 42.9 percent in 1952, the highest union density level of the entire postwar period (Ebbinghaus and Visser 2000: 322). IG Metall, the largest union in the period, had around 1.3 million members in 1950, and membership increased to 1.6 million in 1955 and 1.8 million in 1960 – hardly a sign of weakness and disorganization (Ebbinghaus and Visser 2000: 333). Finally, as I will show, unions were capable of exerting strong political influence in the 1950s, and in some areas they succeeded in achieving policy outcomes that were very close to their ideal policy preference. Thus, the characterization of German unions of the 1950s as weak is simply incorrect.

2. A second explanation for the wage moderation exercised by unions in this period stresses the economic surprise of the unprecedented economic boom. Many German economists seem to favor this explanation. Giersch, Paqué, and Schmieding argue that "unions' wage demands were not particularly cautious and restrained, but [were] persistently outpaced by the actual supply-side expansion and the resulting productivity gains; thus what may have looked ex ante like an aggressive wage policy turned out to be quite moderate in terms of unit labor costs" (Giersch et. al. 1992: 76). They note, however, that it is not possible to test their explanation, which stresses the misguided economic expectations of labor market actors and policy makers, because no quantitative forecasts of the relevant macroeconomic indicators existed in the 1950s. Moreover, it is not clear how a theory that stresses the importance of "economic surprise" can account for wage moderation over such a long period of time. Why did unions not try to retroactively extract compensation for the distributive setbacks of previous wage bargaining rounds once the relevant figures on output and productivity growth had been published? Accounts that stress off-the-equilibrium expectations should predict sharp upward spikes in wage settlements following the publication of data about firms' profitability and output. The linear trend in the evolution of wage increases of the period is not consistent with the economic surprise explanation.

In support of their argument, Giersch and others refer to union publications of the 1950s that advocate an "expansionary wage policy" (*expansive Lohnpolitik*) (Agartz 1950, 1953). The notion of an expansionary wage policy was advanced by Victor Agartz, a researcher at the Institute for Economic Affairs of the DGB. Agartz argued that unions should demand the highest possible wages in their bargaining with employers (Agartz 1953: 245; Markovits 1986: 84; Weinzen 1986). His argument was based on a Keynesian logic: An increase in workers' real incomes would lead to an increase in consumption and employment and would thus benefit society as a whole (Markovits 1986: 84). The 1952 DGB report noted that Agartz's comments led to "lively deliberations within the social policy committee of the DGB but that discussion continued to remain wide open" (DGB 1953: 379–80). Agartz's keynote address at the 1953 DGB Congress elaborated the notion of an expansive wage policy and generated genuine enthusiasm among some of the participants (Pirker 1960: 138–9).

However, Agartz's rise to prominence within the trade union movement was short-lived, demonstrating that an overwhelming majority of unionized workers rejected radical notions of wage militancy. The publication of Agartz's speech was immediately followed by an open rebuttal from Oswald von Nell-Breuning, the "spiritual father of social Catholicism" in Germany, who argued that "Agartz leads unions to political radicalism that could lead to a disintegration of the DGB" (Pirker 1960: 150). Shortly thereafter, the Christian faction of the DGB threatened to break away to form an independent trade union if the organization followed the official line laid out by Agartz and "the radicals" (Pirker 1960: 151). Thus, to maintain the unity of the labor movement, DGB president Walter Freitag had no choice but to sacrifice Agartz, marginalizing him from leadership positions in the German labor movement (Pirker 1960: 154).

Rather than adopt an expansionary wage policy, the German labor movement took a more pragmatic approach to wage determination. In the business report of 1950, published only one year after its founding congress in Munich, the DGB endorsed the concept of an "index-linked wage scale" (*gleitende Lohnskala*). According to such a scale, unions had to consider increases in productivity as well as firms' sales when determining their wages. "For Germany, it is of vital importance to link wage increases to productivity," the DGB report argued. "For this productivity-based compensation [*leistungsgerechte Entlohnung*], both production per hour of work and the market sales of firms have to be considered" (DGB 1951: 312). A formula for the optimal wage policy, known as the Meinhold formula, was elaborated only at the beginning of the 1960s; it called for a "double adaptation of the wage policy to the evolution of prices and productivity" (Bergmann, Jacobi, and Müller-Jentsch 1975: 192; Schauer 1999: 431, 429).

A third explanation for the wage moderation of the 1950s points to the importance of workplace representation, or codetermination, to German unions. As Henry Wallich has argued, "the quest for codetermination . . . distracted some of the union leadership's energies from a more determined pursuit of wage increases" (Wallich 1955: 307). An alternative formulation of this hypothesis is that unions deliberately moderated their wage demands to demonstrate their reliability as social partners to both employers and the Christian Democratic coalition and to influence ongoing debates about the design of institutions of codetermination. While this third explanation can account for wage moderation in the early 1950s, it does not explain the persistence of unions' moderate approach even after workplace representation legislation was adopted by the German parliament.

The enterprise-level representation of workers was a critical policy issue for the German labor movement in the early 1950s. For German unions, concerns about the establishment of workplace democracy went back to the Weimar period: In response to the demands of the socialist trade union federation (the Allgemeiner Deutscher Gewerkschaftsbund), Weimar policy makers introduced the Works Council Act (*Betriebsrätegesetz*) of 1920, which guaranteed the election in large enterprises of consultative bodies consisting of worker representatives (Hirsch-Weber 1959: 77; Thelen 1991: Chap. 3). In the immediate postwar years, German unions sought not just the restoration of the Weimar-era status quo but also the introduction of even more encompassing legislation to guarantee a stronger decision-making role for workers in all important choices made by firms. As union publications in the British and American occupation zones formulated these demands: "We call for co-determination in all sectors of the economy. . . . This includes especially consultation [*Mitwirkung*] of works council in questions of production, control and distribution of goods. . . . All intentions for production and other plans have to be communicated to the works council and have to be decided jointly with the works councils" (Hirsch-Weber 1959: 82).

Initially, the British occupation authorities shifted the policy status quo toward an outcome that was favorable to labor by granting equal representation to workers and employers on company supervisory boards in the steel, iron, and mining sectors. This favorable development prompted German trade unions to advocate for the expansion of the "parity" model

133

of codetermination to all sectors of the German economy. On this issue, however, they faced strong opposition from German employers and the Christian Democratic government of Konrad Adenauer. Beginning in 1950, Christian Democratic policy makers formulated a number of draft bills that attempted to roll back the codetermination legislation of the occupation period (Markovits 1986: 77). The strategy pursued by German trade unions in the struggle over codetermination evolved throughout the period. Initially, unions chose an approach that relied on threats of confrontation and extensive industrial action (Pirker 1960: 213). The threat of a national strike was used in 1951, when it successfully preempted the efforts of Christian Democratic policy makers to enact a bill that would have reduced the role of workers' representatives in the iron and mining industries. After 1951, the DGB leadership switched to a strategy of "constructive cooperation" with the government in the hope of gaining the support of labor-friendly representatives within the Christian Democratic Union (Pirker 1960: 214, 223). Constructive cooperation implied support for other government policy proposals, restraint in the use of the strike weapon, and moderation on the wage front. As a study of the union movement has pointed out, DGB president "Christian Fette was a strong advocate of the policy of constructive cooperation and defended the policy of collaboration with the government" (Pirker 1960: 232). Politically, the Federation of German Trade Unions supported other policies of the Adenauer government, such as the Schumann plan, a decision that led to open conflict between the labor movement and the Social Democratic Party (Markovits 1986: 79). On the economic front, unions exercised strong moderation during the wage bargaining rounds of 1951 and 1952, despite a sharp upswing in profits and production. The strategy of constructive cooperation was ineffective, however, at swaying Christian Democratic policy makers to extend codetermination as established in the iron, steel, and mining sectors to the entire German economy.

Wallich's hypothesis that concern for codetermination was a source of union moderation explains the strategy of the German labor movement during the period between 1950 and 1952. It does not explain the continuation of this moderation, however, after the codetermination issue was resolved by the legislature in 1952. The explanation advanced in this study suggests that unions' concern for social policy acted as an ongoing source of wage moderation. A critical assumption of the model developed in Chapter 1 is that unions' objective function has two components: concern for social policy benefits and services and concern for securing increases

Table 4.1. *Germany: Replacement rates for old-age, unemployment, and sickness insurance, 1950–1960*

	1950	1960
Program		
Old-age insurance		
Average benefits*	61	160
Replacement rate	29%	37%
Unemployment insurance		
Average benefits*	88	204
Replacement rate	41%	47%
Sickness insurance		
Replacement rate[†]	50%	90%

Notes:
*Expressed in current prices.
[†]In the first six weeks of sickness.
Source: Alber 1989, 147.

in real wages. If advances in the level of benefits and services are sufficiently large, the equilibrium strategy of unions will be to moderate wage demands. In the period between 1950 and 1960, social policy transfers grew at a rapid rate. Table 4.1 presents descriptive statistics on the evolution of benefits in the major social insurance programs. (Descriptive statistics for old-age insurance refer to the *Arbeiterrentnerversicherung*, which preceded the pension insurance legislation of 1957.) In the 1950s, the average level of old-age benefits increased by 38 percent while unemployment benefits rose 43 percent. These improvements in social policy benefits paralleled the rate of wage growth (Hockerts 1980: 193). A significant portion of social policy expenditures was financed by federal government revenues, not by social insurance contributions. Total social insurance contributions rose only by 4 percent in the 1950s (Alber 1989: 122). Thus, in contrast to other periods, the growth in the fiscal burden exerted only a small negative impact on the real take-home pay of workers (Hockerts 1980: 193).

The goals and objectives pursued by the DGB in negotiations about social protection evolved during the 1950s. In the immediate postwar years, labor's most significant policy goal was to acquire "policy control" in the institutions that administered social insurance (Hockerts 1980; Manow 2001; Mares 2003). Beginning with the Bismarckian reforms of the 1880s, German institutions of social insurance were administered by representatives of capital and labor. Prior to 1945, labor representatives had a two-thirds majority in the institutions of sickness insurance and half of the seats in the administration of old-age and unemployment insurance. By contrast, accident insurance was administered by employers' representatives alone. Beginning with the founding congress of the DGB in 1949, trade unions demanded workers' "full control...over the administration of all institutions of social insurance" (Hockerts 1980: 135). The unions' view on this issue exceeded in radicalism the demands of the Social Democratic Party, which advocated a "two-thirds majority of labor representatives in all institutions of social insurance" (Hockerts 1980: 135, n. 117). Control over the administration of social insurance was not merely a symbolic issue for the German labor movement. As an observer of the period noted, this was a "question of power" (*Machtfrage*) (Hockerts 1980). Its resolution along the lines demanded by unions could potentially give labor control over enormous amounts of capital, which was flowing through the institutions of social insurance. As Florian Tennstedt (1977) and Philip Manow (2000) have pointed out, participation in the administration of institutions of social insurance was also a source of patronage for trade unions, as unions could distribute thousands of jobs in these institutions. Finally, as these debates were occurring at the same time as deliberations about codetermination, unions believed that an increase in their power within the institutions of social insurance could influence the solution to the codetermination question.

After 1953, concerns about the actual level of social policy benefits began to overshadow in importance these questions of the institutional design of the welfare state. In the immediate postwar years, German trade unions had advocated the introduction of "Beveridgean" social policies with flat-rate benefits. Their policy preferences on this issue changed in the early 1950s, however, as unions began to endorse a return to the "Bismarckian" solution that guaranteed benefits linked to wages. The Action Program adopted at the 1955 DGB Congress demanded "old-age insurance benefits guaranteeing 75 percent of the previous income of the employees" (DGB 1955: 48). An important policy question confronted by policy makers during the period was the question about the mechanism adjusting the level of social policy benefits to rising prices. Seizing on the tremendous opportunity this issue created for unions, a social policy commission appointed by the DGB began to advocate a solution that tied increases in pensions to increases in wages (Hockerts 1980: 313). As the unions argued, Germany could depart from the models implemented in other countries, which indexed social policy benefits only to changes in the price level. If increases in pensions were linked to increases in real wages, pensioners would "fully benefit from the fruits of postwar economic prosperity" (DGB 1955). Unions advocated adjusting pensions to rising wages automatically, without the periodic intervention of lawmakers. Such a method would amplify the economic and political impact of unions' wage choices, causing them to affect not only the economically active population but also the millions of additional citizens who benefited from welfare programs. Critics of the wage-indexation formula argued that it would turn an "army of millions of pensioners into 'supporters' [*Parteigänger*] of trade unions during wage negotiations." The position advocated by unions prevailed, however: The 1957 pension reform endorsed the dynamic pension formula that linked pensions to increases in net wages (Alber 1989: 147).

Thus, the theoretical explanation advanced in Chapter 1, which stresses the importance of unions' concerns about social policy, accounts for the sustained wage moderation exercised by German unions in the 1950s. It also sheds light on the central reasons for unions' discontent and militancy. The most extensive strike waged by the German labor movement in this period was the Schleswig-Holstein strike of 1956–1957. This protracted 16-week confrontation between IG Metall and metalworking employers in northern Germany is an event that has acquired tremendous symbolic value for the German labor movement (IG Metall 1978; Pirker 1960; Manow 2000). Unions' decision to strike was motivated by social policy considerations – the question about the social policy benefits received by workers during periods of sickness. For IG Metall, the strike was more than a routine confrontation. As Otto Brenner, IG Metall's leader, characterized the objectives of the Schleswig-Holstein industrial action, it was a "model case" (*Modelfall*) for the "resolution of social policy issues which have either not been addressed by the legislator or have been resolved extremely unsatisfactorily by trade unions." He explained, "If the strike was successful, it was a demonstration of the fact that social policy was a key object of negotiations among workers and employers, alongside the determination of wages and working time." Given the exemplary importance of the strike, IG Metall chose the region of the confrontation extremely carefully. It targeted a sufficiently large number of firms to inflict major damage on employers, but it was careful not to overextend the lines of the battleground, thus ensuring the availability of sufficient support funds for striking workers (Pirker 1960: 212).

The main object of the confrontation was the question of sick pay (*Lohnfortzahlung im Krankenfall*). IG Metall demanded guarantees of sickness benefits for 6 weeks and the removal of asymmetry in benefits for manual

137

and nonmanual workers (*Angestellte*). A second demand of strikers was the elimination of days with no pay (*Karenztage*) in cases of work-related sickness or disability. Early developments indicated that IG Metall was ready to devote nearly unlimited resources to the resolution of these issues. The conflict was ultimately resolved through the political intervention and mediation of Chancellor Adenauer and Economics Minister Erhard. A wage negotiating agreement between IG Metall and employers in the metalworking industry, concluded in January 1957, resolved some of the issues to the satisfaction of workers, and it was soon followed by the introduction of social policy legislation favorable to the striking workers. The Sick Pay Law of June 1957 introduced some of the most generous social rights in Europe in case of sickness, guaranteeing replacement rates of 65 percent. These benefits could be added to by family subsidies and additional employer subsidies up to a maximum replacement rate of 90 percent (Pirker 1960: 225). To the dissatisfaction of workers, the law did not remove all inequalities in benefits between blue-collar workers and white-collar employees. This equalization was achieved only in 1969, when the Sickness Payment Law (*Lohnfortzahlungsgesetz*) guaranteed white- and blue-collar workers compensation equaling 100 percent of their wages or salaries for the first 6 weeks of sickness.

As Figure 4.2 shows, German trade unions continued to pursue a policy of wage moderation in the early 1960s. With the exception of 1961 and 1962, wage developments lagged behind productivity growth. For some scholars of the German political economy, this poses a puzzle. "To explain union restraint in the 1960s is very difficult," Giersch, Paqué, and Schmieding argue. "No doubt, the unions were rich and radical enough to take a more demanding and radical posture; after all, the unionization rate which had been decreasing over the 1950s now stabilized at about 53 percent. Given the extremely tight labor market conditions prevailing after the 1960s (with the exception of course of the 1966/7 recession), the time would have seemed to be ripe for a major redistributive effort" (Giersch et al. 1992: 155). The evolution of the "social wage" can again account for unions' moderation on the wage front. As a result of the reforms enacted in the late 1950s, total social policy expenditures as a percentage of the GDP increased from 20.7 in 1960 to 26 percent in 1966 (M. Schmidt 1990: 146). Moreover, a number of additional policies guaranteed increases in the take-home pay of workers that compensated them for wage restraint. The 1961 reform of family benefits increased the income supplements of

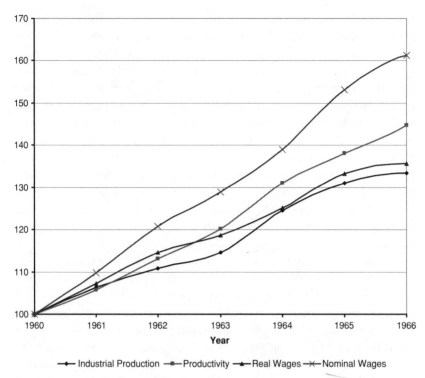

Figure 4.2. Germany: Wages, output, and productivity, 1960–1966. (*Source:* Germany. Statistisches Bundesamt, *Statistisches Jahrbuch für die Bundesrepublik Deutschland*, various years).

families with two or more children. A reform of housing benefits (*Wohngeld*) increased housing subsidies to compensate workers for the rise in rents that followed the liberalization of the housing market (M. Schmidt 1990: 132). In contrast to the reforms of the late 1950s, these policies provided benefits that were not linked to wages, and they had, in effect, a greater redistributive impact. Finally, the level of benefits guaranteed by the major social insurance programs also increased steadily in the early 1960s (Alber 1989: 146–7).

At the same time, German trade unions began to demand additional institutions to ensure better coordination in the formulation of wage, social, and employment policies. The "stylized hypothesis" advanced in the recent literature, which presupposes the existence of coordination between trade unions and the central bank (the Deutsche Bundesbank), does not accurately characterize the policy developments of the early 1960s. Political developments during the 1966 recession, discussed later, demonstrate the absence of coordination between wage setters and monetary authorities. As a DGB report of the period argued, "The Federal Republic lacks a clear and comprehensive process of the formulation of macroeconomic goals. There is no institution with responsibility for all macroeconomic decisions. There is also no institution with clear responsibilities in the formulation of policies aimed at avoiding economic fluctuations. There is no administrative organ that coordinates the economic policies of various ministries, orienting these toward a common goal. It is, therefore, imperative to coordinate the monetary, fiscal and economic policies of the Federal Republic" (DGB 1965: 279–80, 254). Several factors explain unions' growing concern about the absence of policy coordination. The first is their increasing frustration with the absence of an "official bargaining partner" (*ofizieller Verhandlungspartner*) for broad questions of macroeconomic policy (DGB 1965: 279). Given that a commitment to full employment was not enshrined in the *Grundgesetz*, unions hoped that the coordination of fiscal, monetary, and wage strategies would provide better guarantees for the realization of this objective. An additional issue that was a source of constant frustration for the labor movement was its lack of information about the price policies of German firms. In the early 1960s, employers waged numerous public opinion campaigns that attributed growth in prices to the "aggressive" wage behavior of trade unions. Unions attempted to rebut these arguments by attributing inflationary pressures to the price policies of German firms, but they lacked precise information about firms' price setting processes. Thus, the DGB hoped that greater coordination in the policy-making process might facilitate information exchange about both macroeconomic variables and firms' micro-level price and investment decisions.

The first step toward greater coordination was taken with the creation of the Council of Economic Advisors (*Sachverständigenrat*) in 1963 (Shonfield 1965: 294; Flanagan et al. 1983: 279). While the primary goal of this five-member council was to evaluate macroeconomic developments, it was also responsible for publishing data about inequalities in wealth and income (Giersch et al. 1992: 139). The DGB had first advocated the creation of "a neutral institution for the analysis of macroeconomic developments" in 1958, and thus it welcomed the establishment of the council (DGB 1965: 239). Echoing unions' concerns, the council itself regarded the absence of proper coordination between fiscal, monetary, and policy as one of the greatest institutional deficiencies of the Federal Republic. One of its first recommendations, made in 1965, was to establish an arena where unions, employers, and representatives of the central bank and the government would meet on a regular basis (Hardes 1974: 11; Giersch et al. 1992: 136). The 1966 recession added to the urgency of this need. This first recession experienced by the Federal Republic in 1966 resulted from an open conflict between wage developments and monetary policy (Scharpf 1991). In 1966, increases in nominal wages averaged 10.5 percent, and the central bank consequently stepped in and raised interest rates to 5 percent (DGB 1965; Germany Bundesministerium für Arbeit und Sozialordnung 2002: Table 3.3). The resulting decline in economic activity, while appearing modest when judged by later standards, generated a pervasive and somewhat unexplainable sense of panic (Hildebrand 1984: 207). This episode had far-reaching political consequences: It contributed to the introduction of legislation that improved the process of macroeconomic coordination and increased the role of unions in macroeconomic management. While the Erhard government reluctantly agreed to this measure, the policy came into effect only after Erhard had left office.

Policy developments of the Adenauer-Erhard period support the hypotheses advanced in Chapter 1. Throughout the period, German unions exercised significant wage moderation. The wage strategies of the labor movement cannot be understood in isolation from social policy developments: Wage moderation was a rational strategy of unions whose members benefited from significant increases in the level of social policy transfers and services. The reforms introduced in the late 1950s and early 1960s guaranteed the most generous sickness and old-age benefits in Europe. As Manow argues, strictly linking benefits to contributions, the reform put strong premiums on stable career paths, on high incomes and on the early acquisition of skills. It thus came to benefit in particular the core union clientele, the highly qualified core workforce" (Manow 2000: 28). Finally, the indexation mechanism that linked increases in pensions to increases in wages, introduced as part of the 1957 pension reform, benefited unions in two ways. On the one hand, it increased the overall economic impact of the wage choices made by unions. On the other hand, it solved potential problems of "intergenerational equity," guaranteeing that ongoing wage moderation "would not benefit only future generations at the expense of present ones" (Eichengreen 1997: 49; Manow 2000: 48).

Wage Bargaining and Social Policy Developments Under the Grand Coalition, 1966–1969

Ludwig Erhard's resignation in 1966 brought about the first regime change of the Federal Republic. The Social Democratic Party accepted the invitation to participate in a "Black-Red" coalition government, thus returning to power for the first time since 1930. The Grand Coalition government led by Georg Kiesinger represented the entire spectrum of twentieth-century German political orientations, as former members of the National Socialist Party (Chancellor Kiesinger himself) joined former members of the German Communist Party (such as Herbert Wehner) in a government of "reconciliation" (Hildebraud 1984: 266).[3] Despite their different political beliefs, the members of the government agreed about the immediate economic priorities, which included fiscal consolidation and the introduction of measures to overcome the recession (Hildebrand 1984: 275–8).

One of the first policies introduced by the newly elected government was the Stability and Growth Act of 1967 (Hardes 1974). The origin of this legislation can be attributed to Economics Minister Karl Schiller (Social Democratic Party), and it marks a belated effort to inject Keynesian ideas into the German political economy (Allen 1989; Hildebrand 1984: 295). The Stability and Growth Act proclaimed the achievement of full employment (defined as an unemployment rate of 0.8 percent) as a significant policy priority alongside price stability, external equilibrium, and economic growth. More important, it established an institutional arena – "concerted action" (*Konzertierte Aktion*) – in which representatives of the government and the central bank, as well as unions and employers, would meet regularly to coordinate their actions. The explicit mandate of Concerted Action was to formulate appropriate solutions when one of the primary objectives of the Stability and Growth Act was endangered. As a result, Concerted Action meetings had no mandate to initiate new social policies. But by considering the macroeconomic and labor market implications of different social policies, Concerted Action meetings could lead to recommendations for change if the evolution in the level of expenditures endangered macroeconomic objectives. Thus, the Stability and Growth Act established an arena

---

[3] Wehner became minister for German affairs. In the Grand Coalition government, the Social Democratic Party obtained the important economics portfolio (Karl Schiller) as well as the foreign ministry and the position of deputy chancellor, both held by Willi Brandt (Hildebrand 1984: 266).

in which unions, employers, and representatives from various ministries could reach compromises across different policy areas.

The first meetings of Concerted Action were dedicated to the formulation of policies to overcome the 1966 recession. The cause of the recession was diagnosed as insufficient demand, and the participants in the meetings agreed on the introduction of an expansionary budget (Hardes 1974: 18). To stimulate investment, this fiscal expansion included initially favorable depreciation allowances for firms. An additional expenditure program for federal, regional, and local funds was targeted at regions with high unemployment and structural difficulties (OECD Economic Surveys Germany 1968; Hardes 1974). Presiding over this fiscal expansion, representatives of the economics ministry leaned heavily on unions to moderate wage increases in order to eliminate the danger of a wage-price spiral. These pressures were extremely effective. The 1967 wage bargaining round produced wage increases that averaged 2.9 percent, a figure lower than the target of 4 to 5 percent issued by the Council of Economic Advisors (DGB 1969: 289). In response to this moderation, the Bundesbank also agreed to loosen its monetary policy, and it lowered interest rates from 5 to 3 percent (DGB 1969: 245). In combination, these measures led to an extremely swift economic recovery. The economic recession was overcome by the end of 1967. While in 1967 the German economy contracted by 0.1 percent, in 1968 it grew by 5.6 percent (OECD 2000b).

The success of Concerted Action in overcoming the 1966 recession emboldened some of its participants to broaden the objectives of the institution. Trade unions in particular demanded the introduction of policies that could guarantee "redistributive progress" (*verteilungspolitischer Fortschritt*) as part of Concerted Action, including policy changes that would favor low-income groups and legislation that would affect the redistribution of income in German society (DGB 1968: 252, 256). Economics Minister Karl Schiller supported the unions' demands. On several occasions he indicated that future Concerted Action meetings would have to restore "social symmetry" among different economic actors. The notion of social symmetry became the new policy mantra of the period, replacing Erhard's wooden language, but the concept unfortunately remained vague and imprecise. A Concerted Action subcommission on income and redistribution was established to formulate specific proposals for achieving social symmetry (DGB 1965: 254–5). Both employers and representatives of the Bundesbank disapproved of unions' proposals to expand the scope of Concerted Action and to tackle these more ambitious redistributive objectives (Hardes 1974).

As a result, ensuing Concerted Action meetings were afflicted by more fundamental disagreements among the participants.

Social policy legislation of the late 1960s responded to some of the unions' redistributive concerns. As Manfred Schmidt has argued, the initiatives of the Grand Coalition were a "sensational turning point" in postwar social policy development, because they displayed a systematic bias in favor of blue-collar workers. The government first made old-age and unemployment insurance compulsory for white-collar workers by abolishing income ceilings for higher paid *Angestellten*. Next it adopted a financial equalization law that redistributed funds from white-collar employees' old-age insurance reserves to those of blue-collar employees, to the immediate advantage of the latter (M. Schmidt 1990: 134). In 1969, its last year in power, the coalition removed any remaining asymmetry in sickness insurance benefits and eligibility conditions between white- and blue-collar workers. In its effort to push through this important legislation, the Social Democratic Party succeeded in convincing its coalition partners that fulfilling such a long-standing policy demand of unions was important to keep them involved in Concerted Action meetings (Immergut 1986: 64–9).

The changes initiated by the coalition contributed to an overall increase in the level of social protection. The data presented in Figure 4.3 illustrate this positive trend. Aggregate social expenditures as a percentage of total expenditures increased only slightly, from 26 to 27 percent, but the portion of the population covered by social insurance increased by 8 percent (Germany Bundesministerium für Arbeit und Sozialordnung 1998: Table 2.1). Replacement rates for unemployment assistance and insurance and for sickness insurance also rose considerably. The changes responded to unions' distributive concerns by removing some of the asymmetries in social rights among various occupational categories.

These favorable developments in social protection explain why German trade union representatives cooperated in Concerted Action meetings even after the economic recession was overcome. The 1968 wage bargaining round resulted in average wage increases of 4.2 percent (DGB 1968: 290). These increases were lower than the targets formulated by the Council of Economic Advisors and the economics ministry, which recommended a 5 percent wage increase. The unions' sustained wage moderation accounts for the strong performance of the German economy in this period as well as the return of the days of the *Wirtschaftswunder*. The overall level of GDP grew by 5.6 percent in 1968 and by 7.5 percent in 1969, and unemployment decreased to 0.8 percent in 1969, reaching the full employment target of

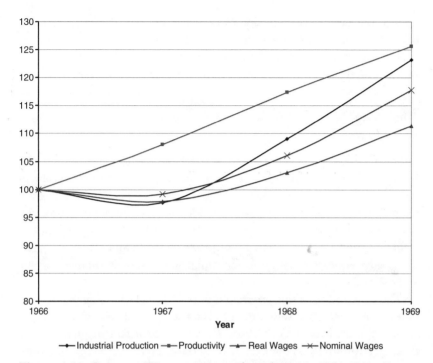

Figure 4.3. Germany: Wages, output, and productivity, 1966–1969. (*Sources:* Germany. Deutsche Bundesbank, *Monatsberichte der Deutschen Bundesbank*, various years; Germany. Statistisches Bundesamt, *Statistisches Jahrbuch für die Bundesrepublik Deutschland*, various years.)

the Stability and Growth Act. Export growth of 17 percent was the engine of the economic expansion, the consequence of a worldwide increase in demand for manufactured goods during the Vietnam War (Scharpf 1991: 122). Fiscal and monetary policies were highly coordinated, stimulating investment and demand without endangering stability (Hardes 1974).

The Grand Coalition governed for only three years. By establishing new arenas of policy coordination, it was remarkably successful in steering the German economy out of its first postwar recession. The coalition also managed to formulate appropriate social policies to ensure sustained wage moderation by German unions. Tensions between unions' demands for the restoration of social symmetry and employers' opposition to the expansion of the prerogatives of Concerted Action did not surface in this period. The efforts of Economics Minister Schiller to expand the scope of Concerted Action fueled unions' hopes. Schiller offered no immediate answer, however, to the question of how the objective of social symmetry could be achieved. These unresolved issues were part of the legacy of the coalition government. Future governments would not have the luxury of postponing the resolution of distributional dilemmas to a future date.

Wage Bargaining and Social Policy Expansion in the Brandt Era, 1969–1974

Following the 1969 elections, the Social Democratic Party became the senior coalition party in Germany, this time leading a coalition government with the Free Democrats (Bracher, Jäger, and Link 1986). In his inaugural address of October 28, 1969, Willi Brandt announced a political program of "internal reforms" (Beyme 1979: 251–81). The list of promises included reforms in the areas of enterprise organization and employee representation, codetermination, vocational training, and sickness insurance (Beyme 1979: 270–2).

The centerpiece of this program was an overhaul of old-age insurance. These policy changes were a direct response to the demands of German trade unions, as the DGB's 1965 *Aktionsprogramm* had defined old-age insurance reform as its political priority (Hockerts 1992: 906). To ensure greater cooperation between the Social Democratic Party and trade unions on questions of social legislation – and "to make his cabinet more attractive to trade unions" – Willi Brandt appointed Walter Arendt, the leader of the mining union (IG Bergbau und Energie), as social policy minister (Hockerts 1992: 908).

Despite such overtures toward the trade unions, the government experienced serious trouble in its relationship with labor. In the fall of 1969, Germany experienced a dramatic surge in wildcat strikes (Flanagan et al. 1983: 264; Müller-Jentsch and Sperling 1978: 265). "The sudden switch of union behavior from moderation to aggressiveness in the late 1960s and early 1970s," Giersch, Paqué and Schmieding point out, "is unique in West German economic history" (Giersch et al. 1992: 157). The strike wave began in the mining industry in Nordrhein-Westfalen in September 1969 and spread quickly to the metal and steel industries of the region. By October 1969, spontaneous strikes were occurring in ship-building, textiles, wood processing, ceramics, and the public sector (DGB 1971: 195–6). In 1969, Germany lost approximately 250,000 working days to strikes, a tenfold increase over 1968 (Germany Bundesministerium für Arbeit und Sozialordnung 2002: Table 3.4). The main reason for the strikes was unions'

146

desire to eradicate some of the distributive setbacks of the 1967 and 1968 wage bargaining rounds. A DGB survey of German workers revealed a pervasive feeling of injustice among workers, as their wages did not improve commensurate with firms' profitability (DGB 1971: 197). By 1969, the patience of the rank and file and the hope of achieving the "social symmetry" promised by the first social democratic government of the Federal Republic had simply run out. As a result of the strikes, unions were able to negotiate much more favorable wage settlements for their members: The 1969 wage bargaining round resulted in wage increases averaging 9.9 percent (DGB 1971). The strike waves also boosted union membership after a decade of stagnation: It grew from 7.8 million members in 1968 to nearly 8.5 million in 1972, a 7 percent increase (Giersch et al. 1992: 157; Ebbinghaus and Visser 2000: 322).

The strike wave of 1969 fundamentally transformed the dynamics of Concerted Action meetings. In the first two years of Concerted Action, the DGB followed the broad recommendations for macroeconomic development of the economics ministry or the Council of Economic Advisors, which tended to formulate extremely conservative predictions about economic growth. Beginning in 1969, however, unions became more reluctant to follow these recommendations. Invoking the principle of *Tarifautonomie*, unions openly disregarded official guidelines for wage settlements. Instead, the DGB began to develop its own independent medium-term economic forecasts (DGB 1971: 170). As a result, unions increasingly came into conflict with representatives of the Bundesbank and the Council of Economic Advisors within Concerted Action meetings (DGB 1971: 172–4).

In 1970 and 1971, external factors increased the importance of wage moderation for the maintenance of macroeconomic stability (Scharpf 1991: 123). Under the system of fixed exchange rates, Germany was importing high levels of inflation from the United States. To stave off inflation, the Bundesbank pursued extremely restrictive monetary policies and revalued the deutsche mark repeatedly. Unions were under stronger pressure to moderate their wage demands. Chancellor Brandt himself called on unions on multiple occasions, while at the same time reiterating the commitment of his administration to greater redistribution through reforms of both the tax system and the system of social protection. But unions resisted the calls for moderation. They attributed price increases to the policies pursued by German firms and were unwilling to accept lower real wages for their members. In 1970, nominal wages grew by 11.9 percent, and the DGB was able to reassure member unions that, "despite strong increases in the level of

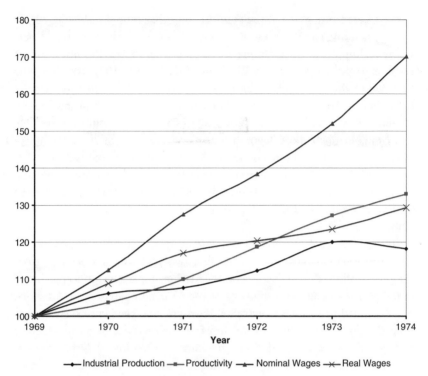

Figure 4.4. Germany: Wages, output, and productivity, 1969–1974. (*Source:* OECD 2000b.)

prices, the real purchasing power of workers increased by more than 8 percent" (DGB 1971: 198, 171). Similarly, in 1971, negotiated wage increases averaged 9.3 percent, leading to real wage increases of 7.7 percent (DGB 1971: 201). In both years, wage increases exceeded productivity increases by 2 percent (Germany Bundesministerium für Arbeit und Sozialordnung 2002). Figure 4.4 illustrates these developments.

Unions agreed to moderate their wage demands beginning in 1972. This date was not accidental: 1972 was the year in which the comprehensive legislation for pension insurance that had been initiated in 1969 was finally adopted. This massive reform package involved a projected increase in old-age expenditures of 186 billion DM to 1986, and it contained a number of additional changes that responded to trade unions' concerns (Hockerts 1992: 904). The law significantly raised benefit levels. It also introduced coverage for the self-employed and women who chose not to work. From the perspective of unions, the most important change was the increased flexibility of the retirement age. The new law allowed for retirement at age 63, 2 years prior to the official retirement age, with no deductions in the level of benefits. Thus, the 1972 reforms improved benefits and eligibility conditions for nearly every subgroup of the German population.

Trade unions welcomed the legislation. "Social policy was particularly successful during the last few years," the DGB announced in 1974. "In no other period has legislation responded to such a great number of union concerns" (DGB 1974: 43). Unions expressed particular enthusiasm about the provisions of the 1972 pension law, which provided a legal resolution to the long-standing policy demands of the labor movement, such as the elimination of the "excessively rigid" official retirement age and better benefits for persons with short employment histories (DGB 1974: 45–6). Invoking the expansion in benefits that resulted from the new legislation, union leaders exerted significant pressure on the rank and file to moderate their wage demands and were successful in restraining the militancy of their members. In 1972, industrial wages increased on average by 8.5 percent, and real wages increased by only 2.8 percent (Scharpf 1991: 123).

The 1972 wage bargaining round remained exceptional, however, with respect to wage developments under the Brandt government. 1973 was another crisis year for the German labor movement (Scharpf 1991). A massive wave of spontaneous strikes affecting firms in nearly all sectors of the German economy challenged the DGB's policy of wage moderation (Jacobi, Müller-Jentsch, and Schmidt 1973; E. Schmidt 1973). Despite the restrictive monetary policy of the Bundesbank, an influx of foreign funds defeated the efforts of German policy makers to stabilize the growth of the money supply. "From the unions' point of view," Fritz Scharpf points out, "the sacrifices they had made on behalf of stabilization were worthless. They had merely increased firms' profits and accelerated wage drift. Because the government was unable to protect the Federal Republic from worldwide inflation, unions had to adjust their inflationary expectations as well. The wage negotiations of 1973 reflected this change of union demands aiming at a substantial redistribution of incomes and anticipating further increases in the rate of inflation" (Scharpf 1991). The wage bargaining round produced nominal wage increases of 10.3 percent. Due to inflation, however, these nominal wage increases translated into real wage increases of 3.5 percent (Bispinck et. al. 1993: 134). The restrictive policy of the Bundesbank contributed to a sharp increase in the number of persons out of work, which doubled from 273,000 to 582,000 between 1973 and 1974.

The 1974 wage bargaining round revealed another weakness of the German wage negotiation system. In the late 1950s, IG Metall had assumed the role of leader in the wage bargaining process, with other unions following the level of wages established in the metalworking sector. One of the consequences of this informal convention was that the needs of the export sector were given higher weight in the wage setting process. This practice, however, rested on an informal agreement, not on a codified rule. In 1974, the Public Sector, Transportation, and Traffic Union (Gewerkschaft Öffentliche Dienste, Transport, und Verkehr, or ÖTV) challenged IG Metall's role and demanded a wage increase of 15 percent supplemented by additional fringe benefits, such as higher vacation pay. The German White-Collar Workers' Union (Deutsche Angestellten Gewerkschaft) followed the lead of the ÖTV and demanded a 14 percent wage hike (Bracher et al. 1986: 110). Both Chancellor Brandt and Finance Minister Schmidt strongly objected to these wage demands and urged the cabinet not to give in. Unions, however, did not respond to their exhortations. As a result of the failed negotiations, the ÖTV called the first national-level strike of the public sector in February 1974. The union was successful in challenging public-sector employers, and public-sector workers obtained wage increases of 11 percent.

This debacle about public union pay was one of the causes that contributed to the downfall of the Brandt government in 1974 (Bracher et al. 1986: 110–12; Giersch et al. 1992: 157). Commenting on the implications of this episode, historians have noted that "the impression created by the capitulation of the state in front of its employees was devastating" (Bracher et al. 1986: 111). In his memoir, Willi Brandt observed that "the 'loss of face' from giving in to union demands turned out even worse than expected" (Brandt 1992: 283). In the aftermath of the "Kluncker round" of 1974 (named after Heinz Kluncker, the president of the ÖTV), the Federation of German Employers Associations (Bundesvereinigung der Deutschen Arbeitgeberverbände) started a massive offensive designed to sway public opinion against unions and to demonstrate that, despite its ties with labor, the Social Democratic Party was unable to control labor militancy (Markovits 1986: 125).

The evolution of wage developments under the Brandt administration supports some of the theoretical propositions advanced in this book. First, as Chapter 1 has demonstrated, the absence of interunion coordination in the wage setting process accounts, in part, for the wage militancy of this period. Second, unions' concern for social policy continued to act as a source of wage moderation. Unions responded to the introduction of the much anticipated pension reform of 1972 with very restrained wage settlements. Third, unions' wage strategies were influenced by the macro-economic policy orientation of the government. In 1973 and 1974, militancy was a rational policy response to the inability of the Bundesbank to control inflationary pressures. The higher nominal wage settlements of these years produced real wage increases that were not particularly excessive. Yet we find an unexplained residual in the wage behavior of unions in the late 1960s and early 1970s: The unprecedented strike waves of 1968 and 1969 demonstrate that concerns about inequality and the distribution of economic resources among capital and labor remained important considerations motivating unions' behavior.

Wage Bargaining and Social Policy Developments Under the Social-Liberal Coalition, 1974–1982

The government of Helmut Schmidt took over under extremely inauspicious circumstances. External conditions, including a worldwide reduction in demand, severely affected Germany's exports, which fell by 11.5 percent in 1975 (OECD 2000b: Table 11.2). Domestically, the Bundesbank pursued an extremely restrictive monetary policy in the hope of preempting higher price increases and simultaneously disciplining the wage behavior of the unions. In late 1973, the Bundesbank reduced increases in the money supply to zero and maintained a policy of tight credit in the following months, thus sending a clear signal to all economic actors that it had abandoned the pursuit of the four goals laid out in 1967's Stability and Growth Act (Scharpf 1991: 132). As a result of the collision between the Bundesbank and the trade unions, the German economy slid into a deep economic recession. Over a period of 12 months the number of persons out of work quadrupled, rising from 270,000 in 1973 to 1.1 million the following year.

The social policy priorities of the Social-Liberal Coalition of 1974, outlined by Schmidt in his inaugural address, differed in important respects from the objectives of the outgoing government. In contrast to the "reform euphoria" of the Brandt government, Schmidt expressed caution about the possibility of expanding social programs. "Reforms are only feasible if they can be financed," he announced. This statement implied that previous growth rates for taxes and social policy expenditures were no longer

151

economically sustainable. Schmidt's inaugural address called for "realism and austerity" in the setting of social policy priorities and the need to "concentrate on the most essential elements, while leaving everything else aside" (Jäger and Link 1986: 13). An internal working document (*Arbeitsprogramm der Bundesregierung*) of the new government announced cutbacks in a number of social programs, an unprecedented event in the Federal Republic (Jäger and Link 1986: 14).

The new government attacked the economic recession with a combination of demand- and supply-side measures. The initial policies pursued in 1975 were Keynesian in orientation. To stimulate demand, the 1975 budget mandated an increase in borrowing at all levels of government (Scharpf 1991: 140). During the same year, an additional fiscal stimulus of 1.7 billion DM was introduced in the form of a "conjunctural program" (*Konjunkturprogramm*) whose goal was to improve the overall labor market situation (Jäger and Link 1986: 452). The main social policy program that was expanded in 1975 was family allowances: Monthly subsidies for children were increased by over 100 percent (Germany Bundesministerium für Arbeit und Sozialordnung 2002: Table 8.17). Additional tax reforms that lowered the tax burden on low-income households played an important role in preempting a real decline in the income and purchasing power of workers. In response to these policies, trade unions returned to a policy of wage moderation. The outcome of the 1975 wage settlements was an increase of 6 percent in the hourly wage rate. As a result of this combination of fiscal expansion and wage moderation, the German economy overcame the recession by the end of 1975. In 1976, the GDP grew at a rate of 5.4 percent (OECD Economic Surveys Germany 1977: 38).

Between 1976 and 1982, the Social-Liberal Coalition oscillated between implementing policies that attempted to consolidate the budget and lower the rate of growth of future social policy commitments and backing policies that offered improvements in the levels of benefits and services. An emphasis on fiscal consolidation dominated between 1976 and 1980 (Jäger and Link 1986: 19). A range of measures introduced in these years, such as the Budget Structural Adjustment Law (*Haushaltsstrukturgesetz*) of 1975, severely curtailed public investment programs (Manow and Seils 2000: 273). Efforts were made to slow growth in health-care expenditures. The gradual diminution of government-financed subsidies to the various subsystems of the German welfare state was an important aspect of the government's policy of fiscal consolidation (Deutsche Bundesbank 1987b: 12–13). The coalition also reduced subsidies to various labor market programs administered by the Federal Employment Office (M. Schmidt 1990: 136). Its austerity policies were successful in slowing down the rate of public expenditures growth: Between 1976 and 1982, the size of the public sector remained virtually unchanged at around 30 percent of the GDP (M. Schmidt 1990: 146). One important consequence of the reduction in fiscal subsidies to the insurance programs was a gradual increase in the level of insurance contributions. Contributions to unemployment insurance rose from 1 percent of the wage in 1974 to 2.3 percent in 1983, while contributions to sickness and old-age insurance increased by less than 1 percent (Germany Bundesministerium für Arbeit und Sozialordnung 2002: Table 7.7).

The policy of fiscal consolidation was followed by a brief Keynesian revival beginning in 1979. At the 1978 Bonn summit, the United States pressured Germany to embrace expansionary fiscal policies and to accept responsibility for helping other industrialized countries overcome the economic crisis that followed the second oil shock. The metaphor used at the summit compared the German economy to a "locomotive" pulling the rest of the countries out of recession (Putnam and Bayne 1984). Reluctantly, Helmut Schmidt accepted this role, although he later bitterly deplored the "locomotive strategy" as the main cause of his domestic political troubles (Jäger and Link 1986). Germany agreed to increase demand by about 1 percent of the GDP (Germany Bundesministerium der Finanzen 1978: 7; Scharpf 1991). Social policy legislation introduced in the late 1970s increased family allowances (though by a smaller amount than in 1974) and maternity leave benefits. A tax relief act lowered income taxes and provided additional tax benefits for housing allowances.

The wage strategies pursued by German trade unions were characterized by significant moderation. Figure 4.5 presents developments in wages, productivity, and output. On average, hourly wages rose by around 5 percent a year (DGB 1981, 1982). Real wages grew at a much slower rate and even declined in 1981 and 1982 by 0.8 percent (Scharpf 1991: 152, Table 7.8.). Unions' wage moderation in this period had several causes. Politically, Helmut Schmidt enjoyed a much closer relationship to unions than his predecessor. He appointed prominent union leaders to his cabinet (5 out of 15 cabinet members belonged to unions) and made sure they were constantly consulted regarding critical policy decisions (Jäger and Link 1986). As Willi Brandt characterized Schmidt's relationship with the unions, "Helmut Schmidt has three coalition partners, the DGB, the FDP and the SPD, in this particular order" (Braunthal 1983: 114). Several policy changes of 1976–1982, such as family allowances and tax credits, compensated

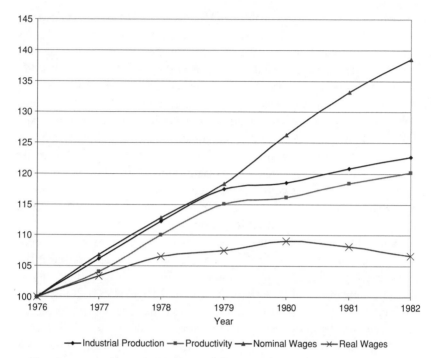

Figure 4.5. Germany: Wages, output, and productivity, 1976–1982. (*Source:* Bundesministerium für Arbeit und Sozialordnung, 1996.)

unions for wage restraint and guaranteed the maintenance of a constant income level for employed persons and their families (Scharpf 1991). A rise in unemployment also had a disciplining effect on the unions' wage behavior.

In contrast to the period before 1973, however, wage restraint was insufficient to restore full employment in the late 1970s and early 1980s. The average unemployment rate between 1975 and 1982 stood at 4.4 percent. The combination of fiscal expansion and wage moderation (pursued in 1975 and 1977) contributed to only a moderate decline in unemployment of 0.1 percent in 1975 and 0.6 percent in 1977 (OECD 2000b). This small decline came at a very high cost, however. To finance fiscal expansion, the deficit increased from 31.2 billion DM in 1977 to 75.7 billion DM in 1981 (Germany Bundesministerium der Finanzen 1986). An important factor that accounted for the decline in the effectiveness of the policy of wage moderation was the growth of the tax wedge. Figure 4.6 contrasts the evolution

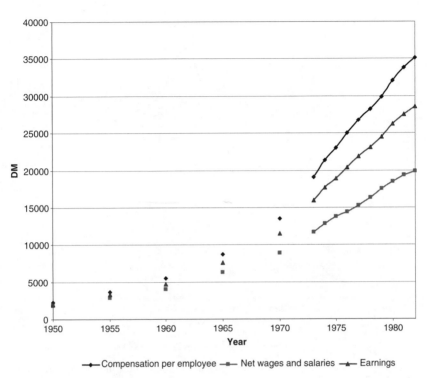

Figure 4.6. The growth of the tax wedge in Germany, 1950–1982. (*Source:* OECD, *Economic outlook: Germany*, various years.)

of net wages and salaries in Germany to the evolution of two additional indicators: total earnings and the total compensation of employees. (Total earnings include, in addition to net wages, the contributions of employees to social security and wage taxes. Total compensation is computed by adding the contribution of employers to social security to total earnings.) In 1950, net wages and salaries represented 80 percent of total compensation. This ratio declined to 72 percent in 1960 and 65 percent in 1970. By 1982, net wages accounted for only 56 percent of total compensation – in other words, almost half of the wage bill was already committed in the form of taxes. This decline in the share of wages as a percentage of total labor costs placed a higher burden on the one instrument unions could affect: wages. Much deeper cuts to wages were required to restore full employment. As the German welfare state matured, the effectiveness of unions' wage policy declined.

Figure 4.7. Germany: Share of foreign labor in total employment. (*Source:* Paqué 1996, 127.)

As a result of this decline in the effectiveness of traditional policy instruments to address the deterioration of Germany's employment performance, policy makers were led to experiment with a new strategy. This approach involved a series of measures that contributed to the reduction of the labor supply, or what Claus Offe has called a "negative labor supply policy" (see Manow and Seils 2000: 273). The first component was stopping the influx of foreign workers. In 1973, German firms stopped hiring new foreign workers, and the German government began efforts to repatriate foreigners living in Germany. As Figure 4.7 illustrates, the share of foreign labor as a percentage of total employment peaked in 1973 at 10.8 percent of the labor force. The second component of this political strategy consisted of the formulation of policies that created incentives for elderly workers to exit the labor market prior to the official retirement age. This strategy was initially extremely appealing both to policy makers and to unions, because it created an alternative to unemployment for an extremely vulnerable labor

156

market group. The costs of this decision, which came in the form of higher levels of payroll taxes that were a consequence of the contraction of the contributory base, became apparent only in the following decades.

German courts took the first step toward the creation of early retirement policies (Jacobs and Schmähl 1988; Mares 2001, 2003). Faced with an increase in the number of unemployed elderly workers, the Federal Social Court modified the entitlement criteria for occupational disability pensions (*Erwerbsunfähigkeitsrenten*). In an influential case of 1969, the Federal Social Court ruled that an occupational disability pension could be granted to a person with a partial disability if no part-time jobs were available (Bundessozialgericht 1970: 176–7). The immediate consequence of the court's decision was the transformation of disability pensions into "disability unemployment compensation" (Jacobs and Schmähl 1988: 202). Some of the risk of unemployment was de facto shifted to other subsystems of the welfare state, such as disability insurance. In the justification prefacing the decision, the court expressed its belief that it was appropriate for pension insurance (via the special occupational disability pensions) to absorb some of the costs of unemployment (Bundessozialgericht 1970: 177).

The second policy instrument that facilitated early retirement in Germany was a provision of the Employment Promotion Act (*Arbeitsförderungsgesetz*), which had been introduced by the Grand Coalition government in 1969. Paragraph 129 of the Act gave unemployed elderly workers the right to a pension 5 years prior to the official retirement age (Germany Bundesanstalt für Arbeit 1985). At the time the policy was formulated, unemployment appeared to be a short-lived problem facing a full-employment economy. The progressive worsening of labor market circumstances increased the attractiveness of the early retirement policy instrument for both firms and employees. Using paragraph 128, large firms began to lay off workers at age 59 and supplement their unemployment compensation for 1 year until the former employees became eligible for early pension benefits at age 60. The use of the Employment Promotion Act became increasingly common between 1970 and 1980 (Mares 2003: 233; Naschold and de Vroom 1994).

Finally, the Pension Reform Act of 1972 created a third pathway to early retirement. This law gave elderly workers the possibility of retiring at age 63 without facing an actuarial deduction in the level of their pension benefits. The Social-Democratic Coalition introduced this law as a response to a long-standing demand of trade unions and without fully anticipating the labor market implications of the measure. In conjunction with the other

157

measures, it created conditions for elderly workers to exit the labor market prior to retirement.

In combination, these policy changes had implications for both labor markets and for the financial equilibrium of Germany's insurance systems. The labor force participation rates of elderly workers experienced a steady, uninterrupted decline. Participation rates of men aged 55 to 64, which stood at 80.1 percent in 1970, fell to 65.5 percent by 1982 (OECD 2000b). As a result, Germany's overall labor force participation rates declined steadily. Total employment stood at 68.8 percent of the working age population in 1970 and dropped to 63.4 percent in 1982 (Scharpf and Schmidt 2000: 342). The growth in the number of labor market outsiders had an unfavorable impact on the financing of Germany's social insurance systems. Given that the largest subsystems of the German welfare state are financed by payroll taxes, reduction of the contributory basis established a vicious cycle in which a growth in the number of labor market outsiders exerted a continuous upward pressure on labor costs.

The negative labor supply-side policies embraced by German policy makers in the late 1970s and early 1980s affected the level of employment by raising social insurance charges. Scholars have developed two competing hypotheses about the impact of these policies on the wage demands of trade unions. The model developed in Chapter 1 hypothesizes that an increase in expenditures going to labor market outsiders is likely to fuel the wage militancy of trade unions, because it reduces the share of social policy services and transfers received by union members. But trade unions' publications advocating the early retirement solution – such as the Food Processing Workers' Union (NGG) – advanced the opposite proposition, arguing that early retirement could lead to a moderation of unions' wage demands, as unions were willing to trade off wage gains in exchange for a reduction in working life (Döding 1982, 1984). A comparison of wage developments in sectors that included early retirement agreements as part of wage negotiations and sectors where no such policy packages were in place shows no significant intersectoral difference in the growth in wages. The introduction of early retirement had no discernible effect on the wage strategies of trade unions.

By 1982, unions' patience with the policies pursued by the Schmidt government had run out. As discussed previously, unions had been a staunch ally of Helmut Schmidt and had negotiated extremely moderate wage settlements to support the efforts of the Social-Liberal Coalition to combat unemployment through fiscal expansion. Negotiations over the 1982 budget, which were known at the time as "Operation 82," led to a confrontation between unions and the government (Jäger and Link 1986: 208). The government made a determined attempt to stop the expansion of the deficit, which had doubled during the previous 4 years. To accomplish this goal, it recommended cutbacks to programs that were important to its Social Democratic constituency, such as unemployment benefits and family allowances, at the same time it raised individual social insurance contributions and consumption taxes (Scharpf 1991: 155). These attacks on the social safety net went too far for trade unions, which decided to show their determination to "topple the budgetary compromise of the government" (Scharpf 1991: 240). An IG Metall publication argued that the new policy developments caused "a deep rift in the relationship between unions and the Social Democratic Party" (Scharpf 1991: 245). Ernst Breit, the president of the DGB, warned that unions would not "contend themselves with verbal protests, but [would] express their opposition through appropriate actions" (Scharpf 1991: 240).

By the time unions announced their opposition to further austerity measures, German Social Democrats had been confronted with another ultimatum, this time from their junior coalition partner, the Free Democrats. In a policy memorandum, Economics Minister Otto von Lambsdorff demanded deeper cuts in social policy benefits than those under consideration by the Social Democrats and recommended at the same time traditional supply-side measures, such as tax cuts, to combat rising unemployment. The Lambsdorff memorandum was a "manifesto of secession," as *Die Zeit* aptly characterized it (10 September 1982). As a result of the leftward shift of unions and the rightward shift of the Free Democrats, Helmut Schmidt was unable to hold his ruling coalition together. The German chancellor chose to manifest loyalty to his traditional political constituency, the trade unions. His rejection of the Free Democrats' demands for additional austerity measures led to the political downfall of the Social-Liberal Coalition in 1983.

The evolution of wage, social policies, and employment outcomes from 1974 to 1982 stands in contrast to the policy developments of previous periods. While German trade unions continued to deliver wage moderation, this moderation was less effective at lowering unemployment than it had been in the past. The loss in effectiveness can be attributed to the growth in payroll and income taxes, which lowered the share of the total wage bill made up by wages. In response to the labor market deterioration, the government began to pursue policies that reduced the labor supply and encouraged early exit from the labor market. While these policies appeared to be an expedient solution, providing generous alternatives to labor market groups that were vulnerable to the risk of unemployment, in the long term they eroded the contributory basis of the German welfare state and pushed up payroll taxes still further.

The Consequences of Welfare State Maturation: Wage and Social Policy Developments, 1982–1990

In 1982 the Christian Democrats returned to power, forming a coalition with the Free Democrats. Using the term that had been introduced into German political discourse by the Lambsdorff paper, the new coalition proclaimed its intention to bring about a "dramatic break" (*Wende*) with the legacy of the Schmidt administration (Wever 1998a; Sturm 1998). Proposed reforms included a reduction in the size of the public sector, privatization, cutbacks in subsidies, tax cuts, and the deregulation of labor markets (Sturm 1998: 184). In addition, the new government pursued a number of changes to the major insurance systems designed to lower (or at least stabilize) the rate of growth of contributions. In the period leading up to German reunification, policies aimed at reducing the rate of growth of total social expenditures were more successful in achieving their objective than the social insurance reforms.

Until 1989, a central goal of the government's fiscal policy was to slow the expansion of the public sector. In his 1982 inaugural address, Helmut Kohl emphasized that his administration wished "to return to a consolidated state through consolidated finances" (Sturm 1998: 183). Its first priority was to lower the rate of growth of the public debt. When the Christian Democratic Party took office, Germany's public debt stood at 667 billion DM, or 40 percent of the GPD. The Social-Liberal Coalition had already initiated efforts to retard its further growth as part of "Operation 82." The Kohl administration implemented policies of fiscal consolidation more vigorously in the first 2 years of its administration in conjunction with the 1983 and 1984 budgets (Jochem 2001: 198). Retrenchment measures introduced cuts to social policy benefits financed out of general taxation, such as policies of child support, cuts to educational assistance for both schoolchildren and students, and limits on the level of public-sector salary and pension growth (Deutsche Bundesbank 1990: 38–9). Additional cuts were brought about through a reduction in capital spending by federal, local, and state governments: Between 1982 and 1984, this spending item was reduced by 20 percent. Financial subsidies, such as public loans at low interest rates and other grants to enterprises, were also reduced. These policies of fiscal consolidation were relatively successful, slowing the average rate of growth of the public debt to 6.1 percent between 1983 and 1989, as compared to 16.6 percent for 1975–1979. From 1982 to 1989, public spending grew at an average rate of 3.2 percent against an 8 percent increase for the period between 1978 and 1981 (Deutsche Bundesbank 1990: 39).

Consolidating the public debt was a fiscal priority in the first 2 years of the Kohl administration. The focus of policy shifted, however, in the following years (Sturm 1998). Beginning in 1985, the central objective of fiscal policy became the gradual reduction of the total tax burden and the restructuring of the tax system (Deutsche Bundesbank 1989: 40; OECD 1985: 15–17). A series of tax reforms introduced between 1986 and 1988 provided overall tax relief of about 50 billion DM (Sturm 1998: 192). The largest part of this tax relief came in the form of subsidies to families with children. The Tax Reduction Act of June 1985 raised children's allowances from DM 432 to DM 2,484 per child, a sixfold increase whose cost was estimated at about 11 billion DM in foregone taxes (Deutsche Bundesbank 1989: 41). Other measures raised the basic allowance but also reduced the tax burden at the higher levels of the marginal tax rate. The Tax Reform Act of July 1988 continued the reforms along the same trajectory: It provided for an additional increase in the basic allowance and children's allowance, which was raised to DM 3,024, but it also lowered the top rate of the income tax by 3 points to 53 percent (Deutsche Bundesbank 1989: 43).

With respect to social protection, the Kohl government engaged in intense efforts to limit the growth of workers' and employers' payroll taxes. It attempted to reverse the trend toward ever-higher labor costs (Jochem 2001). Each measure provided only short-term relief, however, and was followed by a rise in payroll taxes, and thus between 1982 and 1989 the total rate of insurance contributions financing old-age, sickness, and unemployment insurance increased from 34 to 36 percent of the wage bill (Germany Bundesministerium für Arbeit und Sozialordnung 1998: 292). An explanation for the failure of the Kohl government to reduce payroll taxes can be found by analyzing developments in the two largest insurance systems of the welfare state: sickness and old-age insurance.

In comparative terms, Germany devotes a very large share of public expenditures to health care. In 1985, total health expenditures were 8.6 percent of the GDP, making the Federal Republic the world's second largest

161

spender on health care after the United States (OECD Economic Surveys Germany 1990; Deutsche Bundesbank 1991a: 29). Given the size of the health care sector, efforts to reform it occupied a central place on the agenda of the Christian Democratic government (Bandelow 1998; Rosewitz and Webber 1990). The overarching goal of health care reform was to lower the rate of expenditure growth and to maintain overall stability in insurance contributions (*Beitragsstabilität*) (Perschke-Hartmann 1994: 45). The Schmidt government had established a "Concerted Action Group for Germany's Health Sector" that included representatives of unions, employers, health insurance institutions, and suppliers of medical services in addition to government officials. In the first years of the Kohl administration, Labor Minister Norbert Blüm relied extensively on this institution for the formulation of health care reforms. The defining characteristic of the reforms it recommended was their reliance on the statutory health insurance funds to reduce the rising costs of health care (Perschke-Hartmann 1994: 46; Döhler and Manow 1997). The new legislation delegated new competencies to the health insurance funds in the hope that they would use their increase in power to pressure health care providers to lower their costs (Bandelow and Schubert 1998: 116). This was the gist of the Hospital Reform Act (*Krankenhausneuordnungsgesetz*) of December 1984, which increased the decision-making responsibilities of health insurance funds and hospitals for the financing of hospital costs and simultaneously decreased the financial and political involvement of the federal government in these decisions (Deutsche Bundesbank 1985: 30). This approach to health care reform, which reflected the preference of Christian Democratic parties for "subsidiarity" in the provision of social insurance benefits, did not succeed in curbing the rate of growth of health care expenditures. As a result, German policy makers had no choice but to increase contributions to health insurance, which rose by about 2 percent between 1982 and 1988.

Given the failure to contain rising health care costs, all major parties began to discuss plans for a "structural reform" of the German health care system. Their deliberations, which lasted for more than 3 years, culminated in the adoption of the Health Insurance Reform Act (*Gesundheitsreformgesetz*) of 1988 (Perschke-Hartmann 1994). The main goal of this act was to limit health care expenditures to "what is medically necessary and sufficient" (Deutsche Bundesbank 1991a: 26). The law raised the level of co-payments for drugs by 10 percent and modestly reduced some benefits (Bandelow and Schubert 1998: 117). Lawmakers also attempted to pressure pharmaceutical firms to lower the prices of drugs and introduced a "negative list" of drugs that were no longer covered (Deutsche Bundesbank 1991a: 27). Nevertheless, the Health Insurance Reform Act also failed to curtail the growth of health care costs, which fell only temporarily. While in 1989 total expenditures of health care funds decreased by 3 percent, they increased sharply beginning in 1991 (Bandelow and Schubert 1998: 118).

In contrast to health care, reforms in the area of old-age insurance were not motivated by a sense of immediate urgency – over the course of the 1980s, pension insurance funds held a slight surplus as a result of favorable demographic developments – but rather by long-term considerations. Deliberations about pension reform lasted for several years and culminated in the adoption of the 1989 Pension Reform Act (Nullmeier and Rüb 1993). The act changed the indexation in the formula that determined pension benefit levels, shifting the basis from gross wages to net wages. Beginning in 1974, real and nominal pension benefits had grown at a faster rate than the net wages and salaries of workers. This was a consequence of rising social insurance contributions, which led to slower rates of net wage growth as compared to gross wages (Deutsche Bundesbank 1985: 15). The formula change was necessary to keep the rate of growth in pension benefits from surpassing the growth of productivity. The law introduced several deductions in benefits for persons choosing the retirement option prior to the official retirement age but postponed the implementation of these measures to a later time. It also restructured federal subsidies to pension insurance, tying them to increases in contributions. By guaranteeing a steady commitment in federal financing for future rises in expenditures, this measure was intended to act as a brake on the growth of future insurance contributions. Overall, about 20 percent of future pension expenditures would be financed by federal government revenues (Deutsche Bundesbank 1995: 22).

A necessary condition for stabilizing growth in insurance contributions was higher labor force participation rates. Low employment ratios were particularly problematic for the German welfare state, which was heavily dependent on insurance contributions for its financing. In the mid-1980s, Christian Democratic policy makers enacted several reforms in the hope of increasing the labor force participation rates of elderly workers (Mares 2001, 2003; Manow and Seils 2000: 280–1). The central legislative effort in this direction was the Early Retirement Act (*Vorruhestandsgesetz*) of 1984, which aimed to reduce the attractiveness of the early retirement option for both firms and workers. The Early Retirement Act doubled the charges firms faced for laying off elderly workers prior to the official retirement age (from 30,000 DM to 70,000 DM) while at the same time increasing the stringency of eligibility conditions for benefits received by individual workers (Mares 2003: 243). But the act failed to slow the trend toward early exit from the labor market. While it reduced the attractiveness of some of the early retirement pathways, firms turned to substitute instruments available in different subsystems of the welfare state and continued to offer powerful inducement to elderly workers to stop working several years prior to the official retirement age (Manow and Seils 2000: 281; Jacobs, Kohli and Rein 1991: 203). Labor force participation rates of workers aged 55 to 64 stood at 63.1 percent in 1983 and declined to 57.8 percent in 1989 (Scharpf and Schmidt 2000: 350).

This discussion suggests that the inability of the Kohl government to lower social insurance contributions can be traced to factors specific to individual policy areas. The organizational decentralization and fragmentation of sickness insurance institutions posed great challenges to the government's efforts to slow the growth in health care expenditures. In the case of old-age insurance reforms, the multitude of policy pathways that allowed firms to shed elderly workers frustrated the efforts of policy makers to stop the trend toward early exit from the labor market and end what labor minister Norbert Blum called the "financial hemorrhage" of the old-age insurance system. Figure 4.8 examines the consequences of the rise in social insurance contributions on workers' net wages. The gap between the total compensation of workers and net wages continued to increase over this period: In 1983, net wages represented 57.11 percent of employees' total compensation; this ratio had declined to 54.96 percent by 1989. At the end of the decade, nearly 50 percent of the wage bill remained committed in the form of taxes.

Such high nonwage labor costs established rigid constraints for wage bargaining actors in the 1980s. Analysis of successive wage bargaining rounds, however, reveals remarkable levels of wage moderation. Figure 4.9 presents data on the development of wages, output, and productivity between 1982 and 1990, the year of German reunification. Even Bundesbank publications applauded unions' moderation, noting that "the all in all relatively moderate wage rate policy during the period from 1985 to 1989, in which agreed pay rates were raised by over 3 percent per year on a monthly basis and by not quite 4 percent on an hourly basis, boosted enterprises' earnings power and improved their profit expectations, which contributed greatly to the acceleration of investment activity in the West German economy" (Deutsche Bundesbank 1994: 30). Real wages stagnated between 1982 and

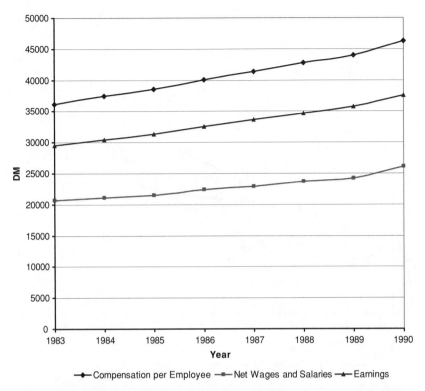

Figure 4.8. Germany: The evolution of payroll taxes and compensation, 1983–1990. (*Source:* OECD, *Economic outlook: Germany*, various years.)

1985 and experienced a slight increase afterward. Throughout the period, increases in real wages lagged behind productivity growth.

The persistence of moderation during this period can be attributed to the stronger constraint imposed by the Bundesbank on the actions of the wage bargaining parties (Hall 1994; Hall and Franzese 1998). As Fritz Scharpf has pointed out, in the late 1970s the Bundesbank gained a first-mover advantage by beginning to announce its money supply goal 1 year in advance of wage bargaining negotiations: "The bank was able to consolidate its strategic gains because neither the unions, nor the federal government were prepared to expend their limited potential for a battle on an institutional issue that no longer seemed critical. It was this fact, rather than the formal provisions of the Federal Bank Act, that allowed the Bundesbank to win a dominant role in the German political economy" (Scharpf 1991). The

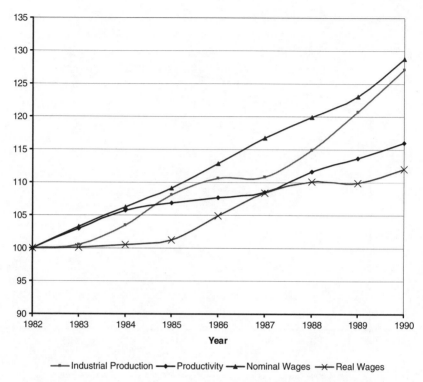

Figure 4.9. Germany: Wages, output, and productivity, 1983–1990. (*Sources:* WSI Mitteilungen 1993, 3:134 (real and nominal wages and productivity); Germany. Bundesministerium für Arbeit und Sozialordnung 2002: Table 3.1.)

effective coordination between wage setting actors and monetary authorities, which has been emphasized in recent studies as an important cause of the moderation of German trade unions, was not a constant throughout the postwar period. It characterizes, however, most accurately the functioning of the German political economy between 1983 and 1989.

The moderate growth in wages was also facilitated by the lengthening of the duration of wage agreements (Kurz-Scherf 1988; Deutsche Bundesbank 1994). While historically the normal length of a wage bargaining agreement was 12 months, the average duration of labor market contracts increased to 16 months in 1984 and to 22 months in 1988 (Kurz-Scherf 1988: 121). These multiyear contracts came into effect in key sectors of the German economy, such as the metalworking industry, textiles, steel, and the public sector (Deutsche Bundesbank 1994: 31). The lengthening of contracts' duration was itself the product of bargaining between unions and employers over reductions in working time. In exchange for a reduction in the working week, unions accepted longer wage contracts and months with no wage increases, the so-called *Null-Monate* (Kurz-Scherf 1988: 124).

Given the high level of payroll taxes, however, the policy of moderation on the wage front was fairly ineffective at reducing unemployment. Between 1983 and 1989, unemployment fell by only 1 point from 9.1 percent in 1983 to 7.9 percent in 1989 (Germany Bundesministerium für Arbeit und Sozialordnung 2002: Table 2.10). In absolute terms, the number of unemployed persons changed very little, hovering slightly above 2 million.

This narrative of the evolution of the nexus between wages and social policy developments in the 1980s has allowed me to test several hypotheses advanced in the literature. The findings support the Soskice-Iversen conjecture that the strong commitment to an anti-inflationary policy of the Bundesbank constrained the militancy of wage bargaining actors. Compared to previous periods, however, the policy of wage moderation was less effective at reducing unemployment in the 1980s. This fact lends support to the proposition of Chapter 1. High payroll taxes eroded the size of the wage bill that was subject to bargaining between unions and employers, and this development, in turn, reduced the employment impact of the policy of wage moderation. While wage moderation had been effective in reconciling high levels of employment and a political commitment to social spending in the first decades of the postwar period, this was no longer the case in the 1980s. Finally, we find no evidence for the hypothesis that an increase in the number of labor market outsiders affected the wage strategies of German trade unions in a direction of greater militancy during this period.

The Aftermath of German Reunification, 1990–1997

The process of reunification created new political challenges for all actors in the German political economy. In an effort to smooth the transfer of West German institutions to the new *Länder*, the Kohl government announced a massive increase in financial transfers from the Federal Republic to the East. The initial financial commitments – made during the negotiations for the Treaty Reestablishing German Unity – were based on unrealistic expectations about the economic conditions of the former Democratic Republic and on belief in the possibility of a painless economic recovery in the East. The transfers included investments in the neglected infrastructure, subsidies to areas with regional or structural disadvantages, and investment grants to private enterprises (Deutsche Bundesbank 1993: 19–20). Between 1990 and 1998, overall transfers to the East stood at an average 6.6 percent of the GDP (Zolnhöfer 2000).

About 40 percent of the financial transfers from West to East Germany were expenditures devoted to labor market and social programs (Bönker and Wollmann 2000). This high share of social policy expenditures can be attributed to two factors. The first is the massive labor market deterioration of the East German *Länder*, whose economic output declined by 15 percent in 1990 and 22 percent in 1991. As a result, open unemployment in the East increased from 10 percent in 1991 to 19.5 percent in 1998. The number of labor market outsiders – defined here as persons of working age who were neither employed nor unemployed – also rose to alarmingly high levels, oscillating between 15 and 16 percent of the population in the 1990s (Burda and Hunt 2001: 6). A variety of labor market programs were extended to cushion economic dislocation, including early retirement, retraining, and job creation programs. Most were financed by the Federal Employment Office, which had an average deficit level of 12 percent between 1991 and 1997 (Deutsches Institut für Wirtschaftsforschung 1997: 727).

The second factor accounting for the high share of social policy expenditures as a percentage of all transfers to the East was the political decision to merge East and West German social insurance institutions (Czada 1998; Zolnhöfer 2000). This politically expedient decision increased social policy transfers received by the citizens of the former Democratic Republic and reassured the reelection of the Christian Democrats. It placed a strong strain, however, on the finances of the various insurance systems. Table 4.2 compares the implications of German reunification for the financial equilibrium of old-age, sickness, and unemployment insurance. As these figures illustrate, the West German old-age and unemployment insurance institutions experienced a surplus in the 1990s. For both these subsystems of the German welfare state, reunification was responsible for their large deficits. Reunification had particularly negative implications for unemployment insurance, which experienced double-digit deficits throughout the decade. By contrast, West German institutions of sickness insurance were in a more precarious financial equilibrium and were consequently less affected by the process of reunification. According to a number of estimates, reunification contributed to an increase in the level of payroll taxes by 3 percent over the 1990s (Bönker and Wollmann 2000).

These developments strained the consensual relationship between monetary authorities, fiscal policy makers, and wage bargaining actors. The

Table 4.2. *Impact of reunification on the financial outlook of the German welfare state: The fiscal balance of several insurance systems*

	1991	1992	1993	1994	1995	1996	1997
Policy							
Old-age insurance							
West	11.2	10.7	0.7	8.8	6.0	11.5	22.3
East	0.7	−1.4	−8.1	−12.6	−15.8	−18.9	−19.0
Total	11.9	9.4	−7.4	−3.8	−9.9	−7.4	3.3
Sickness insurance							
West	−5.6	−9.1	9.1	2.1	−5.1	−4.6	−0.3
East	2.8	−0.3	1.4	0.1	−1.8	−2.1	−1.5
Total	−2.8	−9.4	10.5	2.2	−7.0	−6.8	−1.8
Unemployment insurance							
West	20.4	24.5	15.0	19.5	15.7	11.0	10.4
East	−20.0	−38.0	−38.6	−29.6	−23.1	−26.6	−25.0
Total	0.4	−13.5	−23.6	−10.1	−7.3	−15.7	−14.6

Source: Deutsches Institut für Wirtschaftsforschung 1997.

Bundesbank reacted with a very restrictive monetary policy: It raised the discount rate, which stood at 3.5 percent in 1989, to 8.75 percent in July 1992; in parallel, the Lombard rate was raised from 5.5 percent in 1989 to 9.75 percent in 1992 (Heilemann, Gebhart, and Loeffelholz 1996: 194). As Wendy Carlin and David Soskice characterized the factors influencing the decisions of the Bundesbank officials, "The Bundesbank sought to punish the government for excessive levels of borrowing. Its behavior is likely to have also been influenced by the defeat at the hands of the government over the conversion rate for Ost Mark into Deutschmarks and the failure of its proposals for a revaluation of the D-Mark in the exchange rate mechanism in the wake of reunification" (Carlin and Soskice 1997: 70).

The behavior of German unions in the first year after reunification was characterized by unexpected radicalism. The 1991 wage bargaining round led to wage increases that significantly exceeded growth in productivity or economic output. Several factors account for the rise in union militancy. The first cause was another departure from the postwar norm that gave IG Metall a leading role in wage negotiations. This norm was violated as a result of the decision of the public-sector union ÖTV to act as wage leader in 1991 (Bispinck et al. 1991: 461). A study commissioned by public-sector unions and used by the ÖTV to sway public opinion in its favor showed that over the previous decade wages in the public sector had fallen behind private-sector wages by 10 to 15 percent. In an effort to eradicate this distributive setback, public-sector unions demanded wage increases of 6 percent and succeeded in obtaining them. Agreements negotiated in other sectors matched and sometimes surpassed the public-sector agreement, leading to an average wage growth of 6.6 percent in 1991 (Bispinck et al. 1993: 129).

The militancy of the 1991 wage bargaining round was also a consequence of unions' explicit decision to reject the proposal of German policy makers that unions moderate wages as a "sacrifice" to cushion the costs of reunification. Wulf Mathies, the president of the public-sector unions, argued, for instance, that the "incomes of public sector workers are not a savings bank for national sacrifices" (Bispinck et al. 1991: 460). Two considerations motivated unions' opposition to these proposals: belief that the distribution of the costs of reunification among labor and capital would not be equitable and that labor would be burdened with higher costs. As a publication of unions expressed this view: "A socially acceptable mode of financing of the costs of German unification is not in view. By contrast, the 'solidarity pact' turns out to be an opportunity for welfare state retrenchment, and unions will not be willing to use the wage settlements to correct the 'unsocial' (*unsoziale*) tax and expenditure policy" (Bispinck et al. 1991: 477). Reunification brought about a significant change in the composition of recipients of social policy transfers, swelling the number of "outsiders" who had claims to various programs. This development also lowered unions' willingness to accommodate the increase in transfers to the East with a policy of wage moderation.

In contrast to 1991, wage developments of the following years were characterized by significant moderation. Figure 4.10 summarizes these outcomes and contrasts the evolution of wages, productivity, and output for the period between 1990 and 1997. The return to moderation can be attributed largely to the decision of employers to resist additional wage increases and to their coordinated action in pursuing this goal. The hardline approach of employers was particularly important in the 1993 and 1994 wage bargaining rounds (Bispinck et al. 1993, 1994). In 1993, metalworking employers succeeded in limiting wage growth to increases that were lower than price increases (Bispinck et al. 1993: 136). This settlement was followed by similar settlements throughout the economy, leading to wage developments that lagged behind price developments by 0.7 percent (Bispinck et al. 1994). During the 1994 wage bargaining round, Gesamtmetall called

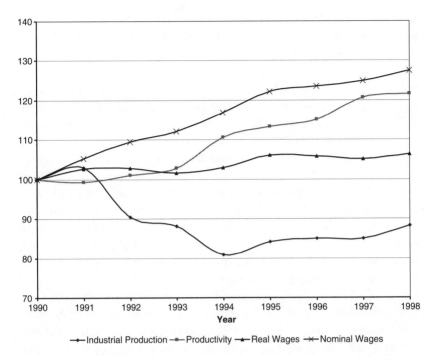

Figure 4.10. Germany: Wages, output, and productivity, 1990–1997. (*Sources:* U.S. Bureau of Labor Statistics 2003 (productivity data); Germany. Bundesministerium für Arbeit und Sozialordnung 2002.)

for a 10 percent reduction in wage costs, while public-sector employers promoted an "outcome of the wage negotiations with a so-called red zero" (Bispinck et al. 1994: 469). While unions deplored this offensive of employers as an "attempt to bring labor on its knees" and "a danger for the social peace," they were unable to resist employers' demands and to secure real wage gains for their members (Bispinck et. al. 1994). In many sectors, the 1994 wage bargaining round ended in a reduction of real wages.

In the following years, German unions made a significant effort to take the political offensive on questions of unemployment. The policy solution proposed by IG Metall leader Klaus Zwickel was the "Alliance for Jobs" (*Bündnis für Arbeit*) (Bispinck et al. 1996: 163). In his initial proposal, announced at the 1996 IG Metall congress, Zwickel committed unions to moderate wage increases in the coming years. In exchange, he demanded from employers a commitment to create 300,000 new jobs as well as opportunities for the long-term unemployed to reenter the labor market, through lower earning jobs (Bispinck et al. 1996: 464). Unions also insisted that the government abandon its attempts to reduce social policy benefits.

These proposals served as the basis for discussion in numerous meetings between unions, employers, and government officials (Heise 1996; Wendl 1997). The Alliance for Jobs proposal failed, however, to cement a long-lasting political agreement among these actors about a sustainable solution to Germany's deteriorating employment performance. Ultimately, the event that triggered the breakdown of the Alliance for Jobs discussions was the government's decision to enact cutbacks in a number of social insurance programs. Emboldened by its success in the 1996 midterm elections, it shifted from cooperating with unions to a more aggressive posture, submitting an austerity package (*Sparpaket*) that attempted to consolidate the budget by lowering replacement rates for several social programs. Of symbolic value for German trade unions was the government's decision to lower compensation for sickness insurance by 20 percent. In protest against this action, IG Metall organized one of the largest demonstrations of the postwar period to coincide with the 40th anniversary of the 1956 Schleswig-Holstein strike. Its protest galvanized public opinion against the Christian Democratic coalition and contributed to the electoral victory of the Social Democrats in 1998.

The return to wage moderation that began in 1992 did not reduce unemployment, which continued to rise in the 1990s, exceeding 3 million in 1994 and 4 million in 1997. The restrictive monetary policy pursued by the Bundesbank in 1991 and 1992 helps to account for the dramatic deterioration of Germany's economic performance in the first years after reunification. But the central structural factor that stymied the effectiveness of wage moderation in lowering unemployment was the high level of payroll taxes. This constraint was an endogenous consequence of the process of welfare state maturation, and it was only marginally intensified by the process of reunification.

Conclusions

The employment performance of the Federal Republic varied dramatically between the period of the economic miracle and decades. The spectacular growth achieved during the first decades of the postwar period was accompanied by low levels of unemployment and expanding labor force

172

Conclusions

participation rates. This economic and employment performance faltered, however, in the mid-1970s. Since then, unemployment has risen at an alarming rate: At its peak in 1997, it stood at 12.7 percent of the labor force. The slow economic recovery of the late 1990s has not resulted in a reduction in unemployment. On the eve of the new millennium, unemployment in Germany continued to exceed 10 percent (Germany Bundesministerium für Arbeit und Sozialordnung 2002).

The dominant explanations that have been formulated by comparative political economy scholars to account for the evolution of Germany's labor market performance examine the mix of strategies pursued by Germany's independent central bank and the DGB. This line of analysis, which began with Scharpf's pathbreaking work, has been refined in recent years by Hall and Franzese, Iversen, and Soskice (Scharpf 1991; Hall and Franzese 1998; Iversen and Soskice 1999, 2000). A problematic implication of this analysis is its inability to explain the persistence of unemployment in Germany in recent decades. Its key explanatory variables – the centralization of the wage bargaining system and the level of central bank independence – have experienced virtually no change in recent decades. Nor can the deterioration of German employment performance simply be attributed to the shock posed by German reunification, as rising unemployment levels preceded German reunification by over a decade. By integrating parameters modeling the level and composition of welfare state transfers into the analysis, and by examining the constraints posed by the welfare state on the behavior of wage bargaining agents, the model developed in this book accounts for the intertemporal deterioration of Germany's labor market performance more effectively than do existing studies.

5

Britain

[handwritten annotation: militant wage behavior of unions + labor unrest contributed to British economic problem]

Most studies that examine macroeconomic policy making in Britain agree that the militant wage behavior of unions and pervasive labor unrest was an important cause contributing to Britain's persistent economic problems in the postwar period and to the relative economic decline of the British economy (Hall 1986; Scharpf 1991). As these studies argue, in Britain income policies were repeatedly attempted but never succeeded. In a recent paper Rhodes summarizes this view, arguing that the political exchange premised on wage moderation in exchange for social policy expansion "was neither developed, nor institutionalized in Britain. One of the peculiarities (at least in the European context) of the British system was the divorce between the labor movement and the social insurance system.... Combined with 'voluntarism' and organizational fragmentation in industrial relations, this helped prevent the development of the notion of the 'social wage' in Britain" (Rhodes 2000: 22).

This characterization of policy making in Britain conflates two factors that might account for the lack of success of policies linking wage moderation to social policy expansion. The first of these concerns the preferences of the labor movement, while the second concerns the structure of the wage bargaining system. Did British trade unions deliberately reject the notion of a "social wage"? Did they show no concern for the expansion of social policy benefits, focusing only on the need to increase the real wages of their members? Did the British labor movement systematically rebuff ideas establishing an equivalence between wages and social policies? Or did income policies fail in Britain as a result of the fragmentation of the wage bargaining system and the inability of trade union leaders to constrain the militancy of the rank and file?

The British case is an ideal testing ground for the micro-level implications of the model developed in Chapter 1 for several reasons. It is a hard test for one of the central hypotheses of this study which suggests that unions' concern for the expansion of social policy benefits and services acts as an important source of wage moderation. The previous chapters demonstrated that this logic was at work in Germany and Sweden, accounting for the wage moderation exercised by unions in these countries in the first two decades of the postwar period. Were the preferences of British labor organizations fundamentally different from the preferences of German or Swedish trade unions, and if so, how can we account for these differences? This chapter will explore these questions, relying on a combination of union publications, minutes of the meetings of the Trades Union Congress (TUC), and secondary sources. The British case is also an important test case for the theoretical argument developed in this book because of the discontinuity in the postwar structure of the wage bargaining system. The British industrial relations system evolved from one that shared important common features with corporatist countries to a fully decentralized system characterized by firm-level wage setting. This provides an ideal setup that allows us to examine the consequences of differences in the design of wage bargaining institutions for the wage choices made by unions.

Wage Developments of the Postwar Years, 1945–1950

In the immediate postwar years, wage policies were negotiated under the shadow of far-reaching new social policies. The policy principles underpinning the reconstruction of the welfare state had been formulated by the wartime coalition government, which included representatives of both Conservatives and Labour. The novel ideas underpinning these policies, such as the commitment to universalism in social protection and to flat-rate benefits, had been expressed for the first time in the British context in a number of policy documents, including the Beveridge report of 1942, the 1944 Butler Education Act, and the White Paper on Employment of 1944 (Brooke 1992). The Labour government elected in 1945 expanded on these ideas and enacted a number of policies, creating the National Health Service and introducing universal social security. In contrast to continental economies, the corporatist organization of social insurance was explicitly abandoned: British unions and employers were given no role in the administration of social insurance.

(handwritten margin note: Britain used contributory financing to fund social programs)

Both the British Labour Party and the TUC supported the basic policy principles of the postwar reforms (Brooke 1992; Howell 1976; Harris 1986). At the 1942 party conference, the Labour Party approved a policy recommendation endorsing ideas resembling the Beveridge report. To establish a sharper distinction between these policies and social assistance, Labour recommended that the new social programs be financed by employers' and employees' contributions. The TUC also welcomed the Beveridge report with relatively few reservations. In a series of documents submitted to Beveridge in December 1941, the Social Policy Committee of the TUC demanded the introduction of an inclusive social insurance scheme covering all the significant risks: old age, unemployment, sickness, accidents, maternity, and widowhood. Unions supported the principle of the minimum standard of living, or the subsistence principle, that was at the core of the Beveridge report (TUC 1942: 224–5). The issue of how to finance social insurance legislation remained more controversial for the British labor movement. Bevanites challenged the principle of contributory financing, advocating instead a tax-financed approach. The controversy was ultimately resolved in favor of contributory financing (Baldwin 1990). British trade unions demanded and successfully secured generous subsidies from the government, covering initially one-third of the costs of the new program. While the welfare reforms contributed to a massive increase in the scope of social insurance coverage, the level of benefits provided by the National Insurance Act were relatively meager. In 1948, standard weekly rates of unemployment, sickness, or retirement benefits were set at 1.30 pounds, approximately 19 percent of the earnings of manual workers (U.K. Government Statistical Service 1988: 256–8).

Analysis of trade union publications from the period suggests that unions established the equivalence between social policy and wages. The notion of the social wage was present in the discourse of the labor movement and informed union strategies. Unions' calculations were straightforward: because the expansion of social policy benefits brought about a real increase in the income of workers, those benefits had a similar status to wages. "Think of what we have achieved in terms of social security, in terms of health services, free meals for children, free milk and better educational facilities," one union publication argued. "That can be assessed at roughly 2 pound 4s per week for the average family" (Whiteside 1996: 90). The expansion of the welfare state was even more remarkable when viewed against the background of interwar unemployment: "The general level of wages has been considerably improved, the cost of living has been kept in close approximation to the means of the average wage earner, expenditure on social services repays in real benefits to the bulk of the population and especially to the wage earner; the number of people in employment has never been so high; the number of unemployed has never been so low" (TUC 1950: 90). Unions acknowledged, moreover, that the massive expansion of government-financed programs removed the need for them to bargain with employers for social policy benefits such as health care or old-age benefits (TUC 1950: 25–6). Consequently, the expansion of benefits strengthened the bargaining position of workers (TUC 1950: 19).

The TUC's acceptance of the equivalence between social policy benefits and wages helped to facilitate the negotiation of income policies between 1947 and 1951. The Labour government first attempted to convince unions to moderate their wage demands in February 1948 (Dorfman 1973: 51–72; R. Jones 1987: 34–47). A government white paper entitled "Statement on Personal Incomes, Costs and Prices" recommended "voluntary restraint in the level of wages" (U.K. Parliament 1948: par. 7a). Unions' cooperation with the policy was by no means automatic. To elicit the help of the TUC, the minister of economic affairs threatened to reduce supplementary income benefits, such as food subsidies (Dorfman 1973: 63–4). The threat proved effective. A special TUC conference endorsed the policy of wage restraint by a relatively wide margin, with 5.6 million members in favor and 4.5 million opposed (TUC 1948: 290). In exchange, unions demanded the continuation of subsidies, the "vigorous enforcement of price controls," and "restraint in profits and dividends." In addition, they asked that "substandard" wages that "fell below a reasonable standard of living" be exempted from the policy of wage restraint (TUC 1948: 10; Dorfman 1973: 66).

In August 1949, the government again approached the General Council of the TUC to demand wage restraint. At this time, "the government hoped to cast the net of the policy rather wide, and in particular to include the 1.5 million workers whose wages were linked directly to the cost of living through 'sliding scales' " (R. Jones 1987: 37–8). Trade unions again cooperated, but this time support for wage restraint was much more limited. At a special executive conference of the TUC in January 1950, supporters of the policy garnered only a narrow majority of 600,000 votes (Whiteside 1996: 92). By late 1950, the government was aware that a third attempt to elicit trade unions' cooperation would fail. Consequently, policy makers began to consider introducing a permanent mechanism for wage regulation. The government elaborated plans to establish a Wages Advisory Council that

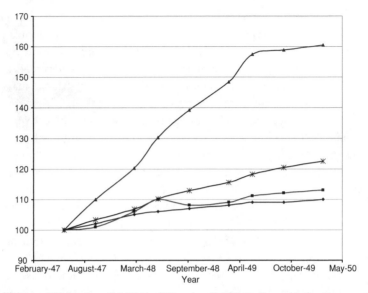

Figure 5.1. Britain: Wage restraint under Labour, 1947–1950. [*Sources:* Dorfman 1978, 78 (wages and prices); U.K. Central Statistical Office 1955 (GDP).]

would formulate official guidelines on pay and productivity (R. Jones 1987: 40). These plans never came to fruition, however, due to Labour's electoral defeat in the fall of 1951.

Wage restraint lasted from 1948 to 1950. As Figure 5.1 illustrates, average growth in wages lagged behind growth in prices and in the GDP. In real terms, "wage increases fell from a yearly average of 8–10 percent during 1945–1948 to an average of 3 percent for the period between March 1948 and September 1949 and then to an average of about 1.4 percent 1 year after devaluation" (R. Jones 1987: 43). Over time, however, the decline in real wages prompted dissatisfaction and concern among the rank and file. By the fall of 1950, the TUC had encountered a wave of resolutions and unofficial strikes that called an end to the policy of wage restraint (Tolliday and Zeitlin 1986; Whiteside 1996: 93). While 1948–1950 saw one of the most successful episodes of wage restraint in postwar British history, its duration was brief.

A few conclusions follow from analysis of the 1948–1950 period. First, it appears that British trade unions shared similar policy preferences with labor movements in other European countries. Like unions in Sweden and

Germany, British trade unions established an equivalence between social policy benefits and wages and were willing to moderate their wage demands in response to the expansion of social protection of the immediate postwar years. Between 1948 and 1950, unions voluntarily agreed to a policy of wage restraint. But the conditions of the immediate postwar years were exceptional. A more adequate test of the theoretical model advanced in Chapter 1 needs to establish whether wage moderation in exchange for social policy expansion functioned under circumstances when increases in the social wage were less dramatic.

Social Policy and Wage Moderation Under the Conservatives, 1951–1964

The Conservative Party did not share the same programmatic commitment to welfare expansion as the Labour Party (H. Jones 1992; Dow 1965; Lowe 1999: 151). While in opposition the Conservatives embraced a more liberal economic approach to questions pertaining to the role of the state in the economy. At the center of their new policy orientation was the belief that high levels of taxation and expenditures had a negative impact on the British economy (H. Jones 1992). Conservatives also opposed the commitment to universalistic and egalitarian social policy benefits that had been at the center of the social policy reforms enacted by the Labour government and embraced policy proposals that envisaged higher levels of targeting to the needy rather than a universalistic distribution of benefits to the entire population.

A number of political factors, however, limited the Conservatives' ability to redesign the British welfare state in line with their liberal orientation. The first constraint was electoral. This limitation was particularly strong between 1951 and 1955. During this period Conservatives presided over a very narrow parliamentary majority, which preempted the passage of any far-reaching policy changes. The popularity of welfare state programs also limited Conservatives' reform options. According to public opinion polls of the period, nearly 80 percent of the population expressed satisfaction with social insurance institutions such as the National Health Service (Lowe 1999). Thus, Conservative policy makers were acutely aware of the potentially strong political repercussions of reductions in social policy expenditures.

The political strategy of British trade unions also constrained the ability of Conservative governments to redesign existing institutions of social protection. In the early 1950s trade unions pursued relative wage moderation. As Flanagan, Soskice, and Ulman have pointed out, this strategy was remarkable not only in comparison to subsequent policy developments in Britain but also from an international perspective (Flanagan et al. 1983: 381–2). With respect to social policies, unions opposed any decline in the real level of benefits and the gradual "residualization" of the welfare state. It was precisely the ability of unions to deliver high levels of wage moderation that made their opposition to social policy cutbacks powerful. As Whiteside argues: "The industrial situation undermined the political feasibility of further cuts in the welfare state. In a tight labor market, attacking the welfare state provoked trouble on the industrial front. . . . For a prime minister eager to keep wages in check, cutting social welfare seemed a potentially expensive economy. The threat of industrial action thus kept the rest of the welfare state intact. In these circumstances, the trade union rank and file came to understand its industrial muscle as primary to the protection of state benefits as well as wages" (Whiteside 1996: 98).

The institutional structure of the wage bargaining system aided the TUC in its pursuit of collective wage restraint. Until the early 1960s the British wage bargaining system was hybrid, with elements of industry-level and firm-level negotiations. On the shop floor, representatives of labor – shop stewards – had some influence over the determination of wages. Industry negotiations between unions and employers' federations determined the basic weekly rates. But the industry level was the main locus of bargaining, and the power of shop stewards was severely constrained (Flanagan et al. 1983: 380; Fellner 1961: 432–6; Clegg 1970: 339). Moreover, the central leadership of the TUC was extremely successful in restraining wage increases and blocking the attempts of more militant unions, such as the Transport and General Workers' Union (TGWU), to achieve wage increases. It was only over the course of the 1960s that the ability of industrial and national union leaders to constrain rank-and-file militancy declined. In that decade, changes in production methods raised the importance of bonus payments for firms and increased the power of shop stewards to the detriment of industrial unions. The pathologies of the British system of industrial relations surfaced in a significant way only beginning in the mid-1960s.

Numerous TUC publications of the 1950s testify to the willingness of the British labor movement to exert wage restraint. In the first meeting of the TUC after the election of the Conservatives, Arthur Deakin, the general secretary of the TGWU, urged unions to observe "reasonableness and the exercise of good sense in the formulation of wage claims" (TUC 1952). In 1954 a motion opposing wage restraint sparked a heated controversy but was ultimately defeated (TUC 1954: 445). "Trade unionists have shown that they are aware that the problems of Britain are their problems and that their own living standards depend on increasing industrial efficiency," a union representative declared. He continued: "Trade unionists have shown too that given a square deal they are willing to accept obligations for the sake of this objective. If, however, the Government or the industrialists by their actions cause trade unionists to reject these obligations, this will do more than turn the clock back in industrial relations: it will jeopardize our whole future" (TUC 1954 quoted in Flanagan et al. 1983: 482).

A second characteristic of the process of wage determination during this period was the rejection by the TUC of government intervention in the wage setting process and the strong defense of voluntarism in industrial relations. Conservative policy makers attempted on two occasions to impose wage freezes, and on both occasions they were defeated. The first of these episodes occurred in 1956, when Prime Minister Anthony Eden attempted to secure trade union cooperation in the form of wage restraint to counteract a severe balance of payments crisis (Dorfman 1973: 73; R. Jones 1987: 50–3; Fishbein 1984: 32). Trade unions strenuously opposed the proposal (Dorfman 1973: 73; Flanagan et al. 1983: 386). A second attempt to impose a wage freeze occurred in 1961, when the Macmillan government introduced a "pay pause" for government employees, hoping to set a standard of restraint for the private sector (R. Jones 1987: 57). The TUC bitterly resisted this policy, adopting a resolution that "deplored the initial step of the government in imposing its will upon public servants and government workers" (TUC 1961: 379; Fishbein 1984: 33; Flanagan et al. 1983: 386; Dorfman 1973: 97–109).

To evaluate the wage policies pursued by unions under the Conservatives, Figure 5.2 compares changes in wages to changes in productivity and output for 1951–1964. Again I take the gap between real wage growth and productivity as a measure of wage moderation. The period between 1950 and 1958 was characterized by relatively moderate wage settlements. This pattern was interrupted in 1958, when a prolonged wave of strikes by public-sector employees concluded with significant wage increases. After 1959, wage growth closely followed the growth rate of the British economy.

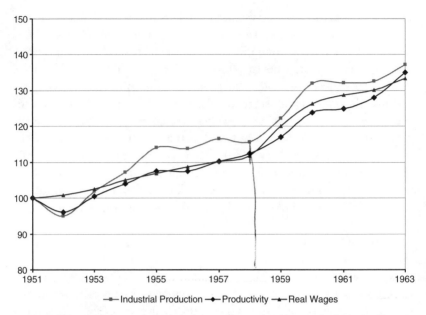

Figure 5.2. Britain: Wages, output, and productivity, 1951–1964. (*Sources:* Flanagan et al. 1983, 368; U.S. Department of Labor, *Handbook of Labor Statistics*, various years.)

"This moderation makes comprehensible the economic performance of the UK during this period," Flanagan, Soskice, and Ulman (1983) explain:

With the benefit of hindsight, the record of an average level of unemployment of 1.8 percent and an average inflation of 3.8 percent was a considerable success.... The Swedish union movement also supported an incomes policy during the early postwar period that ended in a wage explosion, and it also followed this traumatic experience with a bargaining policy characterized by considerable self-restraint. In some respects, however, the British effort, while less effective when judged by the criterion of international competitiveness and balance-of-payments performance, was more remarkable than the Swedish. (Flanagan et al. 1983: 377, 381–2)

The collective wage restraint of British unions increased labor's bargaining power in negotiations over changes in social protection (Whiteside 1996: 98). During this period unions participated in meetings with relevant ministries and were involved in the deliberations of parliamentary and extra-parliamentary commissions. Their participation effectively limited some government proposals for welfare state retrenchment, and it guaranteed a stable expansion of social policy benefits.

182

In the area of social protection, the development of public housing was the highest political priority. In response to the popularity of housing programs, Conservative prime ministers committed themselves to augmenting available houses by 300,000 new homes a year (H. Jones 1992: 284). Between 1951 and 1955 the Conservatives successfully attained and sometimes surpassed these goals. The total number of houses completed rose from 201,000 in 1951, to 248,000 in 1952, to 354,000 in 1954, and to 307,000 in 1957 and 1958 (U.K. Central Statistical Office 1959). Conservatives presided over a reorientation of the goals of housing policies, however. For Labour, the goals of the public provision of housing were universalistic in nature, aiming to provide benefits to all citizens. In contrast, Conservatives attempted to target public housing to the most needy. As a result of this different policy priority, Conservatives reduced public subsidies for "general needs" council housing and increased subsidies for residual housing programs (H. Jones 1992: Chap. 5; Whiteside 1996: 96). Conservatives also attempted to increase the supply of privately available housing: As Figure 5.3 illustrates, the share of houses completed for local housing authorities declined from 244,000 in 1953 to 128,000 in 1961. Finally, the Housing Repairs and Rent Act of 1954 and the Rent Act of 1957 removed rent controls and housing subsidies (H. Jones 1992: Chap. 5).

The TUC opposed these changes to housing policy (TUC 1953: 263; 1954: 458; 1957: 453; 1958: 291). Beginning in 1953, it adopted a number of resolutions that protested the "gradual decay of rent-controlled houses" and the effective increase in rents that was a consequence of the Rents and Repairs Act (1954: 458; 1957: 453). A 1957 TUC resolution called on the Conservative government "to reduce interest rates, to make capital more freely available to local authorities and to reestablish the ratio between private and public housing that existed under the Labour government" (TUC 1958: 291). Policy discussions within the TUC reveal that unions frequently considered demanding higher wages to offset the decline in members' real income that followed from the Conservatives' policies: "Here we have a Government that has the audacity to talk to us of the dangers of inflation, while at the same time passing an Act of this character that is bound to increase the living costs of our members and result in a fresh surge of wage claims" (TUC 1957: 454).

While in office Conservatives also formulated various proposals to reform the National Insurance Act and to top up existing policies with a guarantee of earnings-related benefits. Discussions about the introduction of a national superannuation scheme sparked intense deliberations in

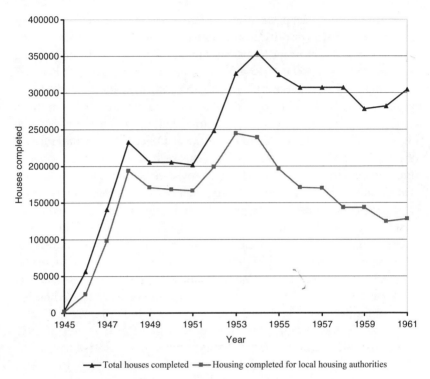

Figure 5.3. Evolution of housing in Britain, 1945–1962. (*Source:* Jones 1992.)

the labor movement about the appropriate mix between public and private social policies. A resolution enacted at the 1958 TUC Congress expressed the "regret that trade unions have hitherto tended to leave exclusively to employers the provision and planning of occupational pension schemes" and urged affiliated unions to "treat the negotiation of adequate pensions as being as much a part of their function as the negotiation of adequate salaries and wages" (TUC 1958: 340). The TUC expressed moderate support for the introduction of the superannuation scheme (TUC 1958: 141–2). Unions welcomed the addition of the second-tier pension system, which harbored the promise of better social protection in old age. They also repeatedly asserted, however, that the introduction of a second-tier pension system should be regarded as a complement to existing institutions; it should not, they insisted, preclude the upgrading of benefits provided by the National Insurance Act (1959).

Between 1951 and 1964 unions frequently expressed concern about the gradual erosion of national insurance benefits. Growing levels of poverty among the elderly suggested to unions that the state's commitment to provide a basic level of subsistence (an important component of the Beveridge report) had been gradually abandoned. On repeated occasions the TUC called on the government to "carry out a fundamental reexamination of the whole question of what constitutes adequate subsistence in presentday circumstances" (TUC 1958: 142). The gradual diminution of social policy benefits was unacceptable in part because similar levels of wage erosion were unthinkable: "Trade unions would never tolerate such a position for one moment in their wage negotiations and we should not tolerate it for the old people, the widows, the injured and the sick" (TUC 1951: 380). During this period, unions succeeded in preventing a reduction of social insurance benefits. National insurance benefits (which included support for retirement, unemployment, and sickness) were raised in 1952, 1955, 1958, and 1961 (U.K. Government Statistical Service 1988). As a result, social policy benefits as a percentage of wages increased slightly from 15.9 percent in 1951 to 18.5 percent in 1952 and 19.7 percent in 1958, followed by a modest decline to 19.1 percent in 1961 (U.K. Government Statistical Service 1988: 257).

An important policy change of the period affected the mode of financing insurance and health service benefits. The most direct result of the Conservatives' policy of fiscal retrenchment was a gradual reduction in subsidies from general taxes to the major subsystems of the British welfare state. The Beveridge report had recommended that around one-third of the costs of old-age insurance be financed by a grant from the treasury (Lowe 1999: 148). Initially the financing of national insurance benefits complied with this recommendation. While in 1947 around 35 percent of the revenue of the National Insurance Fund was financed by a grant from the treasury, this proportion declined to 24 percent in 1950 and to 15 percent in 1961 (U.K. Central Statistical Office 1962). Changes in the financing of health insurance (Fig. 5.4) reveal a similar pattern: In 1950, 87.6 percent of the costs of the National Health Service were financed from general taxation; by the time the Conservatives left office in 1963, this share had been reduced to 77.1 percent (Lowe 1999: 187). The shift in the mode of financing raised individuals' national insurance contributions and eroded the take-home pay of workers.

British trade unions strongly resented these changes in social insurance financing. In 1951 the TUC passed a motion calling for the "restoration of the Exchequer Block grant and the original rate of the Exchequer supplement to contributions" (TUC 1953: 141). Similar concerns were raised

185

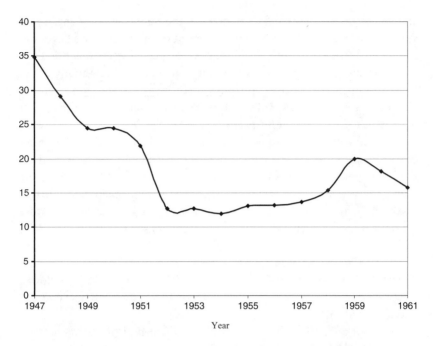

Figure 5.4. Abandoning Beveridge: Changes in the financing of national insurance, 1947–1961. (*Source:* UK. Central Statistical Office. *Annual Abstract of Statistics.*)

virtually every subsequent year (see TUC 1954: 153; TUC 1955: 154). The basic contribution to old-age insurance was increased in 1954, in 1957, and then again in 1960. The TUC "protested strongly against the additional burden which was being put upon contributors" (TUC 1955: 155) and insisted that "the liability for the growing cost of pensions...be fairly apportioned between the whole body of insured contributors, employers and general taxation" (TUC 1959: 143). Unions voiced similar opposition to the increase in health service contributions. According to the unions, rising contributions "impose[d] a further burden on those least able to bear it.... The primary purpose of insurance contributions had been to provide insurance benefits, not to carry rising health care costs" (TUC 1958: 155).

Between 1952 and 1961 Conservative governments were unsuccessful in carrying out their programmatic commitment to reduce taxes and expenditures. Opposition from trade unions caused their retreat from proposals to

186

Table 5.1. *Social policy spending under the Conservatives, 1951–1961*

	1951	1955	1958	1961
Total social expenditures*	13.51	13.44	14.99	16.03
National health service expenditures*	3.86	3.4	3.59	3.94
National insurance expenditures*	5.62	6.09	6.87	7.11
National insurance benefit rates[†]	1.30	2.00	2.50	2.875

Notes:
* Expressed as a percentage of the GDP
[†] Old-age, sickness, and unemployment insurance standard weekly benefits in pounds
Sources:
U.K. Central Statistical Office, *National income and expenditure*, various years; U.K. Government Statistical Service, *Social security statistics*, various years.

introduce cutbacks in existing programs, such as the proposal to introduce an increase in health service charges (TUC 1952: 131). As a result, total social expenditures grew at a rate of around 3 percent yearly. National insurance expenditures increased from 5.62 percent of the GDP in 1951 to 7.11 percent in 1961. By contrast, expenditures on the National Health Service remained at a steady proportion of the GDP. As a result of the increases in the level of national insurance benefits, replacement rates remained at a steady 19 percent under the Conservatives (Table 5.1).

Summing up, the joint evolution of wage negotiation and social policy expansion in Britain from 1950 to 1964 shared many commonalities to policy developments in corporatist economies, such as Germany. In contrast to later periods, British trade unions exhibited significant levels of wage moderation in this period. As Flanagan, Ulman, and Soskice argued, "the restrainers were aided by the existence of wage rounds of industry-wide negotiations in which the rough size of the increases was frequently set by two or three key settlements. And even after 1956, the reasonableness in wage setting was less publicly stated but vigorously pursued" (Flanagan et al. 1983: 380, 377). Unions' moderation on the wage front increased their bargaining position vis-à-vis the government and their ability to demand increases in the social policy benefits while protecting existing programs from cutbacks. Analysis of union publications reveals that the TUC attributed the same status to social policy benefits as to wages (TUC 1958: 340). Unions militated to maintain a constant ratio between insurance benefits and wages, even at the cost of temporary setbacks on the wage front. The TUC strongly opposed cutbacks in the government grant to the National Insurance Fund, largely because this measure pushed up workers'

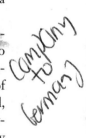

contributions. These developments point to the presence of a tacit political exchange between unions and governments that linked wage moderation to increases in social protection.

The Labour Government, 1964–1970

In the electoral campaign of 1964 the Labour Party pledged to "formulate a national economic plan with both sides of industry operating in partnership with the government" (Craig 1990: 43). The 1964 election manifesto also announced "drastic reforms in our major social services" that would be "costly in money, manpower and resources" (Craig 1990: 51). New institutions of planning and a larger welfare state were to work together to achieve the fundamental political objective of the Labour Party, "the abolition of poverty in the midst of plenty." "This goal can be achieved," the manifesto maintained, "provided Britain wills three things: the mobilization of its resources within a national plan, the maintenance of a wise balance between community and individual expenditure and the education of all its citizens" (Craig 1990: 49).

Labor won in 1964 by a very narrow margin. The centerpiece of the economic strategy of Harold Wilson's government was the introduction of institutions of economic planning. In 1965 the government published a national plan that formulated industrial objectives for a large number of sectors (Opie 1972: 157–77; Graham 1972: 178–217). It established the Department of Economic Affairs to preside over the planning effort and thus curtailed the power of the conservative Treasury Department over economic policy (Fishbein 1984: 38). The goal of the new institutions was to achieve both economic growth and a "planned growth of incomes."

Unions' support was vital to the achievement of Labour's objectives. In 1963, one year prior to its electoral victory, the party had secured informal promises from unions of their future cooperation. A resolution adopted at the Labour Party conference in 1963 announced the objective of a future Labour government to develop "an incomes policy to include salaries, wages, dividends, profits and social security benefits" (Fishbein 1984; Panitch 1976: 52–62). It was supported by important elements of the labor movement, although unions were careful to avoid using the phrase "wage restraint." Frank Cousins put the unions' position this way: "We are spending a good deal of time ensuring that we get a Government that thinks the same things as we do, and when we have succeeded in getting that Government, we shall be talking, as we are now doing, about a planned growth of wages, not wages restraint" (Fishbein 1984: 38).

Labour's approach to wage moderation differed from that of the outgoing Macmillan government. On numerous occasions Labour Party leaders denounced the pay pause of 1961 as "unjust" because it imposed disproportionately high costs on public-sector employees. Several documents from the period, such as the 1965 white paper on prices and incomes and the 1969 white paper entitled "Productivity, Prices and Incomes Policies" indicate that for Labour, wage moderation had important redistributional objectives. These aimed to improve the economic situation of low-earning employees and to reduce existing income differentials, thus complementing the redistributional objectives already being pursued by means of social policy transfers. For Labour leaders, incomes policies were "more than a means to achieve price stability" and "by no means a weapon designed solely as a substitute for devaluation" (Beckerman 1972: 64–65).

Between 1964 and 1969, the Labour government made two efforts to negotiate incomes policies with trade unions. These two episodes differed dramatically in the strategy pursued by the government and in the fiscal and policy inducements offered to trade unions to moderate the level of wage growth. In the first case the government relied on the informal cooperation of trade unions. In the second episode, which lasted from 1966 to 1970, the government attempted to impose a wage freeze unilaterally. The first attempt immediately followed the October 1964 elections. The overtly expansionary fiscal policy of the outgoing Conservative government left in its wake a severe balance of payments deficit. The Wilson government ruled out devaluation and chose instead to attack the problem by containing growth in prices and incomes. It turned to trade unions and pressed the TUC to honor its previous commitment to accept voluntary wage restraint. An agreement with unions and employers was reached with remarkable rapidity in the spring of 1965. The government committed itself to an economic plan that aimed at a yearly productivity growth of around 3.2 percent. Its policy promises were published in a white paper entitled "Prices and Incomes Policy." Unions agreed to link wage increases to increases in productivity and to restrict wage growth to about 3.0–3.5 percent a year. Employers also accepted some guidelines for price increases. To monitor the application of this agreement, the government established an administrative agency (the National Board for Prices and Incomes) that included representatives of the TUC and of employers (Flanagan et al. 1983: 388).

189

To ensure unions' cooperation, the government offered several inducements in the form of tax changes. A budget passed in the final quarter of
1964 announced increases in social insurance benefits (Artis 1972: 274). The
standard benefit rates for old age, sickness, and invalidity were increased
by 18.5 percent (U.K. Government Statistical Service 1988). In February
1965, the government abolished prescription charges that had been introduced by the Conservatives. Finally, a number of important tax changes
were implemented in an effort to redistribute income more equitably. The
Long-Term Capital Gain and Corporation Tax was introduced in April
1965, 2 days prior to the publication of the white paper on prices and
incomes (Artis 1972: 274).

In exchange, the central leadership of the TUC agreed to wage moderation. In April 1965, a special conference of trade unions' executive committees endorsed the policy of wage restraint by a wide margin (TUC 1965). In
practice, however, the policy was not fully observed. In 1965, average weekly
wages rose by 8.5 percent (Flanagan et al. 1983: 368). The most important
reason for the central union leadership's failure to enforce the 3.5 percent
wage norm was institutional in nature. In the mid-1960s, Britain's wage
bargaining system gradually decentralized, and shop stewards consolidated
economic and political power (Clegg 1970: 243–305). They were involved
in the negotiation of all issues in addition to the basic wage rate, such as
overtime rates, piecework rates, and bonuses (Brown 1981; Fishbein 1984:
44; Flanagan et al. 1983: 364). "Shop-stewards, while acting as agents of the
national union in the plant, have seen themselves primarily as work-group
representatives," Flanagan, Soskice, and Ulman explain; "Their ability to
behave independently of national unions is the result, in large part, of their
ability to call unofficial strikes" (Flanagan et al. 1983: 364).

Figure 5.5 summarizes the consequences of the first stage of Labour's
incomes policy. Productivity growth exceeded wage growth only between
1963 and 1964. After 1964, wages grew at a much faster rate than productivity despite policy inducements to unions. Thus, the first attempt of the
Labour government to bring about wage moderation failed.

This failure prompted a change in the government's strategy. Labour
abandoned the approach to incomes policies that relied on the voluntary cooperation of trade unions and turned instead to a policy that relied
on statutory control. At first it established an early warning system that
required advance notification of intentions to increase prices or wages
(TUC 1966: 316). Faced with this unilateral decision, the TUC "accepted
the principle that the government should introduce enabling legislation to

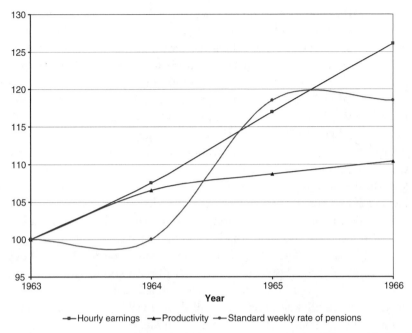

--■--Hourly earnings --▲--Productivity --•--Standard weekly rate of pensions

Figure 5.5. Incomes policy under Labour, stage 1: 1964–1966. [*Sources:* National Institute of Economic and Social Research (UK). *National Institute Economic Review* (hourly earnings and productivity); U.K. Government Statistical Service, *Social security statistics*, various years (pensions).]

give them powers to require notification of pay claims and prices increases" but reiterated the view that "a voluntary incomes policy was much more likely to prove effective and to achieve greater justice and equity than a system based on the use of legislation" (TUC 1966: 319). Early elections called in the spring of 1966 precluded the implementation of the advance notification policy.

Emboldened by a decisive electoral victory in 1966, the Labour government decided to push ahead with statutory control of wage setting. The impetus for this policy development was a sterling crisis in the summer of 1966. The government introduced a mandatory 6-month freeze of wages and prices to be followed by a 6-month period of "severe restraint" during which firms were allowed to increase prices only to allow producers to cover costs over which they "could not exercise full control" (Flanagan et al. 1983: 390). The Prices and Incomes Act of 1966 gave the government the legal authority to block wage increases recommended by trade unions.

191

Extensive rounds of consultations with the TUC preceded the introduction of these measures (TUC 1966: 320–8). In these meetings the government justified its policy by invoking the severity of the nation's economic difficulties and the failure of previous efforts to introduce voluntary wage restraint (TUC 1966: 320). The prime minister emphasized "that the government had acted with the utmost reluctance, but that they had no alternative" (TUC 1966: 322). Unions expressed two objections to this policy. First, they disapproved of the asymmetry in the treatment of wage and price increases: "When they met the Minister later in the day, the General Council's representatives stated that the provisions relating to prices were less onerous than those relating to incomes in that in certain circumstances, including an increase in taxation, prices could be increased while incomes were to be completely frozen during the standstill, and they pointed out that, if prices rose, incomes would not in fact have stood still, but would have fallen back" (TUC 1966: 327). Second, unions voiced "doubts about the practicability of this standstill and gave practical illustrations of the effects which it would have on attitudes among trade unionists, on productivity, and on the prospects of establishing a viable long-term incomes policy" (TUC 1966: 322). Nevertheless, unions decided to support the government. The TUC General Council announced "that the interests both of trade unionists and of the nation as a whole in the current critical situation compelled them to acquiesce in the Government's proposal and to discuss how the problems arising could best be dealt with and what amendments should be made to the Prices and Incomes Bill" (TUC 1966: 323).

Compared to 1964, the fiscal and social policy changes that accompanied this incomes policy were more mixed. Short-term deflationary measures were introduced in response to the severe balance of payments crisis. These policies, which were announced between July and September 1966, included cuts in public-sector investment and a hike in indirect taxation rates (Artis 1972: 273). But at the same time the government introduced the National Insurance Act of 1966, which created supplementary earnings-related benefits for short-term sickness and unemployment (Stewart 1972: 95). As Table 5.2 illustrates, these measures had far-reaching distributional consequences, guaranteeing that insurance benefits rose at the same rate as wages in the late 1960s. Trade unions welcomed the advances in social protection, which had a considerable impact on the standard of living of the lowest quintile of the population. A TUC statement asserted that unions' "acquiescence" to the government's incomes policy was justified

Table 5.2. *Social policy benefits and earnings under Labour, 1963–1969*

	1963	1969
Benefits		
Unemployment, sickness, and retirement benefits (single)	100	148
Retirement pension (married)	100	149
National assistance/supplementary benefit (married couple)	100	150
Earnings (weekly)		
Adult male manual workers	100	154
Adult male administrative, technical, and clerical employees	100	148

Source:
Stewart 1972, 100.

given that "the government had deliberately refrained from attacking the social services" (TUC 1966: 324).

Figure 5.6 presents descriptive statistics on the evolution of wages and productivity for 1966–1970. The 1966 wage freeze was relatively effective while the Price and Incomes Act was in effect. Between July 1966 and June 1967, the hourly wage rate rose by 2.8 percent (Flanagan et al. 1983: 390). But this period of wage restraint was followed by a period of more dramatic wage increases. In 1967, average weekly earnings rose by 5.8 percent; in 1968 they rose by 7.8 percent, and this despite the fact that the government continued to push for zero increase (Flanagan et al. 1983: 391). The main factors accounting for the erosion of this policy can be attributed to the loss of power experienced by union leaders during the wage setting process.

A few conclusions follow from this account of policy developments in the mid-1960s. First, the Labour government made significant efforts to link incomes policies to its broader objectives of expanding social policy benefits and achieving a more egalitarian distribution of incomes. In 1964 and 1966, the government adopted policies guaranteeing significant increases in benefits in exchange for the moderation required from trade unions. On both occasions the central leadership of the TUC supported incomes policies and pressured union members to accept wage restraint. But in either case real moderation in incomes did not last more than a year. While TUC leaders supported the government on both occasions, their failure can be attributed to shop stewards' militancy and to their ability to achieve wage increases that exceeded the recommendations of industrial leaders by wide margins. Thus, beginning in the mid-1960s, the decentralization of the

193

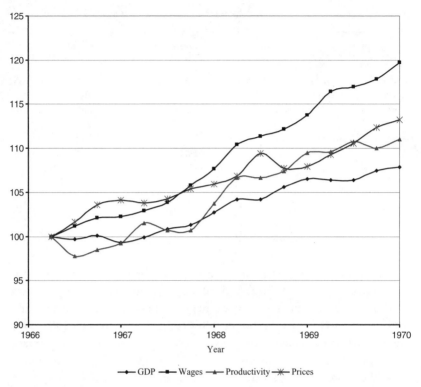

Figure 5.6. Incomes policy under Labour, stage 2: 1966–1970. [*Sources:* National Institute of Economic and Social Research (UK). *National Institute Economic Review.*]

the decentralization

British wage bargaining system limited the successful implementation of the social wage. It is this institutional characteristic of the wage bargaining system – and not the policy preferences of unions – that distinguishes the British economy from the other economies examined in this study.

() what makes Britain different from other country

Conservatives Again, 1970–1974

For the incoming Conservative government, the policy lesson was straightforward: Both efforts to negotiate with unions and attempts to impose wage restraint unilaterally had failed to limit wage growth. During its first 2 years in power, the Heath government thus embraced a new approach that involved a frontal attack on the political and economic power

194

of trade unions. The electoral manifesto of the Conservative Party "rejected the philosophy of compulsory wage control" and instead advocated policies that reduced unions' power (Keegan and Penant-Rea 1979: 180; R. Jones 1987: 84; Scharpf 1991: 74). An additional important electoral promise of the Conservatives was a commitment to a reduction in the level of taxes. As the Conservative manifesto formulated this objective: "Government has been taking an ever increasing slice of people's earnings in taxation. Soaring prices and increasing taxes are an evil and disastrous combination" (Holmes 1997: 67).

The initial strategy of the Heath government, pursued between 1970 and 1972, had two components. In its effort to weaken the collective power of trade unions, conservatives introduced the Industrial Relations Act in August 1971. The act increased the government's power to scrutinize trade union activity by requiring unions to register. The registrar of trade unions and employers' associations could withhold union registration if a union did not guarantee free and open elections (Flanagan et al. 1983: 402). The act also attempted to curtail the power of shop stewards by making them liable for damage resulting from unofficial strike action. Finally, it abolished the closed shop except in cases where unions could prove that 100 percent membership was essential to their survival (Fishbein 1984: 59). Unsurprisingly, the TUC reacted to the provisions of the act with intense hostility. At a special conference held in March 1971, it recommended that unions resist the legislation and urged affiliated unions to refuse appointing representatives to the new institutions created by the act (Fishbein 1984: 63). At the TUC annual conference of September 1971, a majority of members voted to boycott the act (R. Jones 1987: 86). Union opposition was extremely successful in practice, rendering the provisions of the Industrial Relations Act ineffective.

The second component of the government's strategy was the effort to toughen the bargaining stance on the part of the government to reduce wage increases in the public sector. The goal was to limit each successive public-sector wage settlement to an increase lower than the previous year's by 1 percent (Flanagan et al. 1983: 397). This approach, referred to at the time as the "N − 1" strategy, or the strategy of "deescalation," resembled one taken by Conservatives in 1961–1962. It was prompted by alarming growth in public-sector wages in 1970. But the strategy was unsuccessful in practice: A number of unions in the public sector, such as railway workers and the National Union of Mineworkers, challenged the policy and succeeded in obtaining

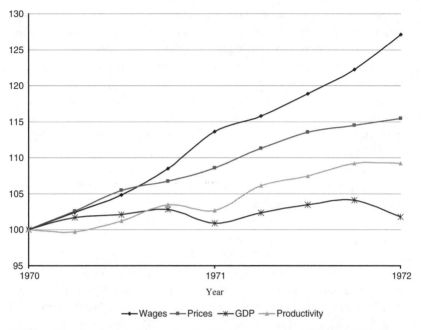

Figure 5.7. Incomes policy under the Heath government, 1970–1972. [*Source:* Flanagan et al. 1983; U.S. Department of Labor, *Handbook of Labor Statistics*, various years (productivity and output).]

wage increases that exceeded the government guidelines by large amounts (R. Jones 1987: 85; Flanagan et al. 1984: 400). By 1972, the deescalation policy had proven to be a major fiasco, and it had to be abandoned.

To honor its electoral commitment to reduce taxes, the government initiated a thorough investigation of public spending. The first budget of the Heath administration, published in 1970, announced a reduction in total public expenditure of 300 million pounds in 1971 and anticipated higher cuts in subsequent years (OECD Economic Surveys United Kingdom 1971: 15). While larger social policy programs were left more or less unaffected, the cuts affected smaller programs, such as food subsidies and school meals. In the area of housing, the government pursued an incremental residualization by encouraging the sale of council houses to tenants and by eliminating control of local authority rents (Holmes 1997: 39; Glennerster 1990: 18–20).

The combination of fiscal cutbacks with a systematic attack on the power of trade unions did not generate the desired economic outcomes (Fig. 5.7).

196

In 1970 and 1971, wages grew at an average of 12.3 percent. The contractionary fiscal policies contributed to an increase in the unemployment rate, which rose from 2.5 percent in 1969 to 3.5 percent in 1971 (Flanagan et al. 1983: 368). These economic developments prompted a dramatic change in the policy orientation of the Heath government, leading to the famous "U-turn" in government policy. Incomes policies returned to the agenda (Flanagan et al 1983: 408; R. Jones 1987: 86). Beginning in July 1972, the government initiated discussions with the TUC and the Confederation of British Industry about the possibility of voluntary restraint of wages and prices. The obstacles to successful accommodation with trade unions, however, had reached an all-time high. The policies introduced during the first 2 years of the Heath administration had enhanced unions' distrust and hostility. Moreover, two of Britain's largest unions, the Amalgamated Union of Engineering Workers and the National Union of Mineworkers, experienced a turn to the left, precluding cooperation with the Conservative government (R. Jones 1987: 89).

To pave the way for negotiations with trade unions, the government abandoned the restrictive fiscal policy of its first 2 years in office (Fishbein 1984: 85; Holmes 1997: 64). Beginning in 1972, it provided a budgetary increase of over 1,200 million pounds. It persuaded the Confederation of British Industry to restrain price increases to 5 percent until July 1972 (Fishbein 1984: 85). In addition, it decided to let the exchange rate float to remove any balance of payments constraints on the pursuit of its policy (Jones 1987: 87). These adjustments brought the trade unions to the negotiating table. Tripartite negotiations involving the government, the Confederation of British Industry, and the TUC took place from spring through fall of 1972.

Unions' initial position during these negotiations built on a resolution adopted by the TUC at its 1972 Congress: "No consideration can be given to any policy on incomes unless it is an integral part of an economic strategy which includes control of rents, profits, dividends and prices, and is designed to secure a redistribution of income and wealth nationally and globally" (TUC 1972: 478). In this spirit, unions emphatically asserted that wage negotiations were inseparable from the negotiation of policies that affected the redistribution of income within British society. They brought three specific social policy demands to the bargaining table. First, they demanded additional increases in pensions and the guarantee of an automatic increase in benefits following price increases (Fishbein 1984: 78). Second, they required legislation addressing persistent poverty. To reduce

197

the number of persons caught in "poverty traps," unions recommended reductions in taxation coupled with an expansion of benefits that were not means-tested, such as family allowances. Finally, unions opposed the freezing of housing rents (R. Jones 1987: 89; Fishbein 1984: 80–81). As Rhodes and other scholars have observed, in the 1972 negotiations, unions "consciously raised the issue of the social wage and linked their agreement to a wage accord with radical welfare concessions" (Rhodes 2000: 33).

The government ignored the social policy concerns raised by trade unions, however. For government representatives, wages were the only issue at stake in these negotiations. They recommended a voluntary limitation in the growth of wages of 2 pounds per week (R. Jones 1987: 88). The government recommended that firms continue price moderation but refused to impose a statutory control on the level of prices. The "carrot" offered to unions in exchange for wage restraint was the government's commitment to a wage growth rate of 5 percent in the coming 2 years (Fishbein 1984). These proposals remained unsatisfactory for trade unions, however. Trade unions reiterated their demands for a change in pension legislation and an increase in the provision of public housing, and they protested the government plan to introduce a regressive value-added tax. Because the government was unwilling to accommodate these demands, the TUC withdrew its delegation from the tripartite meetings in the fall of 1972.

In the wake of the failed negotiations, the government decided to implement a statutory wage freeze. The policy, introduced in November 1972, set an upper ceiling of 8 percent for wage increases (Flanagan et al. 1983: 410). In an effort to induce unions to cooperate, the policy was coupled with additional provisions, such as better financial assistance for low-income rents and a promised boost to pensions to come into effect in October 1973 (Fishbein 1984: 107). To assuage concern about the plight of low-wage workers, unions were given some discretion over the distribution of increases among wage earners (Flanagan et al. 1983: 411). The wage freeze remained in effect until March 1973.

In practice, the statutory incomes policy of the Heath government was extremely ineffective. Weekly earnings rose at an average rate of about 15 percent despite the mandated 8 percent ceiling (Flanagan et al. 1983: 368). The government's expansionary monetary policies militated against the success of the wage freeze. In 1973, increases in the money supply exceeded 20 percent (R. Jones 1987: 97). The spike in oil prices of the fall of 1973 further pushed the aggregate price level upward and made it impossible for firms to respect the guidelines for price changes. As Jones argues, "Incomes policy was being asked to do far too much, in an environment in no way conducive to its successful operation" (R. Jones 1987: 94). In 1974, a long strike by the National Union of Mineworkers challenged the incomes policy and was ultimately successful in bringing down the Conservative government.

In retrospect, the 1973 negotiations over the introduction of an incomes policy were by no means preordained to end in failure. By the spring of 1972, the Conservative government had abandoned its original adversarial approach toward trade unions and made a genuine effort to institutionalize tripartite bargaining. But the Heath government did not appreciate the political importance of social policy considerations to trade unions, and this shortcoming contributed to the collapse of the negotiations (Rhodes 2000: 33). For unions, a critical precondition for the acceptance of wage moderation was more determined government action in the field of social protection, and in particular the extension of benefits to low-income groups. Thus, the failure of the 1973 negotiations can be traced to the government's unwillingness to recognize the linkage unions had established between wages and social policy demands.

The Social Contract, 1974–1979

While in opposition, the Labour Party engaged in a systematic consideration of the policies that could guarantee a stable political exchange with trade unions. The new policy ideas were synthesized in the notion of a "social contract," a term introduced into the party's economic program by Lord Balogh, an advisor to Harold Wilson (Balogh 1970; Fishbein 1984: 115; R. Jones 1987: 99). The painful lesson of previous experience was that statutory incomes policies failed to achieve the desired levels of wage moderation and often triggered a backlash in the form of wage explosion. As Balogh argued, prolonged wage moderation could only be achieved if the government remained committed to systematic reforms in the sphere of social protection (Balogh 1970). The social contract was defined as a "deliberate agreement on economic and social policy" in which the government "introduced systematic economic planning, expanded the social services, extended public ownership of the economy and imposed a heavier tax burden on higher-income earners" (Fishbein 1984: 116). In exchange, unions would collectively agree to moderate their wage claims. As a Labour document put it, unions would "give their free acknowledgement that they had other loyalties than those to their own members in pay bargaining, in return for redistribution and welfare" (Clark 2001: 16).

The social contract occupied a prominent place on the political agenda of the Labour Party. As a consequence, "the commitments to increase benefits for the poor and to higher taxes on those most able to pay were unusually prominent in the February 1974 manifesto" (Gillie 1991: 229). "Only a much fairer distribution of the national wealth," the manifesto stated, "can convince the worker and his family and his trade union that an 'incomes policy' is not some kind of trick to force him, particularly if he works in a public service or nationalized industry, to bear the brunt of the national burden. Government is ready to act – against high prices, rents and other impositions falling most heavily on the low paid and on pensioners – so we believe that the trade unions voluntarily (which is the only way it can be done for any period in a free society), will cooperate to make the whole policy successful" (Craig 1990: 190–1).

The Labour Party manifesto also formulated a number of priorities in the area of social protection. The most urgent goal was to "bring immediate help to existing pensioners, widows, the sick and the unemployed" by increasing benefits "within the first parliamentary session of the government." To take pensioners off means-tested benefits, the government promised to introduce an earnings-related pension. Labour also committed itself to provide child cash allowances and benefits for the disabled. In the area of housing, its goals were to repeal the Housing Finance Act that had been adopted by the Heath government in 1972, to increase subsidies for local authority house building, to extend subsidies for mortgages, and to provide stronger protection against eviction (Craig 1990: 190). Finally, the party proposed improving the progressivity of the tax structure and imposing new wealth and capital gains taxes (Fishbein 1984: 125).

We can distinguish several stages in the political implementation of the social contract (Scharpf 1991: 77). The first of these stages, which lasted until the pound crisis of 1976, was characterized by the sustained efforts of the Wilson government to deliver on its political commitments in the sphere of social protection. The initial budget, published in 1974, was expansionary. It projected an increase in the level of public expenditures of 1,240 million pounds, a staggering 12 percent. The largest items in this budget were increases in spending on housing and food subsidies (R. Jones 1987: 101). Simultaneously, the government introduced significant new social policy legislation. National insurance benefits were uprated by 13 percent, bringing pensions as a proportion of average earnings up to a value equivalent to the previous high, which was reached in 1965 as a result of Labour legislation. To maintain the real value of these benefits in the future, the legislation linked future increases in pensions to higher wages or incomes. Given that between 1975 and 1977 prices rose higher than earnings, social policy benefits as a proportion of earnings grew from 17.5 percent in October 1973 to 21 percent in November 1977 (Gillie 1991: 230). Additional legislation introduced a noncontributory invalidity pension for people with short working histories who were ineligible for existing invalidity benefits. Finally, the government initiated legislation for the introduction of a State Earnings-Related Pension Scheme (SERPS) that added a second-tier pension to the basic flat-rate pension.

External factors aggravated the macroeconomic consequences of this fiscal expansion. The 1973 oil shock contributed to a spike in import prices. Consequently, the aggregate price level rose by an average of 15 percent per year. Faced with these intense inflationary pressures, the government began to exert pressure on unions to deliver their part of the social contract by moderating wage settlements.

In anticipation of the 1974–1975 bargaining round, the central leadership of the British trade unions published a document entitled "Collective Bargaining and the Social Contract" (TUC 1974; Wickham-Jones 1991: 279). This document recommended that negotiators seek agreements that maintained the real wages of union members without pushing for increases. In addition, TUC leaders urged unions to "prioritize negotiating agreements which would have beneficial effects on unit costs and efficiency (that is, to productivity agreements), which would help attain reasonable minimum standards on pay and which would help to eliminate pay discrimination against women, or which would improve nonwage benefits such as sick pay and occupational pension schemes" (Fishbein 1984: 137). The overall tone of the document was marked by significant moderation and by a willingness of unions to deliver their part of the bargain.

Additional sources in the archives of the Labour Party show that support for the social contract among union leaders was genuine and that "unions tried to link the pay policy to social policy pledges" (Clark 2001: 17). But union leaders did not anticipate the virulent opposition of the rank and file to the policy of restraint. As Jack Jones, the president of the Transport and General Workers' Union (TGWU), remembers the period, "When he went round factories workers knew what was happening to prices and dividends and they simply shouted at him for acquiescence in pay policies.... When Jones retired, TGWU members chose Moss Evans to succeed him, who

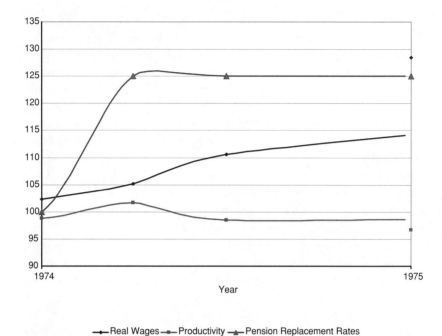

Figure 5.8. The first year of the social contract. (*Sources:* Flanagan et al. 1983; U.S. Department of Labor, *Handbook of Labor Statistics*, various years.)

stood as an anti-pay policy candidate, being more concerned with net wages than pension increases" (Clark 2001: 17).

By 1974, the influence of the general council of the TUC over individual unions was at its nadir. In the 1974 bargaining round, the exhortations of the central leadership of the TUC to additional restraint had no impact on the strategies pursued by affiliated unions. The pay settlements adopted were extremely high. According to a survey of 77 wage settlements (covering around 8 million workers), the average wage increase of the period was 32 percent (Fishbein 1984: 141). To make up for income lost under the Heath government, unions in the public sectors – such as railways and postal and medical services – won particularly large wage increases (Fishbein 1984: 138; Flanagan et al. 1983: 427). By December 1974, it was widely accepted that the social contract had failed. Industrial militancy was on the rise: The number of days lost to strike action had doubled. Britain was on the verge of hyperinflation. Figure 5.8 depicts how hourly wages rose dramatically in 1974 despite the increase in the social wage (pension replacement rates) offered to unions in exchange for moderation.

The dramatic circumstances of the British economy triggered a change in Labour's policy orientation. The government abandoned its expansionary fiscal policy and began to implement a deflationary policy despite the rise in unemployment (Clark 2001; Jackson 1991). A public expenditure white paper published in 1975 recommended cuts of 1 billion pounds in the level of public spending, totaling 2 percent of public spending (Jackson 1991: 77). The cuts were especially deep in defense, capital spending on nationalized industries, housing, and education (Jackson 1991; Artis and Cobham 1991b). An additional white paper published in 1975 recommended the stabilization of "public spending at the 1976/1977 levels and a subsequent decrease in the level of public spending as the economy recovered" (Jackson 1991). This document marked a profound change in the orientation of the British government, anticipating later developments under Thatcher. It interrupted the "postwar expectation of a continuous rise in public spending" and "generated an alternative discourse of public expenditure, which transformed it from healer of the nation to economic villain" (Jackson 1991; Mullard 1987: 149). James Callaghan's announcement at the 1976 Labour conference dramatically characterized the change in policy: "The cosy world where full employment could be guaranteed by the stroke of a chancellor's pen suddenly died" (Clark 2001: 3).

When the government turned to trade unions in the spring of 1975 demanding additional wage moderation, it was unable to offer higher levels of social spending in exchange. Instead, it appealed to unions' concern for egalitarianism and recommended a flat-rate increase in wages of 6 pounds per week. This redistributive wage policy appealed to some concerns about the need to reduce wage differentials and was actively supported by public-sector unions as well as by unions representing lower skilled employees (Scharpf 1991: 77). Wage agreements reached in the following year conformed to this policy, and the rate of growth slowed slightly (Flanagan et al. 1983: 431). In the third quarter of 1976, nominal wages grew by 18.7 percent as compared to 33.1 percent in 1975 (R. Jones 1987: 107). But such an egalitarian wage policy, which did not favor high-skilled workers, was unsustainable for a long period of time. In response to the dissatisfaction of high-skilled unions, the flat-rate wage norm was abandoned in the following year's wage round.

The third attempt of the Labour government to negotiate incomes policies began in 1976. In contrast to the previous two attempts, in which the government offered either significant increases in social policy benefits (in 1974) or an egalitarian policy that advantaged lower earning employees (in 1975), on this occasion Chancellor of the Exchequer Dennis Healey offered unions significant tax cuts in exchange for wage moderation. In justification of this policy, Labour Party leaders argued that the basic tax rates had reached "unsustainable high levels" (Clark 2001: 38; Jackson 1991). The "conditional budget" of 1976 provided for a potential tax cut totaling 1,200 million pounds (Wickham-Jones 1991: 285). However, only 300 million pounds were offered as unconditional tax relief for old people and child allowances (OECD Economic Surveys United Kingdom 1977: 17). The remaining cuts were to be introduced only if the TUC agreed to restrict wage increases to 3 percent. Wage settlements in excess of 3 percent would decrease the amount of the tax relief (Artis and Cobham 1991a: 12). "This was the first budget in British history the implementation of which was contingent on the whims of an extra-parliamentary body," Jones notes. "The *Times* for one suggested that the budget had actually transformed the Trades Union Congress into a sort of 'Second House of Parliament,' a second chamber with power and authority the House of Lords had long since lost" (R. Jones 1987: 108).

After protracted negotiations, the general council agreed to a modified proposal that allowed slightly higher increases in wages. But this consent was to be limited in scope. In 1977, the TUC approved a resolution that expressed its determination to shift away from the strategy of moderation beginning with the 1978 bargaining round: "This Congress welcomes the continued reduction in the annual rate of inflation which has arisen largely as a result of the Trades Union Congress/Government initiative on prices and incomes. It is further encouraged by the response given by the trade union movement to the Social Contract in 1976–1977, and recognizing the sacrifice and restraint shown by all workers during the economic crisis of the last 18 months, supports the view that a planned return to free collective bargaining should begin to take place in 1977" (Flanagan et al. 1983: 433). The general council's decision to abandon wage moderation had two distinct causes. In the last quarters of 1975 and the first quarters of 1976, real earnings had declined by 7 percent, sparking fears among TUC leaders of unrest among the rank and file (Flanagan et al. 1983: 432). Second, as a result of the government's restrictive fiscal and monetary policies, unemployment rose from 2.9 percent in 1974 to 4.3 percent in 1975 and 5.7 percent in 1976 (Scharpf 1991: 78). Many union leaders consequently challenged the Labour government openly, questioning whether it had delivered its part of the social contract (Flanagan et al. 1983: 433).

The relation between unions and the government in the period between 1978 and 1979 was intensely confrontational (Scharpf 1991: 83; Crouch 1982: 90–110). In early 1978, the government established a guideline calling for maximum wage increases of 5 percent and offered in exchange some additional tax concessions. But by this time unions were unwilling to adhere to these guidelines for wage moderation and openly rebelled against the recommendations of the government. Between November 1978 and March 1979 – the so-called Winter of Discontent – Britain lost 29 million working days to strike action (R. Jones 1987: 113). Both private- and public-sector unions participated in this strike. As Fritz Scharpf characterized the consequences of this intense period of confrontation, "wares were not transported, public transportation collapsed, children were not taught, sick people were turned away, and the dead remained unburied" (Scharpf 1991: 87). When the government and unions attempted to reach an agreement on wage moderation and inflation control in February 1979, it was too late. By then public opinion had decisively shifted away from the Labour government, and an overwhelming majority of the electorate supported a Conservative government that pledged to restore order.

In retrospect, the social contract was a bold effort to institutionalize the political exchange involving an increase in the level of transfers and the generosity of social policy benefits in exchange for wage moderation. Analysis of the evolution of the social contract indicates that the strategies pursued by the government differed across the three stages of this policy. In the first stage, the government offered unions fiscal expansion in exchange for wage moderation. The external economic environment was highly unfavorable, however, placing an immense burden on the incomes policy. In the second attempt at negotiation, which occurred between 1974 and 1975, the government did not increase benefits, but instead appealed to unions' concern for redistribution and recommended an egalitarian wage policy. Finally, beginning in 1976, the government offered unions tax relief targeted to distributionally disadvantaged groups. In this period union leaders displayed willingness to cooperate with the policies of the government, but the low institutional capacity of the labor movement prevented this cooperation from resulting in wage restraint.

The Conservative Attack on the Social Wage, 1980–1996

Margaret Thatcher took office in the aftermath of the Winter of Discontent. As a result of her unwavering commitment to a "Gladstonian liberalism" (Beer 2001: 21), Thatcher distrusted all the policies of the postwar settlement: the commitment to full employment, the dedication to welfare state expansion, and organized labor, which she referred to as "the enemy within." Conservatives abandoned efforts to link wage and social policy negotiations and rejected the notion of the social wage (Rhodes 2000: 40). As the 1979 Conservative manifesto expressed this change in policy orientations, "The road to ruin has been paved with such exchanges of promises between the Labour government and the unions" (Dale 2000a). The Conservative strategy of deinstitutionalizing the social wage had two related elements: On the one hand, Thatcher abandoned incomes policies and pursued a series of reforms that weakened the power of organized labor and decentralized wage bargaining; on the other hand, she pursued a series of social policy reforms that limited growth in expenditures and reduced benefits. In contrast to all previous postwar governments, the Thatcher government pursued these reforms without involving unions in the policy-making process.

The Conservative attack on the power of organized labor had three interrelated components. The first element of this strategy was the introduction of industrial relations legislation that tightly circumscribed the ability of trade unions to disrupt economic activities. This legislation was pursued hesitatingly at first and with determination only later on. In 1980 the government adopted the first Employment Act, which set out to eliminate the sources of excess union power. The act prohibited recruitment by unions of new members for the purposes of expanding an industrial dispute, placed severe restrictions on picketing by eliminating the right of workers to picket beyond their place of work, and empowered employers to resist industrial action by making available to them a range of common-law sanctions that had been unavailable before. An additional measure weakening trade unions amended social security laws to limit the payment of supplementary benefits to strikers' dependents if they were receiving strike payments from union funds.

In the Cabinet the position of the more Conservative policy makers who demanded even more far-reaching changes was strengthened after 1981. Thatcher herself pushed for more radical measures against trade unions by invoking the continuing recurrence of strikes, such as the extended conflict in the steel industry of 1981, and additional measures restricting the bargaining power of labor were enacted in 1982. The Employment Act of that year provided a very restricted definition of "lawful" union action and removed the legal immunity that unions had enjoyed against action in court, thereby enabling a trade union to be sued for damages in the case of an unlawful strike for the first time since 1906. The law also restricted the role of closed shops and curtailed the power of shop stewards.

In addition to limiting unions' power to act, a second component of the Conservative strategy was legislation designed to constrain the power of union leaders over their members. The Conservative manifesto of 1979 had formulated Tories' belief that "trade unions are dominated by a handful of extremists who do not reflect the commonsense view of most union members" (Dale 2000a). The underlying principles of the reforms were spelled out in a green paper of 1983 entitled "Democracy in Trade Unions" (U.K. Department of Employment 1983). The Trade Union Act of 1984, which elaborated on the recommendations of this green paper, required more stringent use of pre-strike ballots in an effort to inhibit major strike action. New legal developments followed after the yearlong strike of miners of 1984. The 1988 Employment Act allowed individual workers to appeal against a union's decision to take industrial action if that action had not yet been approved by ballot.

A third element of the strategy by which the Thatcher administration attempted to break the power of organized labor was the privatization of publicly held corporations (Ogden 1994: 67; Parry, Waddington, and Critcher 1997: 174). The unexpected success of the British Telecommunications privatization in 1982 accelerated the government's commitment to privatization (Boix 1998: 173). Important flagship corporations of the British economy, including British Gas, British Airways, Rolls Royce, and British Petroleum, changed ownership in the Thatcher years. Proceeds from privatization rose from 0.2 percent of the GDP in 1983 to 1 percent in 1986–1987 and 1.5 percent in 1988–1989. Publicly held corporations employed 1,849,000 people in 1979, or 7.3 percent of the workforce. By 1992 this figure had declined to 516,000 people, or 2 percent of the workforce (Boix 1998: 174). Numerous studies of union representation in industries that changed ownership in the Thatcher years reveal that privatization significantly eroded the responsibilities of unions (Colling 1994; Ogden 1994; McKinlay and Taylor 1994; Parry et al. 1997). On some occasions private owners refused union recognition entirely, while on others the scope and effectiveness of collective bargaining were severely curtailed by the introduction of contract labor on a massive scale (Parry et al. 1997: 177).

Finally, the unprecedented rise in the unemployment level itself exerted strong disciplining effects on the political and economic demands of trade unions. The macroeconomic policies pursued by Thatcher were characterized by a strict commitment to rigid targets for monetary growth and a related commitment to low public-sector borrowing requirements (Hall 1986). By pursuing these rigid monetary policies, Conservatives succeeded in controlling inflation, which declined from 21.9 percent in August 1980 to 3.7 percent in May 1983 (King and Wood 1999: 381). But the consequence of these extremely austere macroeconomic policies was a steady rise in unemployment, from 4.5 percent in 1979 to a peak of 11.8 percent in 1985 (Scharpf and Schmidt 2000: 341).

The Thatcher government's policies, taken as a whole, were, according to Crouch, "probably the most single-minded and sustained attack on the position of a major and previously legitimate social force to have been undertaken anywhere under modern democratic conditions" (Crouch 1996: 120). The consequence of these reforms was a steady decline in the power of organized labor (Waddington 1992; King and Wood 2001). In 1979 union membership stood at 13.3 million (Dunn and Metcalf 1996: 77). It declined to 8.9 million in 1992 and to 7.9 million in 1996, the year the Conservatives left office. These changes represented a 20 percent decline in union density from 57.3 percent in 1979 to 36.4 percent in 1995 (Ebbinghaus and Visser 2001: 745). The trend affected blue- and white-collar workers and public- and private-sector unions alike. The organizations most seriously affected by the decline were the TGWU, which lost 50 percent of its members between 1979 and 1992; the Amalgamated Engineering and Electrical Union, which lost 47 percent; and the National Union of Teachers (Ebbinghaus and Visser 2001).

One of the explicit objectives of these labor market reforms was the transformation of wage setting institutions and the shift to a bargaining system in which pay rates were established at the firm level. The Conservative manifesto had explicitly formulated the party's objective to abolish the industry-level bargaining that was still common in Britain in the 1970s: "Pay bargaining in the private sector should be left to the companies and workers concerned. At the end of the day, no one should or can protect them from the results of the agreements they make" (Dale 2000a). The strategy of labor market decentralization and deregulation was effective: A

Workplace Industrial Relations Survey points to the decline of multiemployer bargaining in the 1980s (Ingram, Wadsworth, and Brown 1999: 34). By the mid-1980s there were in excess of 30,000 bargaining units in Britain, as opposed to a few hundred in the previous decades. The decentralization of wage setting brought about mixed results with respect to the restoration of wage moderation. In the 1980s wage increases rose faster than prices, and it was only during the mid-1990s that the government was able to achieve "its heart's desire on pay" (Metcalf and Milner 1995). Between 1980 and 1991, the average level of wage increase was 6.8 percent; it declined to 3.76 percent between 1992 and 1996 (Ingram et al. 1999: 37; National Institute Economic Review, various years). There remained, however, significant sectoral differences in wage increases: Pay raises in low-productivity service sectors were much lower than in the manufacturing sector.

Another important consequence of the labor market deregulation pursued by Thatcher was the rise in inequality. The combined labor market and welfare state reforms eroded most of the gains in equality achieved in the postwar period. The Gini coefficient stood at 0.248 in 1979, the year Thatcher was elected, but had increased to 0.329 by 1996. An analysis of the evolution of the relationship of the bottom decile of income earners to the top decile (the 90/10 ratio) depicts a similar trend. The greatest increase in inequality occurred between 1984 and 1991, and it was followed by a slow decline in the 90/10 ratio from its peak of 4.3 in 1991 to 3.9 in 1996. While debate persists about the factors responsible for this rise in inequality, estimates attribute about 30 percent of the growth in inequality to the decline in union density.

In concert with labor market reforms, Thatcher waged a systematic attack on virtually all institutions of the welfare state. In every electoral campaign between 1979 and 1992, the Conservative Party announced its opposition to the "over-powerful state" and its commitment to "lower taxation." "We are the only Party that believes in lower taxation," Conservatives proclaimed. "Lower taxation, by increasing take-home pay without adding to industry's costs, improves competitiveness and helps with jobs. High taxes deprive people of their independence and make choices for them" (Dale 2000a). While Conservatives shared the belief that high taxes were one of the main causes of the British economic malaise, the British tax burden was not particularly large by international comparison. In 1980, total taxation as a percentage of the GDP stood at 32.2 percent, while the OECD average was 35.5 percent (Scharpf and Schmidt 2000: 360). Public social expenditures stood at 18.3 percent of the GDP, a figure that was more than 1 percent below the OECD average (Scharpf and Schmidt 2000: 364). Nor were social policy replacement rates particularly generous in international comparison. When Thatcher took office in 1979, old-age insurance provided a replacement rate corresponding to 22 percent of the average wage of male workers. Replacement rates for sickness and unemployment benefits were lower, standing at about 18 percent of male workers' average wage (U.K. Government Statistical Service 1988: 257).

Conservatives aimed to reduce overall social policy expenditures – by capping the growth rate of future expenditures and by encouraging private provisions – as well as the generosity of social policy benefits. The Thatcher government pursued these goals unilaterally, without any consultation with unions. The Social Security Act of 1980, which was one of the first policies enacted by the new Conservative government, changed the indexation of the basic pension (TUC 1980: 82–5). From 1973 to 1980, pension benefits had been indexed either to higher prices or to wages, but in practice the growth in benefits was linked to wage growth. The 1980 act instead linked benefit growth to rising prices in an attempt to minimize the effects of any gains on the wage front. In practice, the adjustment had far-reaching implications, eroding benefits by about 20 percent over a 10-year period (Pierson 1994: 59). Although the TUC strongly opposed these changes and "deplored the Government's systematic attack on the social wage," unions were unable to influence the details of the new legislation or to preempt the reductions in benefits (TUC 1981: 90–1).

The most dramatic cuts to old-age protection were introduced as part of the Social Security Act of 1986 (Bonoli 2001: 249; TUC 1986: 84–6). The main target of this act was the State Earnings-Related Pension Scheme (SERPS): It lowered SERPS benefits from 25 to 20 percent and simultaneously changed the formula for determining the level of benefits, basing the pension on lifetime average earnings rather than on an employee's best 20 years. Additional provisions made it easier for occupational pension schemes to contract out of SERPS and encouraged contracting out via personal pensions (Araki 2000: 612; TUC 1986: 84). These changes fell short of abolishing SERPS entirely, which was the government's initial intention announced in a 1985 green paper entitled "Reform of Social Security" (U.K. Department of Health and Social Services 1985). But they had a profound impact on the character of old-age protection in Britain, limiting future expenditures on old-age benefits. Several studies have pointed out that, compared to estimates of growth made prior to the passage of the 1986 act, SERPS expenditures are likely to decline by 50 percent by 2021 (Pierson 1994: 63–64; Fry, Smith, and White 1990). The number of persons contracting out of SERPS and setting up private pensions, moreover, increased to 4 million, or about 15 percent of the working population, in 1990 (Pierson 1994: 63).

Despite Thatcher's efforts to privatize the health services, the National Health Service changed relatively little under her government (Pierson 1994: 132–51; Döhler 1990; Giaimo 2002). A policy recommendation to shift from tax financing to contribution-based financing formulated in 1981 generated public outcry and had to be immediately withdrawn (Döhler 1990: 211). Other proposals to shift to mandatory private insurance were also abandoned. Ultimately the government attempted to contain health care expenditures by introducing "internal markets" in the provision of health services. As a result of these changes, which split purchasers from providers, hospitals had to compete with each other for the patients of district health authority purchasers (Giaimo 2002: 346). Conservatives nevertheless remained successful in limiting the rate of growth of future health care expenditures by introducing "standstill budgets" that allowed only minimal rates of growth: Between 1979 and 1996, health service expenditures rarely grew by more than 1 percent in any given year.

In an effort to reduce dependence on social policy benefits, both Thatcher and her successor, John Major, introduced policies that strengthened the compulsion to accept employment as a precondition of the receipt of benefits (Wood 2001; King 1995). "Workfare policies," which "induced people to accept lower paid jobs than they would have done if 'passive' cash benefits had been available," went hand in hand with attempts to deregulate the lower end of the labor market. The Job Seeker's Allowance, which was directed at the unemployed, removed beneficiaries' right to refuse jobs on the basis of wages or conditions of employment, aiming to create an infinitely elastic labor supply. Other policies raised the level of child benefits received by working mothers in an effort to bring single mothers back into the labor market (Grover and Stewart 1999: 76).

How far-reaching were the changes to the British welfare state introduced by the Conservative governments? How did they affect the overall financing of the British welfare state? Table 5.3 presents aggregate data on the evolution of social policy expenditures and revenues. Contrary to Thatcher's aspirations, public social policy expenditures as a percentage of

Table 5.3. *Social policy spending under the Conservatives, 1980–1996*

	1980	1985	1990	1996
Social expenditures as percentage of GDP				
UK	18.3	21.1	19.6	22.8*
OECD (18)	19.9	21.8	22.6	24.7*
Taxation as percentage of GDP				
UK	35.2	37.5	36.6	36
OECD (18)	36.4	38.3	39.2	39.9
Social security contributions as percentage of GDP				
UK	7.4	6.7	6.2	6.2
OECD (18)	9	9.7	10	10.7

Notes:
*Data for 1995

Source:
Schmidt and Scharpf 2000a, 364.

the GDP did not decline under the Conservatives (Scharpf and Schmidt 2000: 364). They stood at 18.3 percent in 1980, the year Thatcher took office, and reached 22.8 percent in 1996. In comparative terms, this 3 percent rise in the level of social policy expenditures ranks below much larger increases in countries such as Norway and Finland and falls below the OECD average by 1 percent. Total taxation as a percentage of the GDP also increased only modestly, from 35.2 percent in 1980 to 37.8 percent in 1986 and falling back to 35.3 percent in 1997 (360). The virtual standstill in taxation growth stands in contrast to the trend across OECD countries, where taxation as a percentage of the GDP increased from 36.4 percent in 1980 to 40.9 percent in 1996.

The policy changes introduced by Conservative governments between 1980 and 1996 were a systematic assault on the power of organized labor and the public commitment to social protection. Their goal was to deinstitutionalize the political exchange between the government and unions that was premised on expansion in social benefits and services in exchange for unions' commitment to wage moderation (Rhodes 2000). Reforms in the sphere of social protection enacted by these administrations were negotiated with no involvement of labor in the policy-making process. As the above analysis has shown, Thatcher's government was more successful at weakening the power of organized labor than at privatizing major social policy programs.

Welfare State and Labor Market Reforms Under New Labour

While in opposition, the Labour Party made a considerable effort to weaken its political link to the trade union movement (McIlroy 1998; Glyn and Wood 2001: 216). This decision was based on the perception that the 1992 electoral defeat had been the result of the identification by the electorate of the Labour Party as the party representing solely the interests of trade unions. At its 1993 conference, the party reduceds unions' share of the vote in elections of party leaders. A number of additional decisions severely curtailed the role of trade unions in the party's internal decision-making procedures and in the process of policy formulation. Tony Blair summarized the new relationship of his party to the trade unions: "Nobody seriously believes in this day and age that the business of the Labour Party is to be the political arm of the trade union movement. . . . In government you cannot operate like that. It wouldn't be right, anyway" (McIlroy 1998: 2000).

Policy developments after Labour's electoral victory reveal a growing political distance between the Labour Party and trade unions. Despite the passage of a motion at the 1994 and 1995 meetings of the TUC for a "repeal of all anti-trade union legislation passed by the Tories," the Blair government accepted the Thatcherite status quo almost entirely (TUC 1994: 242–254, TUC 1995: 34; Smith and Morton 2001; Hay 1999). The centerpiece of the government's industrial relations legislation was summarized in the white paper "Fairness at Work," which became the basis for the Employment Relations Act of 1999 (U.K. Department of Trade and Industry 1998). Despite union opposition, the government took no action to repeal "legislation on the closed shop (Employment Act 1988, 1990) ballots and notices prior to industrial action (Trade Union Act 1984, Trade Union Reform and Employment Rights Act 1993), unofficial action (Employment Act 1990), elections for certain trade union offices, right to join a trade union of one's choice (Trade Union Reform and Employment Rights Act), and the rights of members in specific circumstances not to be disciplined by unions according to rules (Employment Act 1988) will remain" (Smith and Morton 2001: 121; on unions' demands to repeal the Thatcher legislation, see TUC 2000: 67). As the preface to this white paper states the thrust of the new approach, "The days of strikes without ballots, mass picketing, closed shops and secondary action are over" (U.K. Department of Trade and Industry 1998: 3). "For New Labour 'partnership' between capital and labour" would replace "the notion of conflict between employers and employees" (U.K. Department of Trade and Industry 1998: 2). Specific legal provisions intended to bring about workplace harmony and cooperative industrial relations included a limited recognition of unions coupled with measures that excluded autonomous unions and explicitly allowed employers to offer financial inducements to workers to opt out of collective agreements (Smith and Morton 2001: 121). "In offering new rights," the government announced, "we will demand that employees in turn accept their responsibilities to cooperate with employers" (U.K. Department of Trade and Industry 1998: 14).

In his foreword to the "Fairness at Work" white paper, Tony Blair asserted, "Even after the changes we propose, Britain will have the most lightly regulated labor market of any leading economy in the world" (U.K. Department of Trade and Industry 1998: 4). This goal – a dubious achievement for a Labour government – testifies to the dramatic shift that had taken place in the programmatic orientation of the Labour Party. The only significant legislation that sought to reverse some of the labor market consequences of the Conservative period involved the introduction of a minimum wage. The Labour government began to consider introducing minimal wage legislation as early as 1997. While the impetus for the change can be attributed in part to trade union pressure, unions were not formally involved in the decision-making process (Glyn and Wood 2001: 217). An independently appointed Low Pay Commission formulated the policy recommendations that were ultimately adopted: The legislation established a minimum wage of 3.60 pounds per hour for workers aged 22 and older and 3 pounds for workers aged 18 to 21. The adult rate was raised to 3.70 pounds in October 2000 and to 4.20 pounds in October 2001. This was significantly less than the 5 pounds per hour demanded by some public-sector unions and was initially lower than the 4 pound rate advocated by the TUC. As a result, the legislation met with significant protest from trade unions. Existing econometric estimates of its impact suggest that it has reduced wage inequality only modestly, as only 6 to 7 percent of the workforce is affected by the law (Dickens and Mannings 2002). The levels of wage inequality inherited by the New Labour government have changed very little since it was elected, the minimal wage legislation notwithstanding. The 90/10 ratio stood at 4.064 in 1997, the year New Labour took office, and declined only marginally to 4.039 in 2001. This is a very high level of inequality in international terms; it is, in fact, high even by postwar British standards.

New Labour's acceptance of the industrial relations status quo has precluded a concerted approach to wage negotiation. Britain now also lacks the institutional environment appropriate for more extensive negotiations linking wage restraint to social policy reform. As the TUC bluntly complained about the absence of systematic consultation between the government and unions on major reforms, "There is little value in conversation with the government, if their minds are made up and there is no scope for changes in the policy" (Bach 2002: 328). So far, a stable macroeconomic environment and a tough bargaining approach on the part of employers has led to wage restraint. There are no indications that Britain will move away from firm-level wage setting. As Glyn and Wood have argued, "Given the weakness of unions in wide sections of the private sector and the employers' hostility on their freedom of maneuver, attempting to steer them towards coordinated bargaining would be very difficult, but it seems that political considerations – fear of appearing to favor union power and corporatism – have dictated a prohibition even on discussion of the issue" (Glyn and Wood 2001: 209).

The Blair government has also refrained from engaging in a massive fiscal expansion and reorientation of the British welfare state. In this case, the most important constraint on government action has been its commitment not to raise new taxes (Glyn and Wood 2001: 210). This commitment was reiterated on numerous occasions. The 1997 electoral manifesto pledged that "there will be no return to the penal tax rates that existed both under Labour and Conservative governments in the 1970s. . . . The myth that the solution to every problem is increased spending had been comprehensively dispelled. . . . The level of public spending is no longer the best measure of the effectiveness of government action in the public interest. . . . New Labour will be wise spenders, not big spenders" (Dale 2000b: 354–5). A "code for fiscal stability" announced by the treasury in 1998 elaborated the two fiscal rules that the government pledged to follow: It would borrow only to invest, not to fund current spending, and it would set the ratio of net public-sector debt to GDP at a "stable and prudent level," defined as 40 percent of the GDP (U.K. Treasury 1998). Thus, the government's optimal debt target is much lower than the 60 percent target set by the Maastricht Treaty. Between 1997 and 2001, public expenditure as a percentage of the GDP averaged less than 40 percent, as compared to 44 percent for the 1979–1997 period (Mullard 2001: 310). New Labour's commitment to fiscal prudence has preempted major welfare reforms. Despite the call from trade unions to index growth in pension benefits to earnings rather than prices, Labour refused to introduce legislation to this effect. Similarly, the government has resisted unions' demands to abolish the Job Seekers' Allowance and increase unemployment benefits.

Acting within its self-imposed fiscal rules, New Labour nevertheless presided over a change in the distribution of resources between various social policy programs. Expenditures on health care experienced the fastest rate of change and grew by an average of 4.7 percent, while education spending grew at an annual rate of 3.8 percent (Glyn and Wood 2001: 212). These allocations reflect the government's two most important commitments: to make education "Labour's number one priority" and to "save and modernize the NHS [National Health Service]" (Dale 2000b: 382). An increase in expenditures on health care is expected in the new few years, as the government committed itself in the 2001 election campaign to raise health care spending to the level of the European Union (EU) average by 2006 (Bach 2002: 324). By contrast, expenditures on defense contracted by 0.6 percent, and social security spending grew by only 1 percent a year.

One important policy priority of the Labour government is to address social exclusion and marginalization by introducing policies that reinsert previously excluded groups into the labor market. The policy mantra of New Labour is that labor market participation should be the basis for citizenship and that "work is the best way out of poverty" (Glyn and Wood 2001). The centerpiece of Labour's welfare-to-work scheme are "New Deal" policies (Glyn and Wood 2000; Bell, Blundell, and Van Reenen 1999). These policies were initially targeted at young people who had claimed unemployment benefits (Job Seekers Allowance) for over 6 months, but they were later extended to other "problematic" labor market groups, such as persons on disability and lone parents. New Deal policies present several options to these persons situated in a very precarious relationship to the labor market: a full-time job for 26 weeks (subsidized with 60 pounds per week); a job within the voluntary sector or with an environmental task force (offering a wage higher than unemployment benefits); or entry into full-time education and training for a period of 12 months without loss of benefits (Bell et al. 1999: 7). Such policies are financed by a windfall tax on privatized utilities. The distinctive characteristic of this policy is the element of compulsion: The option of continuing to draw unemployment benefits is explicitly ruled out, and sanctions are applied to individuals who refuse to comply with the policies. Additional tax changes complement the New Deal and aim to improve incentives for people at the lower end of the labor market to seek work rather than rely on social policy benefits. The Working Family Tax Credit, introduced in October 1999, is designed to provide a minimum income guarantee to all low-earning families with children in full-time employment and is provided as a tax relief to these families (Oppenheim 2000: 81–82). The Disability Person's Tax Credit and another credit for individuals over the age of 50 provide similar tax relief to vulnerable labor market groups.

The range of policies adopted under the rubric of Labour's New Deal bear important similarities to initiatives under way in many other continental European countries. Such programs aim at the activation of groups previously excluded from the labor market, such as the long-term unemployed, lone parents with small children, elderly workers who have claimed long-term disability benefits, and others caught in "poverty traps." If such efforts are successful and sustainable over the long term, they will generate higher tax revenues and will lower social policy expenditures devoted to labor market outsiders. In the present austerity context, characterized by efforts to contain growth in social policy expenditures, additional funds could then be redirected to social programs that have suffered from a slow attrition of resources. By entering the labor market, moreover, the former outsiders will exert a downward pressure on wages, which can allow an expansionary demand management policy to generate additional employment at very low costs in terms of inflation (Glyn and Wood 2001). There are, however, significant differences in the approaches to the question of welfare state reform pursued by the Labour administration that distinguish Britain from the other countries examined in this study. New Labour – out of either strategic foresight or resignation – has accepted the distinct "institutional equilibrium" of a liberal market economy, which is characterized by deregulated labor markets and low wage labor costs (Hall and Soskice 2001; Wood 2001). None of the reforms it has introduced so far challenge Britain's institutional equilibrium by attempting to reintroduce corporatist-style institutions. Industrial relations reforms have not strengthened trade unions, and no attempt has been made to reestablish tripartite consultation. This testifies to the far-reaching political impact of the Thatcherite reforms.

Conclusion

Students of the British welfare state have often asserted that the notion of a social wage was "neither developed nor institutionalized in Britain" (Rhodes 2000: 23). The analysis developed in this chapter demonstrates, however, that the *quid pro quo* of social policy expansion in exchange for better benefits and services was not entirely absent in Britain. In the first decades of the postwar period, both Labour and Conservative governments expanded social benefits or services in order to offer unions incentives to moderate wage demands. On several occasions these policies were relatively successful. Analysis of trade union publications has also revealed the willingness of union leaders to engage in this political exchange. Thus, the social policy preferences of the British labor movement in the first decades after the Second World War were in no way different from the preferences of unions in Germany or Sweden.

The most important obstacle to the functioning of the political exchange in Britain was the institutional fragmentation of the wage bargaining system and the multiplication of the wage bargaining agents. The authority of union leaders over their members eroded gradually beginning in the 1960s. This was a consequence in part of the prolonged moderation exercised by unions in the previous decade (Whiteside 1996). This erosion undermined the ability of unions to deliver their part of the political bargain and restrain wage growth. In the 1970s various efforts to negotiate a social contract remained unsuccessful.

The reforms enacted by Conservative governments beginning in 1980 systematically decoupled wage negotiations from changes in social protection policies. These reforms were relatively successful in weakening the collective power of unions and removed labor from the policy-making process. Upon its return to power, the Labour Party made no effort to restore the earlier political exchange but accepted the Thatcherite status quo virtually unchanged. The present-day absence of this political exchange is the result of policy failures of earlier decades and of conservative reforms. However, this political exchange has not been entirely absent in Britain during the postwar period.

Conclusion: New Social Pacts in Contemporary Europe

In recent years "social pacts," or tripartite agreements between governments, unions, and employers, have reemerged as a crucial political institution for the formulation of economic and social policy reforms (Fejertag and Pochet 1997, 2000; Regini 2000; Traxler 2000; Hassel 1999; Ebbinghaus and Hassel 2000; Berger and Compston 2002). In many economies these new social pacts continue the existing tradition of corporatist consultation and negotiation. In The Netherlands, a recent agreement signed by the government and unions entitled "the New Course" follows the reform trajectory initiated by the pathbreaking Wassenaar Accord of 1982 (Hemerjick, Van der Meer, and Visser 2000; Visser and Hemerjick 1997). In both Denmark and Norway, policy makers have initiated a series of negotiations with their social partners explicitly linking changes in social policies to guarantees of wage restraint by the labor movement (Lind 1997). Following the electoral victory of the Social Democratic Party in March 1995, Finnish social partners accepted the terms of a centralized agreement involving the moderation of wage demands in exchange for tax reforms (Kiander 1997: 139). And immediately after assuming power, the Red-Green coalition government in Germany reinitiated tripartite discussions with unions and employers as part of the "Alliance for Jobs" (Bispinck 1997; Bispinck and Schulten 2000).

Social pacts are playing a prominent role even in economies whose governments have a weak history of cooperation and consultation with trade unions. In these cases, a series of far-reaching reforms of wage bargaining institutions has attempted to create the necessary preconditions for new political exchanges. In Ireland, the "social partnership" was launched in 1987 with the Program for National Recovery. Since 1987, Irish policy makers and trade unions have concluded three additional social partnership agreements. According to many observers, the policy changes negotiated as part of these agreements, in conjunction with sustained wage moderation, have contributed to the economic revival of the Irish economy in recent years (O'Donnell and O'Reardon 1997, 2000; Baccaro 2002; Baccaro and Simoni 2002). In Italy, a reform of wage bargaining institutions undertaken in July 1993 laid the foundation for the subsequent deepening of "social concertation" (Negrelli 1997, 2000; Baccaro 1999; Regini and Regalia 1997). In the last decade, finally, social pacts have been initiated in both Spain and Portugal (Perez 2000a, 2000b; Barreto and Naumann 1998; Da Paz and Naumann 1997, 2000; Royo 2002).

What explains the emergence of new social pacts in recent years? What are the common policy objectives of these pacts? What is the policy content of these agreements, and in what ways does it differ from policy agreements of earlier periods? Finally, how should one assess the effectiveness of the new social pacts? Examination of these questions allows me to review the main implications of this book's theoretical argument for the dynamics of social policy reform in recent years. At the center of the tripartite negotiations between governments and the social partners are policy mixes that involve a combination of wage moderation and changes in the financing and distribution of social policy benefits. As such, the new social pacts have much in common with the tripartite political exchanges that have figured prominently in many European economies in the postwar period. What is new about the social pacts are the policy constraints faced by the actors in their negotiations. The high fiscal burden and the dense array of preexisting social policies constrain the menu of available policy solutions. At the same time, high payroll taxes reduce the impact of wage moderation on unemployment.

I will begin by summarizing the contribution of this book to the literature on wage determination in advanced industrialized economies. The following section will analyze the consequences of the growth in the fiscal burden for the policy options available to unions and governments in the new social pacts. Finally, I will conclude by considering three areas of reform central to social pacts: wage bargaining institutions, taxation, and policies that attempt to improve participation in the labor market.

The Theoretical Argument

This book has developed a theoretical framework that examines the conditions that facilitate the emergence of a political exchange between unions and governments premised on unions' moderation of their wage demands in return for the expansion of social policy benefits and services. Such a political exchange was central to welfare state expansion in the first years of the postwar period, allowing many economies to reconcile commitment to full employment with social protection. The model developed in this book has identified the key political and institutional variables that affect unions' incentives to pursue wage moderation. It has also explored the key factors influencing the effectiveness of labor movement wage policies in lowering unemployment. Finally, it has showed how the growth of the tax wedge constrains the effectiveness of wage moderation.

The theoretical model developed in this book adds to a familiar set of models of wage determination in advanced industrialized economies. The building block of the analysis is the Calmfors-Driffill model, which explores the impact of differences in labor market institutions – more precisely, differences in bargaining authority centralization – on unions' incentive to deliver wage moderation (Calmfors and Driffill 1988). This analysis predicts a U-shaped relationship between wage bargaining system centralization and wage moderation. Unions' incentive to exercise wage moderation is high in either extremely centralized or extremely decentralized labor markets. In the former, high levels of competition in product markets does not allow individual firms to raise relative prices in response to an increase in wages. In this context, higher wage demands are likely to result in losses in employment, which creates a strong incentive for wage moderation. In highly centralized labor markets, unions face incentives to internalize their militancy, as increases in wages are likely to result in employment losses for the entire economy. By contrast, wage moderation is less common in economies with intermediately centralized wage bargaining institutions, where the effects of unions' monopoly power outweigh their incentives to internalize some of the costs of their militant wage behavior. Generally, the Calmfors-Driffill model has been successful in explaining cross-national variation in the employment performance of European economies.

The model developed in Chapter 1 integrates the findings of a recent literature that demonstrates that unions' wage choices are influenced by their government's macroeconomic policy orientation (Scharpf 1991; Iversen 1999; Soskice and Iversen 1999). As these studies argue, unions have a greater incentive to moderate their wage demands in the presence of a monetary authority that adheres to a low inflation target. In response to militant wage settlements, such a nonaccommodating monetary authority will reduce the real money supply. Hence, wage bargainers will have an incentive to exercise wage restraint. Unions' behavior will differ, however, if the monetary authority is accommodating and seeks to avoid a reduction in real demand. Under these conditions, an increase in wages and prices will have little effect on the real money supply, and unions will face stronger incentives to exercise wage militancy (Soskice and Iversen 1999, 2000). The theoretical framework of the book integrates this theoretical logic advanced by Soskice and Iversen. Both the quantitative and qualitative results presented in this book support these theoretical claims.

This book has extended the Calmfors-Driffill and Soskice-Iversen models by demonstrating that the wage choices made by unions and the equilibrium level of unemployment also depend on the level and structure of welfare state commitments. I have focused on two policy parameters modeling cross-national differences in policies of social protection: taxation levels and the composition of social policy transfers. This richer model, which incorporates social policy characteristics into existing wage bargaining models, accounts for both cross-national and intertemporal differences in the employment performance of OECD economies. Future research might extend the analysis advanced in this book by modeling the impact of additional variables that capture cross-national differences in institutions of social protection, such as the level of insurance coverage or the mix between private and public social policies, on the wage strategies of unions.

The starting assumption of the analysis is that social policy concerns are an important motivation of trade unions. In this model, unions' utility comprises an element capturing the benefits and services received by their members. This assumption distinguishes my model from most wage bargaining models, which assume that unions have utilitarian preferences. As Chapter 1 demonstrates, this additional assumption leads to equilibrium predictions of higher levels of wage moderation and lower levels of unemployment than the Calmfors-Driffill model. The magnitude of the employment effect that follows from this additional wage moderation increases as a function of wage bargaining system centralization. This result supports the informal conjecture of the corporatist literature that concerns for social policy benefits have acted as an important source of moderation for the labor movement (Katzenstein 1985; Esping-Andersen 1990). The "wage moderation effect" explains why the expansion of the welfare state in the first decades of the postwar period was associated with very low costs in terms of employment.

The gradual development and maturation of the welfare state, however, has undermined the effectiveness of the postwar political exchange. This book has focused on two important mechanisms by which welfare state growth has affected the equilibrium choices of unions and firms, and consequently the level of unemployment. The first effect is the result of an increase in taxes: First, higher taxes lower firms' demand for labor; second – as this book has repeatedly emphasized – higher taxes also reduce the effectiveness of wage moderation. As wages come to constitute only a small portion of the total wage bill, even a significant reduction in wage demands has only a modest impact on employment. Chapters 3 and 4 provided empirical support for this hypothesis.

Changes in the structure and composition of social policy expenditures are also likely to undermine the effectiveness of the political exchange. An increase in benefits received by labor market outsiders will lower the net utility of union members from social policy transfers and undermine the willingness of individual workers to accept wage restraint. Chapter 2 presented econometric support for the proposition that an increase in expenditures devoted to labor market outsiders adversely impacts employment. The qualitative chapters, moreover, found *some* (but weaker) evidence relating increases in social policy expenditures devoted to labor market outsiders to heightened union militancy. The unexpected wage militancy of the German labor movement at the beginning of the 1990s can be attributed to the massive increases in social policy transfers to nonunion members following reunification.

Implications for the Politics of New Social Pacts

The qualitative chapters of the book examined the linkages between wage and social policy developments in economies with different levels of wage bargaining system centralization. One cannot understand the major turning points in the wage policies pursued by labor movements or the mix between militancy and restraint without specifying key developments in the policies of social protection. I have also shown that the nexus between wages and social policy developments has undergone a gradual change as welfare states have matured. In the first decades of the postwar period – under conditions of low taxes and low levels of transfers to labor market outsiders – unions' wage moderation was the critical variable accounting for the presence of a virtuous cycle between full employment and increases

223

in social policy transfers and services. The magnitude of the impact of wage moderation on employment varied considerably between countries and was shaped by both the institutional characteristics of a given country's wage bargaining system and the character of its government's macroeconomic policy.

The growth of welfare states has altered the constraints faced by these actors during these political exchanges. One important consequence of welfare state maturation has been the reduction in the importance of wages as a percentage of the total wage bill. In Belgium, Italy, Germany, The Netherlands, and Finland, wages comprise only 50 percent of the total compensation. The share of wages as a percentage of total compensation is higher in Ireland, Denmark, and Norway, where it stands at around 70 percent of the total labor costs (Svenskt Näringsliv 2003: 7).[1] One consequence of this development is that unions effectively bargain over a much smaller share of the total wage bill. This erodes the ability of wage moderation to reduce unemployment.

At the center of new social pacts are efforts to identify areas of reform – such as taxation and social insurance financing – that can diminish the policy constraints imposed by mature welfare states. Examples of these changes are tax changes and other changes in the financing of social insurance that attempt to lower the wedge between gross and net wages. Other social policy reforms attempt to decrease the number of labor market outsiders and reverse the decline in labor force participation rates. Such changes are introduced together with reforms of labor market institutions in the direction of greater wage bargaining system centralization, thus strengthening the incentives for unions to deliver wage moderation. In the remainder of this chapter I will discuss recent efforts to bundle such policy changes as part of new social pacts.

One area of reform that is central to social pacts is the creation of institutional preconditions for wage moderation through reforms of the wage setting process. Wage moderation is regarded as a lever that can influence a variety of other policy goals, including the improvement of a country's competitive position, the reduction of labor costs, and the limitation of growth in the public-sector wage bill (Ebbinghaus and Hassel 2000). In recent years

---

[1] Data are for 1998. The specific country statistics are as follows. Pay for wages as a percentage of compensation costs: Belgium, 50.5 percent; Denmark, 76.6 percent; Finland, 57.6 percent; Germany, 55.9 percent; Ireland, 75.7 percent; Italy, 52.9 percent; The Netherlands, 56.8 percent; Norway, 70.5 percent; Switzerland, 64.7 percent; Sweden, 60.2 percent (Svenskt Näringsliv 2002).

policy makers have experimented with a variety of policy changes attempting to limit wage growth. One strategy involves changing the guidelines for wage bargaining actors in the determination of wages, while another focuses on moving toward greater wage bargaining centralization.

Policy developments in Ireland illustrate the first strategy. In this case, wage bargaining actors jointly agreed to modify the informal guidelines for wage growth (Baccaro 2002; Baccaro and Simoni 2002). Beginning in the 1970s, agreements concluded by foreign multinational corporations became the reference point for centralized wage agreements. The wage bargaining rounds of the 1970s were also notably egalitarian: A number of the resulting agreements' provisions, such as special increments favoring the low paid or provisions for minimally acceptable wage increases, contributed to a significant compression of wage differentials. The social partnership agreements negotiated in the 1990s dramatically transformed wage setting norms. As Baccaro and Simoni characterized these policy developments: "Social partnership linked wage increases in the economy as a whole to productivity gains and ability to pay of the most traditional, labor intensive and presumably more highly unionized domestic portions of the manufacturing sector. In doing so, it injected robust doses of competitiveness in the industries dominated by foreign MNCs, whose productivity skyrocketed, while wage increases grew barely in line with the rest of the economy" (Baccaro and Simoni 2000).

In other cases, policy makers have attempted to limit wage increases by using external standards such as productivity increases or the labor cost developments of their most important trading partners as the upper ceiling for wage growth. In the 1990s formal guidelines designed to keep wage increases below productivity increases were established in Italy, Belgium, Denmark, and Finland (Ebbinghaus and Hassel 2000: 67). In Portugal, a formula agreed on in 1996 mandated that wage growth should not exceed one-half of increases in productivity. Several countries have also tried to use average wage developments in the most important European economies as the baseline for their wage developments. Chapter 3 discussed the role played by the "Edin norm" – which reflected the expected average wage growth in EU countries in Swedish wage negotiations of the 1990s. Belgian policy makers made a similar effort: Their 1996 law of competitiveness used the average forecast of pay increases in Germany, The Netherlands, and France as a ceiling for wage growth (Hassel and Ebbinghaus 2000: 66).

A number of countries have introduced more far-reaching changes in their wage bargaining institutions in an effort to improve coordination.

These institutional changes have figured prominently in economies with a tradition of conflictual industrial relations, such as Spain and Italy. In Italy, first steps in the direction of wage bargaining reform were taken as part of the Interconfederal Agreement of July 1993 (Negrelli 1997, 2000). The agreement attempted to limit the number of bargaining agents and delimit their responsibilities. Within the new framework for collective bargaining set by the agreement, wages were to be determined in collective agreements at the sectoral level (Regalia and Regini 1998: 477; Regini and Regalia 1997). In the hope of limiting the effects of interunion rivalry on wage developments, policy makers also established some informal, nationally set wage guidelines. By contrast, firm-level negotiations were limited to issues of company productivity, product quality, and profitability (Negrelli 1997: 49). In December 1998, the three largest Italian union confederations – CGIL, CISL, and UIL – and Confindustria, the main association representing employers signed another agreement that reconfirmed this wage bargaining structure (Baccaro 2002: 7).

Spain has also undertaken fundamental reform of its wage bargaining institutions, beginning with a 1997 agreement on collective bargaining signed by employers and the nation's two trade union federations, Unión General de Trabajadores and Comisiones Obreras. The main objective of the agreement was the "rationalization of the structure of collective bargaining, so as to mitigate its degree of atomization." To this end, the agreement expanded the policy responsibilities of national sectoral bargains while simultaneously specifying the distribution of policy responsibilities among national and local bargaining agents. Issues such as wage increases, occupational classifications, and overall work reductions remained the sole prerogatives of sectoral agreements (Perez 2000b: 355).

In both Italy and Spain, recent efforts to centralize the wage setting process have enjoyed the political support of broad cross-class alliances comprising both trade unions and key sectors of the business community. To individual union leaders, these reforms promise to expand their authority and improve their ability to preempt the challenges of more militant members. As Perez argues, "fragmented bargaining, particularly in a tight money context, undermined the ability of national labor confederations to mediate between the interests of workers across sectors and thus act as strategic actors in the economy" (Perez 2000b). In Italy, the confederal union's ability to respond to the economic crisis of the early 1990s was challenged by the independent unions that were largely behind the large public-sector increases that drove wage bargaining in 1990 and 1991" (Perez 2002: 1218).

An increase in wage bargaining centralization has also been supported by important sectors of employers, not by labor-based organizations alone. Business support has been particularly important to the reemergence of national concertation in Italy and Spain (Baccaro 1999; Perez 2002). In Italy, the move to recentralize wage bargaining was promoted by large manufacturing firms, such as Fiat and Zanussi, and by sectoral associations of employers, such as the Employer Federation of the Chemical Industry (Baccaro 1999). During the 1993 wage bargaining negotiations, Confindustria, the association of large manufacturing firms, attempted to establish "a complete centralization of wage bargaining in the form of a single locus of collective bargaining at the national level" (Perez 2002). In Spain, both the confederation of employers in the metal sector (Confemetal) and the association representing Catalan employers (Fomento de Trabajo) were engaged in sustained efforts to centralize wage bargaining negotiations leading up to the 1997 wage bargaining round (Perez 2002: 1217). The most important reason for employers' support for wage bargaining centralization was the desire to achieve greater levels of moderation. In the 1980s wage settlements were excessive in both Italy and Spain as a consequence of the dominant role of both public-sector unions and unions in sheltered sectors, such as utilities, in the wage setting process. The reasons for employers' support of centralization of wage negotiations during the 1990s parallel employers' support for policy changes that led to the creation of centralized wage bargaining institutions in the interwar period (Swenson 1991).

The heavy burden imposed by existing payroll taxes blunts the effectiveness of wage moderation in lowering unemployment. To enhance the impact of wage restraint on unemployment, unions' promises of moderation are explicitly linked to additional changes that modify social insurance policies and attempt to control the rate of growth of nonwage labor costs. One avenue of reform by which policy makers have attempted to mitigate some of the constraints imposed by the mature welfare state has been the reform of taxation. Two types of policy changes have been on the reform agenda of new social pacts in recent years. One avenue of reform is to increase unions' incentive to moderate wages by reducing the wedge between gross and net wages. Another has considered more far-reaching reforms in the mode of social insurance financing in order to improve the actuarial soundness of existing policies.

As O'Donnell and O'Reardon argue, "the exchange of moderate wage increases for tax reductions has remained an important feature of Irish social partnership" (O'Donnell and O'Reardon 2000: 237). The initial social partnership agreement was preceded by a number of influential policy documents that underscored the need for a reduction of personal tax rates and for an expansion of the tax base. As part of the 1987 Program for National Recovery, the Irish Trade Union Congress agreed to limit wage increases to 3 percent. In exchange, the government agreed to reform the tax system, guaranteeing an increase in the take-home pay of workers. The combination of small nominal wage increases, low inflation, and tax reduction led to an increase in real disposable wages between 1988 and 1999.

Social pacts in a number of other countries involved similar policy exchanges. In The Netherlands, a tax reform enacted in 1990 partially integrated social security charges and income taxes while broadening and lowering the tax rate (Visser and Hemerjick 2000). Unions responded to these reforms, which increased the purchasing power of workers, with extremely moderate wage policies. The coalition led by Prime Minister Wim Kok carried out similar policy changes. A number of agreements signed by the government, employers, and union confederations included additional tax changes that were designed to reduce the wedge between gross and net wages (Slomp 2002: 236). The 1996 social pact in Portugal involved income tax cuts for low-wage employees in exchange for unions' promises of wage moderation. In 1999, the Finnish government also introduced income tax cuts that were conditional on restrained wage agreements in the private sector.

Other tax reforms negotiated as part of the new social pacts attempt to strengthen the fiscal foundation of social insurance institutions and reduce the rate of growth of future social insurance contributions. This remains a notable achievement of the Agreement on the Consolidation and Rationalization of the Social Security System that was concluded by the Spanish government and the major labor unions in October 1996 (Guillen 1999; Perez 2000a). In an effort to maintain the financial equilibrium of the pension system, the agreement introduced a clearer distinction among the various sources of financing for old-age benefits. It committed all revenues raised through payroll taxes exclusively to the financing of the contributory pensions while directing revenues raised through general taxes to the financing of minimum pensions and other forms of old-age assistance for elderly individuals who fail to qualify for contributory old-age insurance. The reform also created a reserve fund for the contributory pension, which accumulates any surplus in contributions (Perez 2000b: 352). Taken together, these reforms were expected to alleviate some of the future growth of the tax burden while at the same time maintaining the same level of protection for the elderly.

In Germany, the Red-Green coalition government undertook a series of changes of the tax structure. A special working group on tax policy was established within the Alliance for Jobs. The novel policy idea at the center of these reforms was the substitution of more "employment-friendly" ecological taxes for income and social security taxes. To this end, taxes on electricity, mineral oil, and fuel were raised while social security contributions to old-age insurance were lowered. Simultaneously, the government scheduled a step-by-step reduction in the income tax rate, leading to a projected reduction in the basic tax rate from 25.9 percent in 1999 to 15 percent in 2005 (Bispinck and Schulten 2000).

In the short term, these reductions in taxation have been relatively effective in bringing unions to the bargaining table and enhancing the incentives for them to deliver moderate wage settlements. The long-term implications of the policies are more problematic, however. To be sustainable, any reduction in taxes must be accompanied by changes in the provision of benefits and services, and possibly also by reductions in the quality of social protection. As of now, very few economies have introduced policy changes that are sustainable over the long term.

A final component of the social pacts is policies that attempt to improve the labor market participation of groups hitherto excluded from the labor market. These efforts reflect unease about the growing social exclusion and segmentation that has accompanied the labor market deterioration of the last two decades. In many economies, programs of labor market activation stand in contrast to the negative labor supply policies pursued in previous decades. A number of policy efforts attempt to end the bifurcation of the labor market between a group of privileged labor market insiders and a group of outsiders by creating incentives for companies to hire workers who have been previously unemployed. By improving the ratio between contributors and recipients of social policy transfers, labor supply reforms are likely to have a desirable impact on the financial outlook of many continental European welfare states. They may also have indirect beneficial consequences for wage negotiation. The reduction of nonwage labor costs is also expected to weaken the tax constraint imposed by the welfare state on employment, allowing a moderate wage policy to translate into improved employment gains.

Nearly all social pacts include policy provisions that attempt to improve the skill qualifications of the long-term unemployed. In Belgium, tripartite negotiations have established some insurance funds that provide support for the vocational training of unemployed workers and other high-risk groups. These funds are jointly managed by sectoral associations of unions and employers and are financed by contributions from wages (Arcq 1997: 100). In Germany, one of the first policy initiatives of the Red-Green coalition was the formulation of the Alliance for Jobs, Training and Competitiveness, which aims to increase the number of additional opportunities for vocational training (Bispinck and Schulten 2000). In The Netherlands, recent collective agreements include training provisions targeted to groups with precarious employment histories.

To improve the labor market integration of outsiders, other reforms include changes in collectively agreed payments and in labor market legislation that increase the incentives for firms to create new jobs. In Germany, discussions about the necessary reforms needed to extend low-wage employment were a prominent element on the agenda of the Alliance for Jobs. The policy that was ultimately adopted recommended the introduction of public subsidies that lowered social insurance contributions for low-wage occupations. Such public subsidies have recently been introduced in several West and East German Länder.

Dutch trade unions have shown the greatest willingness to exchange some of the rights of core workers for higher overall labor market participation rates. In 1996, Dutch labor market actors concluded the Flexibility and Security Agreement, or the "flexicurity" agreement (Hemerjick et al. 2000: 267). The goal of this agreement is to increase workers' incentive to accept part-time employment by improving some of the employment rights of persons in atypical employment. The agreement counterbalanced advances in employment rights, however, with measures that reduced the protection of "core" workers against dismissal (Wilthagen 1998: 15). The flexicurity agreement became the basis for legislation enacted in January 1999 (Hemerjick et al. 2000: 267; Wilthagen, Tros, and von Lieshout 2003: 18).

New social pacts clearly combine the right mix of policies. In a large number of countries, policy makers, trade unions, and ordinary citizens attach very high hopes to these policy initiatives. While the combination of changes to wage bargaining institutions and social policies that is at the center of new social pacts may restore employment growth, we should carefully calibrate our expectations about how much wage moderation can actually accomplish given the high fiscal constraints imposed by mature welfare states.

References

Agartz, V. 1950. "Die Lohnpolitik der deutschen Gewerkschaften." *Gewerkschaftliche Monatshefte* 1: 441–7.

———. 1953. "Beiträge zur wirtschaftlichen Entwicklung 1953: Expansive Lohnpolitik." *WWI-Mitteilungen* 6: 245–7.

Agell, J., P. Englund, and J. Sodersten. 1996. "Tax reform of the century: The Swedish experiment." *National Tax Journal* 49(4): 643–64.

Alber, J. 1989. *Der Sozialstaat in der Bundesrepublik*. Frankfurt: Campus.

Aldrich, J. 1982. "The earnings-replacement rate of old-age benefits in twelve countries, 1969–1980." *Social Security Bulletin* 45: 3–11.

Alesina, A. 1989. "Politics and business cycles in industrial democracies." *Economic Policy* 8: 55–98.

Alesina, A., and R. Perotti. 1997. "The welfare state and competitiveness." *American Economic Review* 87(5): 921–39.

Allen, C. 1989. "The underdevelopment of Keynesianism in the Federal Republic of Germany." In *The political power of economic ideas*, ed. P. Hall, pp. 264–89. Princeton, NJ: Princeton University Press.

Alm, S. 2001. *The resurgence of mass unemployment: Studies of social consequences of joblessness in Sweden in the 1990s*. Stockholm: Swedish Institute for Social Research.

Anderson, K. 1998. "The welfare state in the global economy: The politics of social insurance retrenchment in Sweden, 1990–1998." Ph.D. diss., University of Washington.

Araki, H. 2000. "Ideas and welfare: The Conservative transformation of the British pension regime." *Journal of Social Policy* 29(4): 599–621.

Arcq, E. 1997. "Collective labour relations and social pacts in Belgium." In *Social pacts in Europe*, ed. G. Fajertag and P. Pochet, pp. 97–102. Brussels: European Trade Union Institute.

Aronsson, T., and J. R. Walker. 1995. "The effects of Sweden's welfare state on labor supply initiatives." SNS Occasional Paper no. 64, SUS, Stockholm.

———. 1997. "The effects of Sweden's welfare state on labor supply incentives." In *The welfare state in transition: Reforming the Swedish model*, ed. R. Freeman, R. Topel, and B. Swedenborg, pp. 203–59. Chicago: University of Chicago Press.

Artis, M. 1972. "Fiscal policy for stabilization." In *The Labour government's economic record, 1964–1970*, ed. W. Beckerman, pp. 262–99. London: Duckworth.

Artis, M., and D. Cobham. 1991a. "The background." In *Labour's economic policies, 1974–1979*, ed. M. Artis and D. Cobham, pp. 1–18. Manchester: Manchester University Press.

———. 1991b. *Labour's economic policies, 1974–1979*. Manchester: Manchester University Press.

Assouline, M. 1998. "L'impact macro-economique d'une baisse des cotisations sur les bas salaires." *Travail et Emploi* 73: 41–65.

Aukrust, O. 1977. "Inflation in the open economy: A Norwegian model." In *World-wide inflation: Theory and recent experience*, ed. L. B. Krause and W. A. S. Salant, pp. 109–51. Washington, DC: Brookings.

Baccaro, L. 1998. "The organizational consequences of democracy: labor unions and economic reforms in contemporary Italy," Ph.D. dissertation, MIT.

———. 1999. *Il sistema italiano di concertazione sociale: Problemi aperti e prospettive di evoluzione*. Cambrige, MA: MIT Press.

———. 2002. "What is dead and what is alive in the theory of corporatism." Working paper, International Institute for Labor Studies, Geneva.

———, and M. Simoni. 2002. "The Irish social partnership and the 'celtic tiger' phenomenon." Working paper, International Institute for Labor Studies, Geneva.

Bach, S. 2002. "Public sector employment relations reform under Labour: Muddling through on modernization." *British Journal of Industrial Relations* 40(2): 319–39.

Bade, R., and M. Parkin. 1982. "Central bank laws and monetary policies." Working paper, Department of Economics, University of Western Ontario, London, Ont.

Baldwin, P. 1990. *The politics of social solidarity: Class bases of the European welfare state 1875–1975*. New York: Cambridge University Press.

Balogh, T. 1970. *Labour and Inflation*. London: Fabian Society.

Bandelow, N. 1998. *Gesundheitspolitik: Der Staat in der Hand einzelner Interessengruppen?* Opladen: Leske und Budrich.

———, and K. Schubert. 1998. "Wechselnde Strategien und kontinuierlicher Abbau solidarischen Ausgleichs: Eine gesundsheitspolitische Bilanz der Ara Kohl." In *Die Ara Kohl*, ed. G. Wever, pp. 113–28. Opladen: Leske and Budrich.

Barreto, J. and R. Naumann. 1998. "Industrial relations under democracy." In *Changing industrial relations in Europe*, ed. A. Ferner and R. Hyman. Malden, MA: Blackwell.

Barro, R., and D. Gordon. 1983. "A positive theory of monetary policy in a natural rate model." *Journal of Political Economy* 91: 589–610.

Beck, N., and J. Katz. 1995. "What to do (and not to do) with time series: Cross-section data in comparative politics." *American Political Science Review* 89(3): 634–47.

Beer, S. 2001. "New Labour: Old liberalism." In *New Labour: The progressive future?*, ed. S. White, pp. 18–31. London: Palgrave.

Bell, B., R. Blundell, and J. Van Reenen. 1999. "Getting the unemployed back to work: The role of targeted wage subsidies." Working paper W99/12, Institute for Fiscal Studies, London.

References

Benner, M. 1997. *The politics of growth: Economic regulation in Sweden, 1930–1994.* Lund, Sweden: Arkiv.

———, and T. B. Vad. 2000. "Sweden and Denmark: Defending the welfare state." In *Welfare and work in the open economy: Diverse responses to common challenges,* ed. F. Scharpf and V. Schmidt, pp. 399–466. New York: Oxford University Press.

Berger, S., and H. Compston, eds. 2002. *Policy concertation and social partnership in Western Europe: Lessons for the 21st century.* New York: Berghahn.

Bergmann, J., O. Jacobi, and W. Müller-Jentsch. 1975. *Gewerkschaften in der Bundesrepublik: Gewerkschaftliche Lohnpolitik zwischen Mitgliederinteressen und Systemzwangen.* Frankfurt: Campus.

Bergström, W. 1992. "Party program and economic policy: The Social Democrats in government." In *Creating social democracy: A century of the Social Democratic Labor Party in Sweden,* ed. K. Misgeld, K. Molin, and K. Amark. University Park: Pennsylvania State University Press.

Bertola, G. 1990. "Job security, employment and wages." *European Economic Review* X: 851–86.

Beyme, K. von. 1979. *Die grossen Regierungserklärungen der deutschen Bundeskanzler von Adenauer bis Schmidt.* Munich: Carl Hansen.

Birch Sørensen, P., ed. 1998. *Tax policy in the Nordic countries.* London: Macmillan.

Bispinck, R. 1997. "The chequered history of the Alliance for Jobs." In *Social pacts in Europe: New dynamics,* ed. G. Fajertag and P. Pochet, pp. 63–78. Brussels: European Trade Union Institute.

———, and T. Schulten. 2000. "Alliance for Jobs: Is Germany following the path of competitive corporatism?" In *Social pacts in Europe: New dynamics,* ed. G. Fajertag and P. Pochet, pp. 187–218. Brussels: European Trade Union Institute.

———, et al. 1991. "Mehr Geld für Niedrigverdiener." *WSI Mitteilungen* 44(8): 457–66.

Bispinck, R., et al. 1993. "Kampf gegen die 'Tarifwende': Die Tarifbewegungen 1992 in den alten Bundeslanderns." *WSI Mitteilungen* 46(3): 129–41.

———, et al. 1994. "Tarifbewegungen im 1. Halbjahr in West – und Ostdeutschland." *WSI Mitteilungen* 47(8): 469–80.

———, et. al. 1996. "Vom Lohnstreik zum 'Bündnis fur Arbeit.'" *WSI Mitteilungen* 49(3): 141–65.

Björklund, A., and B. Holmlund. 1989. Effects of Extended Unemployment Compensation in Sweden. Stockholm: Swedish Institute for Social Research.

Blanchard, O. 1990. "Thinking about unemployment." Unpublished manuscript. Massachusetts Institute of Technology.

——— and J. Wolfers. 2000. "The role of shocks and institutions in the rise of European unemployment: the aggregate evidence." *Economic* J. XY 110 (March): C1–C33.

Boeri, T., A. Brugiavini, and L. Calmfors, eds. 2001. *The role of unions in the 21st century.* Oxford: Oxford University Press.

Bofinger, P., and S. Fasshauer. 1998. "Reduzierung der Sozialausgaben statt Kombilohn." *Wirtschaftsdienst* 78(9): 519–28.

Boix, C. 1998. *Political parties, growth and equality: Conservative and social democratic economic strategies in the world economy.* Cambridge: Cambridge University Press.

Bönker, F., and H. Wollmann. 2000. "Sozialstaatlichkeit im Übergang: Entwicklungslinien der bundesdeutschen Sozialpolitik in den Neunzigerjahren." *Leviathan* 4: 514–37.

Bonoli, G. 2001. "Political institutions, veto points and the process of welfare state adaptation." In *The new politics of the welfare state*, ed. P. Pierson, pp. 238–65. Oxford: Oxford University Press.

Bourguignon, F., and D. Bureau, ed. 1999. *L'architecture des prélèvementss en France: Etat des lieux et voies de reforme.* Paris: La Documentation Francaise.

Bracher, K. D., W. Jäger, and W. Link. 1986. *Republik im Wandel 1969–1974. Die Ära Brandt.* Stuttgart: Deutsche Verlagsanstalt.

Brandt, W. 1992. *My life in politics.* New York: Viking.

Braunthal, G. 1983. *The West German Social Democrats, 1969–1982: Profile of a party in power.* Boulder, CO: Westview.

Brooke, S. 1992. *Labour's war.* Oxford: Clarendon Press.

Brown, W., ed. 1981. *The changing contours of British industrial relations: A survey of manufacturing industry.* Oxford: Basic Blackwell.

Browne, E., and J. Dreijmanis. 1982. *Government coalitions in Western democracies.* New York: Longman.

Bruno, M., and J. Sachs. 1985. *Economics of worldwide stagflation.* Cambridge: Harvard University Press.

Buechtemann, C. 1991. "Does (de-) regulation matter? Employment protection in West Germany." In *Beyond Keynesianism: The socio-economics of production and full employment*, ed. E. Matzner and W. Streeck, pp. 111–36. Cambridge: Edward Elger.

———. 1993. "Employment security and deregulation: The West German experience." In *Employment security and labor market behaviour: Interdisciplinary approaches and international evidence*, ed. C. Buechtemann, pp. 272–96. Ithaca, NY: ILR Press.

Burda, M., and J. Hunt. 2001. "From reunification to economic integration: Productivity and the labor market in East Germany." *Brookings Papers on Economic Activity* 1: 1–92.

Burtless, G. 1987. "Taxes, transfers and Swedish labor supply." In *The Swedish economy*, ed. B. Bosworth, pp. 185–250. Washington, DC: Brookings.

Calmfors, L. 1993. "Centralization of wage bargaining and macroeconomic performance: A survey." *OECD Economic Studies* 21: 161–191.

———. 1994. "Active labour market policy and unemployment: A framework for the analysis of crucial design features." OECD Working papers 2, no. 40, Organization for Economic Co-operation and Development, Paris.

———, ed. 1990. *Wage formation and macroeconomic policy in the Nordic countries.* Oxford: Oxford University Press.

Calmfors, L., and J. Driffill. 1988. "Coordination of wage bargaining." *Economic Policy* 6(1): 14–61.

Calmfors, L., and A. Forslund. 1990. "Wage formation in Sweden." In *Wage formation and macroeconomic policy in the Nordic countries*, ed. L. Calmfors, pp. 63–130. New York: Oxford University Press.

References

Calmfors, L., and the SNS Economic Policy Group. 1986. *Getting Sweden Back to Work*. Stockholm: SNS Förlag.

Cameron, D. 1978. "The expansion of the public economy: A comparative analysis." *American Political Science Review* 72(4): 1243–61.

————. 1984. "Social democracy, corporatism, labor quiescence and the representation of economic interests in advanced capitalist society." In *Order and conflict in contemporary capitalism*, ed. J. Goldthorpe, pp. 143–78. New York: Oxford University Press.

Carlin, W., and D. Soskice. 1997. "Shocks to the system: The German political economy under stress." *National Institute Economic Review* 159: 57–76.

Castles, F., and P. Mair. 1984. "Left-right political scales: Some 'expert' judgements." *European Journal of Political Research* 12(1): 83–8.

Clark, T. 2001. "The limits of social democracy? Tax and spend under Labour, 1974–1979." Working paper 01/04, Institute for Fiscal Studies, London.

Clasen, J. 2001. "Social insurance and the contributory principle: A paradox in contemporary British social policy." *Social Policy and Administration* 35(6): 641–57.

Clegg, H. A. 1970. *The system of industrial relations in Great Britain*. Oxford: Basic Blackwell.

Colling, T. 1994. "Privatisation and the management of IR in electricity distribution." *Industrial Relations Journal* 22(1): 117–29.

Craig, F. 1990. *British general elections manifestos, 1959 to 1987*. Aldershot, U.K.: Dartmouth Publishing.

Crouch, C. 1982. *The politics of industrial relations*. London: Fontana.

————. 1985. "Conditions for trade union wage restraint." In *The politics of inflation and economic stagnation: Theoretical approaches and international case studies*, ed. L. Lindberg and C. Maier, pp. 105–39. Washington, DC: Brookings.

————. 1993. *Industrial relations and European state traditions*. Oxford: Clarendon Press.

————. 1996. "Atavism and innovation: Labour legislation and public policy since 1979 in historical perspective." *Historical Studies in Industrial Relations* 2: 111–24.

————, and A. Pizzorno, eds. 1978. *The resurgence of class conflict in Western Europe since 1968*. 2 vols. London: Macmillan.

————, and W. Streeck, eds. 1997. *Political Economy of Modern Capitalism*. London: Sage.

Cukierman, A. 1992. *Central bank strategy, credibility and independence: Theory and evidence*. Cambridge, MA: MIT Press.

Cukierman, A., and F. Lippi. 1999. "Central bank independence, centralization of wage bargaining, inflation and unemployment – Theory and some evidence." *European Economic Review* 43(7): 1395–434.

Cukierman, A., S. Webb, and B. Neyapti. 1992. "Measuring the independence of central banks and its effect on policy outcomes." *World Bank Economic Review* 6(3): 353–98.

Culpepper, P. 2003. *Creating Cooperation: How States Develop Human Capital in Europe*. Ithaca, NY: Cornell University Press.

Czada, R. 1998. "Vereinigungskrise und Standortdebatte." *Leviathan* 1: 24–59.

Dale, I. 2000a. *Conservative Party general election manifestos*. London: Routledge.
———. 2000b. *Labour Party general election manifestos, 1900–1997*. London: Routledge.
Danthine, J.-P., and J.-C. Lambelet. 1987. "The Swiss recipe: Conservative policies ain't enough." *Economic Policy* 5: 149–74.
Da Paz, M., and R. Naumann. 1997. "Social Dialogue and Social Pacts in Portugal," In *Social pacts in Europe: New dynamics*, ed. P. Pochet and G. Fajertag. Brussels: European Trade Union Institute.
———. 2000. "Social pacts in Portugal: From comprehensive policy programmes to the negotiation of concrete industrial relations reforms?" In *Social pacts in Europe: New dynamics*, ed. P. Pochet and G. Fajertag, pp. 45–62. Brussels: European Trade Union Institute.
Daveri, F., and G. Tabellini. 2000. "Unemployment, growth, and taxation in industrial countries." *Economic Policy* 15: 47–101.
Davidson, A. 1994. *A home of one's own: Housing policy in Sweden and New Zealand from the 1840s to the 1990s*. Stockholm: Almqvist and Wiksell.
De Foucauld, J.-B. 1995. *Le financement de la protection sociale*. Paris: La Documentation Francaise.
Dehez, P., and J.-P. Fitoussi. 1992. *Revenu minimum, allocations-chomage et subventions a l'emploi: Un modele macroeconomique simple*. Paris: OFCE.
Deutsche Bundesbank. 1985. "Recent trends in the finances of the statutory health insurance institutions." *Monthly Report of the Deutsche Bundesbank* 37(1): 27–37.
———. 1987a. "Changes in the structure of the public authorities' debt." *Monthly Report of the Deutsche Bundesbank* 39(4): 13–22.
———. 1987b. "The finances of the statutory pension funds since the beginning of the eighties." *Monthly Report of the Deutsche Bundesbank* 39(4): 12–21.
———. 1989. "Trends in tax revenue since 1986." *Monthly Report of the Deutsche Bundesbank* 41(8): 40–48.
———. 1990. "The expenditure of the central, regional and local authorities since 1982." *Monthly Report of the Deutsche Bundesbank* 42(7): 35–46.
———. 1991a. "Recent trends in the finances of the statutory health insurance institutions." *Monthly Report of the Deutsche Bundesbank* 43(1): 25–36.
———. 1991b. "Trends in public sector debt since the mid-1980's." *Monthly Report of the Deutsche Bundesbank* 43(8): 32–41.
———. 1993. "Public financial transfers to Eastern Germany in 1991 and 1992." *Monthly Report of the Deutsche Bundesbank* 45(1): 15–22.
———. 1994. "The trend in agreed pay rates and actual earnings since the mid-eighties." *Monthly Report of the Deutsche Bundesbank* 46(8): 29–44.
———. 1995. "The finances of the statutory pension insurance funds since the beginning of the nineties." *Monthly Report of the Deutsche Bundesbank* 47(3): 17–31.
Deutsches Institut für Wirtschaftsforschung. 1997. "Vereinigungsfolgen belasten Sozialversicherung." *Wochenbericht* 64: 723–9.
DGB (Deutscher Gewerkschaftsbund). 1951. *Geschäftsbericht des Bundesvorstandes des Deutschen Gewerkschaftsbundes, 1950–1951*. Düsseldorf: Bundverlag.

References

————. 1953. *Geschäftsbericht des Bundesvorstandes des Deutschen Gewerkschaftsbundes, 1952–1953.* Düsseldorf: Deutz.

————. 1955, 1965, 1968, 1969, 1971, 1974. *Geschäftsbericht des Bundesvorstandes des Deutschen Gewerkschaftsbundes.* Düsseldorf: Hans-Böckler Haus.

————. 1981. *Geschäftsbericht des Bundesvorstandes des Deutschen Gewerkschaftsbundes, 1980–1981.* Düsseldorf: Deutz.

————. 1982. *Geschäftsbericht des Bundesvorstandes des Deutschen Gewerkschaftsbundes, 1981–1982.* Düsseldorf: Deutz.

Dickens, R., and A. Mannings. 2002. "Has the national minimum wage reduced UK wage inequality?" Working paper, Center for Economic Performance, London School of Economics, London.

Döding, G. 1982. "Uberzeugendes Handeln is gefragt." *Die Mitbestimmung* 4–5: 157–8.

————. 1984. "Das gewerkschaftliche Ziel verkurzter Lebensarbeitszeit." *Die Mitbestimmung* 6: 232–33.

Döhler, M. 1990. "Der National Health Service in der Ara Thatcher." In *Thatcherismus: Eine Bilanz nach zehn Jahren,* ed. R. Sturm, pp. 199–222. Bochum, Germany: Universitatsverlag Brockmeyer.

————, and P. Manow. 1997. *Strukturbildung von Politikfeldern: Das Beispiel bundesdeutscher Gesundheitspolitik seit den 50er Jahren.* Opladen, Germany: Leske und Budrich.

Dorfman, G. 1973. *Wage politics in Britain, 1945–1967.* Ames: Iowa State University Press.

Dow, J. 1965. *The management of the British economy, 1945–1960.* Cambridge: Cambridge University Press.

Dunn, S., and D. Metcalf. 1996. "Trade union law since 1979." In *Contemporary industrial relations: A critical analysis,* ed. I. Beardwell, pp. 66–98. Oxford: Oxford University Press.

Ebbinghaus, B., and A. Hassel. 2000. "Striking deals: Concertation in the reform of Continental European welfare states." *Journal of European Public Policy* 7(1): 44–62.

Ebbinghaus, B., and J. Visser. 2000. *Trade unions in Western Europe since 1945.* London: Macmillan.

Edgren, G., K.-O. Faxen, and C.-E. Odhner. 1973. *Wage formation and the economy.* London: Allen and Unwin.

Edlund, J. 2000. "Public attitudes towards taxation: Sweden, 1981–1997." *Scandinavian Political Studies* 23(1): 37–65.

Eichengreen, Barry. 1997. "Institutions and economic growth: Europe after World War II." In *Economic growth in Europe since World War II,* ed. N. Crafts and G. Toniolo, pp. 38–72. New York: Cambridge University Press.

Elmeskov, L., J. P. Martin, and S. Scarpetta. 2000. "Key lessons for labour market reforms: Evidence from OECD countries' experience." *Swedish Economic Policy Review* 5(2): 205–52.

Elvander, N. 1972. *Svensk Skattepolitik 1945–1970: En studie i partiers och organisationenfunktioner.* Stockholm: Raben & Sjögren.

237

———. 1979. "Collective bargaining and incomes policy in the Nordic countries." *British Journal of Industrial Relations* 12: 425–31.

———. 1983. Die Gewerkschaftsbewegung in Schweden: Geschichte, Programm, politische Beziehungen. In *Gewerkschaften in den Demokratien Westeuropas*, vol. 2, ed. H. Ruehle and H.-J. Veen, pp. 327–402. Munich: Ferdinand Schoningh.

———. 1988. *Den svenska modellen: Löneförhandlingar och inkomstpolitik, 1982–1986.* Stockholm: Allmänna Förlaget.

———. 1992. *Labour market relations in Sweden and Great Britain: A comparative study of local wage formation in the private sector during the 1980s.* Uppsala, Sweden: Uppsala University Department of Economics.

———, and B. Holmlund. 1997. *The Swedish bargaining system in the melting pot: Institutions, norms and outcomes in the 1990s.* Solna, Sweden: Arbetslivinstitutet.

———, and B. Holmlund. 2001. "Gøsta Rehn, the Swedish model and labor market policies." In *Gøsta Rehn, the Swedish Model and labour market policies*, ed. H. Milner and E. Wadensjo, pp. 13–49. London: Aldershot.

Esping-Andersen, G. 1985. *Politics against markets: The social democratic road to power.* Princeton, NJ: Princeton University Press.

———. 1990. *The three worlds of welfare capitalism.* Princeton, NJ: Princeton University Press.

———. 1999. *Social foundations of postindustrial economies.* Oxford: Oxford University Press.

———. 2001. "Who is harmed by employment regulation?" In *Why deregulate labour markets?*, ed. G. Esping-Andersen and M. Regini. Oxford: Oxford University Press.

Estevez-Abe. M. 1999. "Welfare and capitalism in postwar Japan." Ph.D. diss., Harvard University.

———, T. Iversen, and D. Soskice. 2001. "Social protection and the formation of skills: A reinterpretation of the welfare state." In *Varieties of capitalism: The institutional foundations of comparative advantage*, ed. P. Hall and D. Soskice, pp. 145–83. Oxford: Oxford University Press.

European Commission. 1997. "Effective taxation and tax convergence in the EU and the OECD." Memo 5/1997, Directorate General II of the European Commission, Brussels.

Eurostat (Statistical Office of the European Communities). 1997. *Structures of the taxation systems in the European Union, 1970–1995.* Luxemburg: Eurostat.

Fajertag, G., and P. Pochet, eds. 1997. *Social pacts in Europe.* Brussels: European Trade Union Institute.

———, eds. 2000. *Social pacts in Europe: New dynamics.* Brussels: European Trade Union Institute.

Farber, H. 1986. "The analysis of union behavior. In *Handbook of labor economics*, vol. 2, ed. O. Aschenfelter and R. Layard, pp. 1039–89. Amsterdam: North Holland.

Fellner, W. 1961. *The problem of rising prices.* Paris: OECD

Fishbein, W. H. 1984. *Wage restraint by consensus: Britain's search for an incomes policy agreement, 1965–1979.* Boston: Routledge.

238

References

Flanagan, R. J., D. Soskice, and L. Ulman, eds. 1983. *Unionism, economic stabilization and incomes policies: European experience*. Washington, DC: Brookings.

Flora, P., and J. Alber. 1983. *State, economy and society in Western Europe 1815–1975: A data handbook in two volumes*. Frankfurt: Campus.

Franzese, R. 1999. The interaction of credibly conservative monetary policy with labor- and goods-market institutions: A review of an emerging literature. Manuscript, University of Michigan, Ann Arbor.

———. 2002. *Macroeconomic policies of developed democracies*. New York: Cambridge University Press.

Freeman, R. 1988. "Labor market institutions and economic performance." *Economic Policy* 6: 64–80.

Fry, V., S. Smith, and S. White. 1990. *Pensioners and the public purse*. London: Institute for Fiscal Studies.

Fulcher, J. 1991. *Labour movements, employers and the state: Conflict and cooperation in Britain and Sweden*. Oxford: Clarendon Press.

Garrett, G. 1998. *Partisan politics in the global economy*. New York: Cambridge University Press.

Germany. Bundesanstalt für Arbeit. 1985. *Arbeitsförderungsgesetz mit angrenzenden Gesetzen, Verordnungen und BA: Regelungen*. Nuremberg: Bundesanstalt für Arbeit.

Germany. Bundesministerium der Finanzen. 1978. *Finanzbericht*. Bonn: Bundesministerium der Finanzen

———. 1978. *Finanzbericht*. Bonn: Bundesministerium der Finanzen

———. 1986. *Finanzbericht*. Bonn: Bundesministerium der Finanzen

———. 1987. *Finanzbericht*. Bonn: Bundesministerium der Finanzen.

Germany. Bundesministerium für Arbeit und Sozialordnung. 1996. Statistisches Taschenbuch. Bonn: BMAS.

———. 1998. *Sozialbericht*. Bonn: BMAS.

Germany. Bundessozialgericht. 1970. *Entscheidungen des Bundessozialgerichts*. Koln: Carl Heymans.

Germany. Deutsche Bundesbank. Various Years. *Monatsberichte der Deutschen Bundesbank*. Frankfurt: Deutsche Bundesbank.

Germany. Statistisches Bundesamt. Various years. *Statistisches Jahrbuch für die Bundesrepublik Deutschland*. Stuttgart: W. Kohlhammer.

———. 2002. *Statistisches Taschenbuch*. Bonn: Arbeits und Sozialstatistik.

Germany. Statistisches Bundesamt. Various years. *Statistisches Jahrbuch fur die Bundesrepublik Deutschland*. Wiesbaden: Kohlhammer.

Giaimo, S. 2002. *Markets and medicine: The politics of health care reform in Britain, Germany and the United States*. Ann Arbor: University of Michigan Press.

Giersch, H., K.-H. Paqué, and H. Schmieding. 1992. *The fading miracle: Four decades of market economy in Germany*. New York: Cambridge University Press.

Gillie, A. 1991. "Redistribution." In *Labour's economic policies, 1974–1979*, ed. M. Artis and D. Cobham, pp. 229–47. Manchester: Manchester University Press.

Glennerster, H. 1990. "Social Policy since the second world war." In *The state of welfare: The welfare state since 1974*, ed. J. Hills, pp. 11–27. Oxford: Clarendon Press.

Glyn, A., ed. 2001. *Social democracy in neoliberal times: The Left and economic policy since 1980*. Oxford: Oxford University Press.

———, and S. Wood. 2001. "New Labour's economic policy." In *Social democracy in neoliberal times: The Left and economic policy since 1980*, ed. A. Glyn, pp. 200–22. Oxford: Oxford University Press.

Golden, M. 1993. "The dynamics of trade unionism and national economic performance." *American Political Science Review* 87(2): 439–54.

———, P. Lange, and M. Wallerstein. 1998. "Union centralization among advanced industrial societies: An empirical study." Dataset available at http://www.shelley.polisci.ucla.edu/data, version dated July 28, 2004.

Goldthorpe, J., ed. 1984. *Order and conflict in contemporary capitalism*. New York: Oxford University Press.

Goodman, A., and A. Shephard. 2002. "Inequality and living standards in Britain: Some facts." Briefing Note 19, Institute for Fiscal Studies, London.

Gould, A. 1996. "Sweden: The last bastion of social democracy." In *European welfare policy: Squaring the welfare circle*, ed. V. George and P. Taylor-Gooby, pp. 72–94. New York: St. Martin's.

Gourevitch, P., ed. 1984. *Unions and economic crisis: Britain, West Germany and Sweden*. Boston: Allen and Unwin.

Graham, A. 1972. "Industrial policy." In *The Labour Government's economic record 1964–1970*, ed. W. Beckerman, pp. 178–217. London: Duckworth.

Grilli, V., D. Masciandaro, and G. Tabellini. 1991. "Political and monetary institutions and public financial policies in the industrial countries." *Economic Policy* 13(3): 341–92.

Grover, C., and J. Stewart. 1999. "'Market workfare': Social security, social regulation and competitiveness in the 1990s." *Journal of Social Policy* 28(1): 73–96.

Grubb, D., and W. Wells. 1993. "Employment regulation and patterns of work in EC countries." *OECD Economic Studies* 21(1): 7–58.

Guillen, A. M. 1999. "Pension reform in Spain, 1975–1997: The role of organized labor." Working Paper 99/6, European University Institute, San Domenico, Italy.

Hadenius, A. 1976. *Facklig organisationsutveckling: En studie av Landsorganisationen i Sverige*. Stockholm: Raben and Sjogren.

———. 1981. *Spelet om skatter: Rationalistisk analys av politiskt beslutsfattande*. Stockholm: Norstedt.

Hall, P. 1986. *Governing the economy*. Oxford: Oxford University Press.

———. 1994. "Central bank independence and coordinated wage bargaining: Their interaction in Germany and Europe." *German Politics and Society* 31(1): 1–23.

———, and R. Franzese. 1998. "Central bank independence, coordinated wage bargaining and European monetary union." *International Organization* 52(2): 505–35.

———, and D. Soskice, eds. 2001. *Varieties of Capitalism: The institutional foundations of comparative advantage*. New York: Oxford University Press.

Hardes, H.-D. 1974. *Einkommenspolitik in der BRD: Stabilität und Gruppeninteressen; Der Fall Konzertierte Aktion*. Frankfurt: Herder und Herder.

References

Harris, J. 1986. "Political ideas and the debate on social welfare, 1949–1955." In *War and social change*, ed. H. J. Smith. Manchester: Manchester University Press.

Hassel, A. 1999. "Bündnisse für Arbeit: Nationale Handlungsfähigkeit im europäischen Regimewettbewerb." Discussion paper 99/5, Max Planck Institute for the Study of Societies, Köln, Germany.

———. and B. Ebbinghaus. 2000. "From means to ends: Linking wage moderation and social policy reform" In *Social pacts in Europe: New dynamics*, ed. P. Pochet and G. Fajertag. Brussels: European Trade Union.

Hay, C. 1999. *The political economy of New Labour: Labouring under false pretenses?* Manchester: Manchester University Press.

Headey, B. 1970. Trade Unions and National Wage Policies. *Journal of Politics* 32: 407–39.

Heilemann, U., H. Gebhart, and H. D. von Loeffelholz. 1996. *Wirtschaftspolitische Chronik der Bundesrepublik 1960 bis 1995*. Stuttgart: Lucius und Lucius.

Heise, A. 1996. "Bündnis für Arbeit: Wie eine kooperative Wirtschaftspoplitik auch aussehen könnte." *WSI-Mitteilungen* 49(5): 303–15.

Hemerjick, A. Van Der Meer, M. and J. Visser. 2000. "Innovation through coordination: Two decades of social pacts in the Netherlands." In *Social pacts in Europe: New dynamics*, ed. G. Fajertag and P. Pochet. Brussels: European Trade Union Institute.

Hemerjick, A., and J. Visser. 2000. *The Dutch miracle: Job growth, welfare reform and corporatism in the Netherlands*. Amsterdam: Amsterdam University Press.

Herschel, W. 1973. "Zur Enstehung des Tarifvertragsgesetzes." *Zeitschrift fur Arbeitsrecht 2*.

Hibbs, D. 1977. "Political parties and macroeconomic policy." *American Political Science Review* 71(4): 1467–87.

———. 1992. "Partisan theory after fifteen years." *European Journal of Political Economy* 8(2): 361–73.

Hildebrand, K. 1984. *Von Erhard zur grossen Koalition, 1963–1969*. Stuttgart: Deutsche Verlagsanstalt.

Hirsch-Weber, W. 1959. *Gewerkschaften in der Politik: Von der Massenstreikdebatte zum Kampf um das Mitbestimmungsrecht*. Köln: Westdeutscher Verlag.

Hockerts, H. 1980. *Sozialpolitische Entscheidungen im Nachkriegsdeutschland: Alliierte und deutsche Sozialversicherungspolitik 1945 bis 1957*. Stuttgart: Klett-Cotta.

———. 1992. "Vom Nutzen und Nachteil parlamentarischer Parteienkonkurrenz: Die Rentenreform 1972." In *Staat und Parteien*, ed. K. D. Bracher, pp. 903–34. Berlin: Humblot.

Hollingsworth, R., and R. Boyer, eds. 1997. *Contemporary capitalism: The embeddedness of institutions*. New York: Cambridge University Press.

Holmes, M. 1997. *The failure of the Heath government*. London: Macmillan.

Holmlund, B. 1983. "Payroll taxes and wage inflation: The Swedish experience." *Scandinavian Journal of Economics* 85(1): 1–15.

Huber, E., and J. Stephens. 2001. *Development and crisis of the welfare state: Parties and policies in global markets*. Chicago: University of Chicago Press.

Huber, E., C. Ragin, and J. Stephens. 1997. Comparative Welfare States Dataset. Available at http://www.lisproject.org/publications/welfaredata/welfareaccess .htm, updated April 2004.

Howell, D. 1976. *British Social Democracy: A study in development and decay*. London: Croom Helm.

IG Metall, ed. 1978. *Streik der Metaller Schleswig Holstein 1956/57*. Frankfurt: Dokumentation.

Immergut, E. 1986. "Between state and market: Sickness benefits and social control." In *Public/private interplay in social protection*, ed. M. Rein and L. Rainwater, pp. 57–148. Armonk, NY: M.E. Sharpe.

———. 1992. *Health politics: Interests and institutions in Western Europe*. New York: Cambridge University Press.

Ingram, P., J. Wadsworth, and D. Brown. 1999. "Free to choose? Dimensions of private sector wage determination." *British Journal of Industrial Relations* 37(1): 33–49.

IMF (International Monetary Fund). 2003. "Unemployment and labor market institutions: Why reforms pay off." In *IMF World Economic Outlook: April 2003, 129–50*. Washington, DC: International Monetary Fund.

Iversen, T. 1998. "Wage bargaining, hard money and economic performance: Theory and evidence for organized market economies." *British Journal of Political Science* 28: 31–61.

———. 1999. *Contested economic institutions: The politics of macroeconomics and wage bargaining in advanced democracies*. New York: Cambridge University Press.

Jackman, R., R. Layard, and S. Nickell. 1996. "Combating unemployment: Is flexibility enough?" Discussion paper 293, Center for Economic Performance, London School of Economics, London.

Jackson, P. 1991. "Public expenditure." In *Labour's economic policies, 1974–1979*, ed. M. Artis and D. Cobham. Manchester: Manchester University Press.

Jacobi, O., W. Müller-Jentsch, and E. Schmidt, eds. 1973. *Gesellschaften und Klassenkampf: kritisches Jahrbuch 1973*. Frankfurt: Fischer.

Jacobs, K., and W. Schmähl. 1988. "Der Übergang in den Ruhestand: Entiwicklung, offentliche Diskussion und Moglichkeiten seiner Umgestaltung." *Mitteilungen aus dem Arbeitsmarkt und Berufsforschung* 2: 196–205.

Jacobs, K., M. Kohli, and M. Rein. 1991. "Germany: The diversity of pathways." In *Time for retirement: Comparative studies of early exit from the labor force*, ed. M. Kohli, A.-M. Guillemard, and H. van Gunstern, pp. 181–221. New York: Cambridge University Press.

Jäger, W., and W. Link. 1986. *Republik im Wandel, 1974–1982: Die Ara Schmidt*. Mannheim, Ger.: Brockhaus.

Jochem, S. 2001. "Reformpolitik im deutschen Sozialversicherungsstaat." In *Wohlfahrtsstaatliche Politik: Institutionen, politischer Prozess und Leistungsprofil*, ed. M. G. Schmidt, pp. 193–226. Opladen, Germany: Leske und Budrich.

Johannesson, J. 1981. "On the composition of Swedish labor market policy." In *Studies in labor market behaviour: Sweden and the United States*, ed. G. Elliason, B. Holmlund, and F. Stafford, pp. 67–97. Stockholm: Almqvist and Wiksell.

References

————, and I. Persson-Tanimura. 1984. *Labour market policy under reconsideration: Studies of the Swedish labour market and the effects of labour market policy.* Stockholm: Swedish Ministry of Labor.

Johnston, T. L. 1962. *Collective bargaining in Sweden.* London: Allen and Unwin.

Jones, H. 1992. *The Conservative Party and the welfare state, 1942–1955.* London: London School of Economics.

Jones, R. 1987. *Wages and employment policy, 1936–1985.* London: Allen and Unwin.

Kalbitz, R. 1979. *Aussperrungen in der Bundesrepublik: Die vergessenen Konflikte.* Köln: Europaische Verlagsanstalt.

Katzenstein, P. 1985. *Small States in World Markets: Industrial Policy in Europe.* Ithaca, NY: Cornell University Press.

Kautto, M. 2000. *Two of a kind? Economic crisis, policy responses and well-being during the 1990s in Sweden and Finland.* Stockholm: Ministry of Health and Social Affairs.

————. 2001. "Moving closer? Diversity and convergence in financing of welfare states." In *Nordic welfare states in the European context*, ed. M. Kautto, J. Fritzell, B. Hvinden, J. Kvist, and H. Uusitalo. London: Routledge.

Keegan, W., and R. Penant-Rea. 1979. *Who runs the economy? Control and influence in British economic policy.* London: Temple-Smith.

Kenworthy, L. 2001. "Wage-setting measures: A survey and assessment." *World Politics* 54(1): 57–98.

————. 2002. "Corporatism and Unemployment in the 1980's and 1990's." *American Sociological Review* 2002: 267–88.

Kiander, J. 1997. "The 1995 social pact in Finland: wage restraint through incomes policy." In *Social pacts in Europe: New dynamics*, ed. G. Fajertag and P. Pochet, pp. 135–44. Brussels: European Trade Union Institute.

King, D. 1995. *Actively seeking work? The politics of unemployment and welfare policy in the United States and Great Britain.* Chicago: University of Chicago Press.

————, and S. Wood. 1999. "The political economy of neo-liberalism: Britain and the United States in the 1980s." In *Continuity and change in contemporary capitalism*, eds. H. Kitschelt, P. Lange, G. Marks, and J. Stephens, pp. 371–97. New York: Cambridge University Press.

Kitschelt, H., P. Lange, G. Marks, and J. Stephens, eds. 1999. *Continuity and Change in Contemporary Capitalism.* New York: Cambridge University Press.

Korpi, W. 1981. "Workplace bargaining, the law and unofficial strikes: The case of Sweden." *British Journal of Industrial Relations* 16: 355–68.

Kurz-Scherf, I. 1988. "Tarifrunde 1987: Bilanz der Tarifbewegungen." *WSI Mitteilungen* 41(3): 133–50.

Kydland, F. E., and E. C. Prescott. 1977. "Rules rather than discretion: The inconsistency of optimal plans." *Journal of Political Economy* 85: 473–86.

Lange, P. 1984. "Unions, workers and wage regulation: The rational bases for consent." In *Order and conflict in contemporary capitalism*, ed. J. Goldthorpe, pp. 98–123. Oxford: Clarendon Press.

————, and G. Garrett. 1985. "The politics of growth: Strategic interaction and economic performance in the advanced industrial democracies 1974–1980." *Journal of Politics* 47: 792–827.

Leisering, L. 1999. "Der Deutsche Sozialstaat." In *50 Jahre Bundesrepublik Deutschland: Rahmenbedingungen – Entwicklungen – Perspektiven*, ed. T. Ellwein and E. Holtmann, pp. 181–92. Wiesbaden: Westdeutscher Verlag.

Lind, J. 1997. "EMU and collective bargaining in Denmark." In *Social pacts in Europe: New dynamics*, ed. G. Fajertag and P. Pochet, pp. 145–55. Brussels: European Trade Union Institute.

Lindbeck, A. 1975. *Swedish economic policy*. London: Macmillan.

LO. 1951. *Protokoll: 14: e ordinarie kongressen*. Stockholm: LO.

———. 1953. *Trade unions and full employment: Report to the 1951 congress*. London: Allen and Unwin.

———. 1976. *Landsorganisationens 19: e Ordinarie Kongres*. Stockholm: LO.

———. 1991. *Landsorganisationens 22a ordinarie kongress 8–14 juni 1991*. Stockholm: LO.

Lowe, R. 1999. *The welfare state in Britain since 1945*. New York: St. Martin's.

Lynch, J., and K. Anderson. 2004. "Internal institutions and the policy preferences of organized labor: The effects of workforce aging on unions' support for pension reform." Unpublished manuscript.

Manow, P. 2000. "Wage coordination and the welfare state: Germany and Japan compared." Working Paper 00/7, Max Planck Institute, Köln.

———. 2001. "Capitalist production, social Protection." Manuscript, Max Planck Institute for the Study of Societies.

———, and E. Seils. 2000. "Adjusting badly: The German welfare state, structural change and the open economy." In *Welfare and work in the open economy*, vol. 2, ed. F. Scharpf and V. Schmidt, pp. 264–307. Oxford: Oxford University Press.

Mares, I. 2001. "Enterprise reorganization and social insurance reform: The development of early retirement in France and Germany." *Governance* 14: 295–318.

———. 2003. *The politics of social risk: Business and welfare state development*. New York: Cambridge University Press.

———. 2005. "Wage bargaining in the presence of social services and transfers." *World Politics* 57.

———. Forthcoming. "Labor market institutions and economic performance: What have we learned during three decades of research?" In *The consequences of democratic institutions*, ed. H. Kitschelt.

Markovits, A. 1986. *The politics of the West German trade unions*. Cambridge: Cambridge University Press.

———, and C. Allen. 1983. "Trade unions and the economic crisis: The West German case." In *Unions and economic crisis: Britain, West Germany and Sweden*, ed. P. Gourevitch, A. Martin, G. Ross, C. Allen, and A. Markovits, pp. 89–188. London: Allen and Unwin.

Martin, A. 1984. "Trade unions in Sweden: Strategic responses to change and crisis." In *Unions and economic crisis: Britain, West Germany and Sweden*, ed. P. Gourevitch, A. Martin, G. Ross, C. Allen, and A. Markovits, pp. 190–359. London: Allen and Unwin.

———. 1985. "Wages, profits and investment in Sweden." In *The politics of inflation and economic stagnation*, ed. L. Lindberg and C. Maier, pp. 403–66. Washington, DC: Brookings.

References

Mas-Colell, A. 1995. *Microeconomic theory*. New York: Oxford University Press.

McIlroy, J. 1998. "The enduring alliance? Trade unions and the making of New Labour." *British Journal of Industrial Relations* 36: 536–64.

McKinlay, A., and P. Taylor. 1994. "Privatisation and industrial relations in British shipbuilding." *Industrial Relations Journal* 25(2): 293–304.

Meidner, R. 1969. "Active manpower policy and the inflation-unemployment dilemma." *Swedish Journal of Economics* 3: 161–83.

Mendoza, E., A. Razin, and L. L. Tesar. 1994. "Effective tax rates in macro-economics: Cross-country estimates of tax rates on factor incomes and consumption." *Journal of Monetary Ecoomics* 34: 297–323.

Metcalf, D., and S. Milner, eds. 1995. *New perspectives on industrial disputes*. London: Routledge.

Middlemas, K. 1991. *Power, competition and the state: The end of the postwar era*. London: Macmillan.

Misgeld, K., K. Molin, and K. Åmark, eds. 1992. *Creating social democracy: A century of the Social Democratic Labor Party in Sweden*. University Park: Pennsylvania State University Press.

Mullard, M. 1987. *The politics of public expenditure*. London: Croom Helm.

———. 2001. "New Labour, new public expenditures." *Political Quarterly* 72: 310–34.

Müller-Jentsch, W., and H.-J. Sperling. 1978. "Economic development, labour conflicts and the industrial relations system in West Germany." In *The resurgence of class conflict in Western Europe since 1968*, vol. 1, ed. C. Crouch and A. Pizzorno, pp. 257–306. New York: Holmes and Meier.

Naschold, F., and B. de Vroom, eds. 1994. *Regulating employment and welfare: Company and national policies of labor force participation rates at the end of worklife in industrial countries*. Berlin: Walter de Gruyter.

National Institute of Economic Research (Sweden). 1992. *The Swedish economy*. Stockholm: National Institute of Economic Research.

National Institute of Economic and Social Research (UK). Various Years. *National institute economic review*. London: National Institute of Economic and Social Research.

Nautz, J. 1998. "Das deutsche Tarifvertragsrecht zwischen Interventionismus und Autonomie." In *Entstehung des Arbeitsrechts in Deutschland: Aktuelle Probleme in historischer Perspektive*, ed. H. Nutzinger, pp. 71–121. Marburg: Metropolis.

———. 1999. "Die Entstehung des Tarifvertragsgesetzes: Historische, politische und juristische Hintergrunde." *WSI Mitteilungen* 52(7): 437–44.

Negrelli, S. 1997. "Social pacts and flexibility: Towards a new balance between macro and micro industrial relations: The Italian experience." In *Social Pacts in Europe: New dynamics*, ed. P. Pochet and G. Fajertag, pp. 45–62. Brussels: European Trade Union Institute.

———. 2000. "Social pacts in Italy and Europe: Similar strategies and structures, different models and national stories." In *Social pacts in Europe: New dynamics*, ed. P. Pochet and G. Fajertag. Brussels: European Trade Union Institute.

Nickell, S. 1997. "Unemployment and labor market rigidities: Europe versus North America." *Journal of Economic Perspectives* 11: 55–74.

245

————, and R. Layard. 1999. "Labour market institutions and economic performance." In *Handbook of labour economics*, vol. 3, ed. O. Ashenfelter and D. Card. Amsterdam: North Holland.

Noe, C. 1970. *Gebändigter Klassenkampf: Tarifautonomie in der Bundesrepublik Deutschland: Der Konflikt zwischen Gesamtmetall und IG Metall vom Frühjahr 1963.* Berlin: Duncker und Humblot.

Nullmeier, F., and F. Rüb. 1993. *Die Transformation der Sozialpolitik: Vom Sozialstaat zum Sicherungsstaat.* Frankfurt: Campus.

O'Donnell, R., and C. O'Reardon. 1997. "Ireland's experiment in social partnership, 1987–1996." In *Social pacts in Europe: New dynamics*, ed. G. Fajertag and P. Pochet, pp. 79–95. Brussels: European Trade Union Institute.

————. 2000. "Social partnership in Ireland's economic transformation." In *Social pacts in Europe: New dynamics*, ed. G. Fajertag and P. Pochet, pp. 237–56. Brussels: European Trade Union Institute.

OECD. 1994. *The OECD jobs study: Evidence and explanations.* Paris: OECD.

————. 1997. *Employment outlook.* Paris: OECD.

————. 1999a. *Employment outlook.* Paris: OECD.

————. 1999b. *Benefit systems and work incentives.* Paris: OECD.

————. 2000a. *Effective average tax rates on capital, labour and consumption goods: Cross-country estimates.* Paris: OECD

————. 2000b. *Historical statistics.* Paris: OECD.

————. 2000c. *Tax burdens: Alternative measures.* Paris: OECD.

————. Various years. *Economic surveys: Germany.* Paris: OECD.

————. Various years. *Economic surveys: Sweden.* Paris: OECD.

————. Various years. *Economic surveys: United Kingdom.* Paris: OECD.

Ogden, S. 1994. "The reconstruction of industrial relations in the privatized water industry." *British Journal of Industrial Relations* 32(1): 67–84.

Öhman, B. 1974. *LO and labour market policy since the Second World War.* Stockholm: Bockforlaget Prisma.

Olson, M. 1982. *The rise and decline of nations: Economic growth, stagflation and social rigidities.* New Haven, CT: Yale University Press.

Olsson, S. E. 1990. *Social policy and welfare state in Sweden.* Lund, Sweden: Arkiv Forlags.

Opie, R. 1972. "Economic planning and growth" In *The Labour Government's economic record 1964–1970*, ed. W. Beckerman. London: Duckworth.

Oppenheim, C. 2000. "Enabling participation: New Labour's welfare-to-work policies." In *New Labour: The progressive future?*, ed. S. White, pp. 77–92. London: Palgrave.

Palme, J., Åke Bergmark, Olof Bäckman, Felipe Estrada, Johan Fritzell, Olle Lundberg, Ola Sjöberg, and Marta Szebehely. 2002. "Welfare trends in Sweden: Balancing the books for the 1990s." *Journal of European Social Policy* 12(4): 329–46.

Palme, J., and I. Wannamo. 1998. *Swedish social security in the 1990s: Reform and retrenchment.* Stockholm: Cabinet Office and Ministers.

Panitch, L. 1976. *Social democracy and industrial militancy.* Cambridge: Cambridge University Press.

References

Paqué, K.-H. 1996. "Unemployment and the crisis of the German model: A long-term interpretation." In *Fighting Europe's unemployment in the 1990s*, ed. H. Giersch, pp. 123–55. New York: Springer-Verlag.

Parry, D., D. Waddington, and C. Critcher. 1997. "Industrial relations in the privatized mining industry." *British Journal of Industrial Relations* 35(2): 173–96.

Perez, S. 2000a. "From decentralization to reorganization: Explaining the return to national bargaining in Italy and Spain." *Comparative Politics* 32(4): 437–58.

———. 2000b. "Social pacts in Spain." In *Social pacts in Europe: New dynamics*, ed. G. Fajertag and P. Pochet, pp. 343–63. Brussels: European Trade Union Institute.

———. 2002c. "Monetary union and wage bargaining institutions in the EU: Extrapolating from some member states' experiences." *Comparative Political Studies* 35(10): 1198–227.

Perschke-Hartmann, C. 1994. *Die doppelte Reform: Gesundheitspolitik von Blum zu Seehofer*. Opladen, Germany: Leske und Budrich.

Pierson, P. 1993. "When effect becomes cause: policy feedback and political change." *World Politics* 45: 595–628.

———. 1994. *Dismantling the welfare state? Reagan, Thatcher and the politics of retrenchment*. New York: Cambridge University Press.

———. 1996. "The new politics of the welfare state." *World Politics* 48: 143–179.

Piketty, T. 1998. "L'impact des incitations fianciers au travail sur les comportements individuals: Une estimation pour le cas francais." *Economie et Prevision* 132–3: 1–35.

Pirker, T. 1960. *Die blinde Macht: Die Gewerkschaftsbewegung in Westdeutschland*. Munich: Mercator.

Pontusson, J. 1992. *The limits of social democracy: Investment politics in Sweden*. Ithaca, NY: Cornell University Press.

———, and P. Swenson. 1996. "Labor markets, production strategies and wage bargaining institutions: The Swedish employer offensive in comparative perspective." *Comparative Political Studies* 29(2): 223–50.

Putnam, R., and N. Bayne. 1984. *Hanging together: Cooperation and conflict in the seven-power summits*. Cambridge, MA: Harvard University Press.

Quinn, D., and C. Inclan. 1997. "The origin of financial openness." *American Journal of Political Science* 41(3): 777–813.

Regini, M. 2000. "Between deregulation and social pacts." *Politics and Society* 28(1): 5–33.

———, and I. Regalia. 1997. "Employers, unions and the state: The resurgence of concertation in Italy?" *West European Politics* 20: 210–30.

Rhodes, M. 2000. "Restructuring the British welfare state: Between domestic constraints and global imperatives." In *Welfare and work in the open economy*, ed. F. Scharpf and V. Schmidt, pp. 19–68. Oxford: Oxford University Press.

Rosewitz, B., and D. Webber. 1990. *Reformversuche und Reformblockaden im deutschen Gesundheitswesen*. Frankfurt: Campus.

Rowthorn, R. 1992. "Centralization, employment and wage dispersion." *Economic Journal* 102: 506–23.

Royo, S. 2002. "'A new century of corporatism'? Corporatism in Spain and Portugal." *West European Politics* 25(3): 77–104.

Rueda, David. Forthcoming. "Insider-outsider politics in industrialized democracies: The challenge to Social Democratic Parties." *American Political Science Review.*

SAF. 1978. *Direct and total wage costs for workers: International survey.* Stockholm: SAF.

SAP. 1981. *Framtid for Sverige.* Stockholm: SAP.

———. 1989. *90 – talsprogrammet.* Stockholm: SAP.

Scarpetta, S. 1996. "Assessing the role of labour market policies and institutional settings on unemployment: A cross-country study." *OECD Economic Studies* 26: 43–98.

Scharpf, F. 1991. *Crisis and choice in European social democracy.* Ithaca, NY: Cornell University Press.

———, 1998. *Governing in Europe: How effective? How democratic?* Oxford: Oxford University Press.

———. and V. Schmidt, eds. 2000. *Welfare and work in the open economy.* New York: Oxford University Press.

Schauer, H. 1999. "Tarifpolitik und Sozialreform: Stationen bundesdeutscher Tarifgeschichte." *WSI Mitteilungen* 7: 426–44.

Schelkle, W. 2000. "Subsidizing low earnings: German debates and U.S. experiences." *Vierteljahresschrift für Wirtschaftsforschung* 69(1): 1–16.

Schmidt, E. 1973. "Spontane Streiks, 1972–1973." In *Gewerkschaften und Klassenkampf: Kritisches Jahrbuch 1973*, ed. O. Jacobi, W. Müller-Jentsch, and E. Schmidt, pp. 30–42. Frankfurt: Fischer.

Schmidt, M. G. 1990. "Sozialpolitik." In *Politik in der Bundesrepublik Deutschland*, ed. K. V. Beyme and M. G. Schmidt, pp. 126–49. Opladen, Germany: Westdeutscher Verlag.

Schmitter, P. 1979. "Still the century of corporatism?" In *Trends towards corporatist intermediation*, ed. P. Schmitter and G. Lehmbruch, pp. 7–52. Beverly Hills, CA: Sage.

———. 1981. "Interest intermediation and regime governability in contemporary Western Europe and North America." In *Organizing interests in Western Europe*, ed. S. Berger. New York: Cambridge University Press.

Schönhoven, K. 1987. *Die Deutschen Gewerkschaften.* Frankfurt: Suhrkamp.

Shonfield, A. 1965. *Modern capitalism: The changing balance of public and private power.* Oxford: Oxford University Press.

Siebert, H. 1997. "Labor market rigidities: at the root of unemployment in Europe." *Journal of Economic Perspectives* 11: 37–54.

Slomp, H. 2002. "The Netherlands in the 1990s: Towards 'flexible corporatism' in the Polder model." In *Policy concertation and social partnership in Western Europe: Lessons for the 21st century*, ed. S. Berger and H. Compston, pp. 235–48. New York: Berghahn.

Smith, P., and G. Morton. 2001. "New Labour's reform of Britain's employment law: The devil is not only in the details but in the values and policy too." *British Journal of Industrial Relations* 39(1): 119–38.

References

Soskice, D. 1990. "Wage determination: The changing role of institutions in advanced industrialized countries." *Oxford Review of Economic Policy* 6(4): 36–61.

————, and T. Iversen. 1999. "Monetary integration, partisanship and macroeconomic policy." Paper presented at the 95th Annual Meeting of the American Political Science Association, Atlanta, September 2–5, 1999.

————. 2000. "The nonneutrality of money with large price or wage setters." *Quarterly Journal of Economics* 115(1): 1–20.

Stephens, J. 1996. "The Scandinavian welfare states: Achievements, crises, prospects." In *The welfare state in hard times: National adaptations in global economies*, ed. G. Esping-Andersen, pp. 32–65. Thousand Oaks, CA: Sage.

Stewart, M. 1972. "The distribution of income." In *The Labour government's economic record, 1964–1970*, ed. W. Beckerman. London: Duckworth.

Sturm, R. 1998. "Die Wende im Stolperschritt: Eine finanzpolitische Bilanz." In *Die Ara Kohl*, ed. G. Wever, pp. 183–200. Opladen, Germany: Leske und Budrich.

Summers, L., J. Gruber, and R. Vergara. 1993. "Taxation and structure of labor markets: The case of corporatism." *Quarterly Journal of Economics* 108(2): 385–411.

Svenskt Näringsliv. 2002. *Internationell Utblick: Löner och arbetskraftskostnader*. Stockholm: Svenskt Näringsliv.

Swank, D. 2000. "Political Strength of political parties by ideological group in capitalist democracies." Dataset available at http://www.marquette.edu/polisci/Swank.htm.

————. 2002. *Global capital, political institutions and policy change in developed welfare states*. New York: Cambridge University Press.

Sweden. Ministry of Economic Affairs. 1981. *The 1980 medium term survey of the Swedish economy*. Stockholm: Ministry of Economic Affairs.

Sweden. Ministry of Finance. 1966. *The Swedish economy 1966–1970 and the general outlook for the seventies*. Stockholm: Fritzes.

————. 2000. *The long-term survey of the Swedish economy, 1999/2000*. Stockholm: Fritzes.

Sweden. Productivity Commission (Produktivitetsdelegationen). 1991. *Drivkrafter för produktivitet och välstånd: Produktivitetsdelegationen betänkande*. Stockholm: Allmänna förlag.

Sweden. Statistical Office (Statistika Centralbyrån). Various Years. *Statistical yearbook of Sweden*. Stockholm: SCB.

Sweden. Welfare Commission (Kommitten Välfärdsbokslut). 2002. *Welfare in Sweden: The balance sheet for the 1990s*. Stockholm: Ministry of Health and Social Affairs.

Swenson, P. 1989. *Fair shares: Unions, pay and politics in Sweden and West Germany*. Ithaca, NY: Cornell University Press.

————. 1991. "Bringing capital back in, or social democracy reconsidered." *World Politics* 43(3): 379–399.

————. 2002. *Capitalists against Markets: The making of labor markets and welfare states in the United States and Sweden*. New York: Oxford University Press.

Tennstedt, F. 1977. *Soziale Selbstverwaltung: Geschichte der Selbstverwaltung in der Sozialversicherung*. Bonn: Verlag der Ortskrankenkassen.

Thelen, K. 1991. *Union of parts: Labor politics in postwar Germany*. Ithaca, NY: Cornell University Press.

———. 1994. "Beyond Corporatism: Toward a new framework for the study of labor in advanced capitalism." *Comparative Politics* 27: 107–24.

———. 2000. "Why German employers cannot bring themselves to dismantle the German model." In *Unions, employers and central banks: Macroeconomic coordination and institutional change in social market economies*, ed. T. Iversen, J. Pontusson, and D. Soskice, pp. 138–69. New York: Cambridge University Press.

———. 2001. "Varieties of Labor Politics in the Developed Democracies." In *Varieties of capitalism: The institutional foundations of comparative advantage*, ed. P. Hall and D. Soskice, pp. 75–103. Oxford: Oxford University Press.

———, and I. Kume. 1999. The rise of nonliberal training regimes: Germany and Japan compared. *Journal of Japanese Studies* 25: 33–64.

Tolliday, S., and J. Zeitlin. 1986. *Shop floor bargaining and the state*. Cambridge: Cambridge University Press.

Tranøy, B. 2000. "Bad timing: Recommodificaton, credit reform and crises of coordination in Norway and Sweden in the 1980s and 1990s." In *Globalization, Europeanization and the end of Scandinavian social democracy?* ed. R. Geyer, C. Ingebritsen, and J. Moses, pp. 45–61. New York: St. Martin's.

Traxler, F., S. Blaschke, and B. Kittel. 2001. *National labour relations in internationalized markets: A comparative study of institutions, change, and performance*. Oxford: Oxford University Press.

Traxler, F. 2000. "National pacts and wage regulation in Europe: A comparative analysis." In *Social Pacts in Europe: New Dynamics*, ed. P. Pochet and G. Fajertag. Brussels: European Trade Union Institute.

Traxler, F., and B. Kittel. 2000. "The bargaining system and performance: A comparison of 18 OECD countries." *Comparative Political Studies* 33(9): 1154–90.

Trehörning, P. 1993. *Measures to combat unemployment in Sweden: Labor market policy in the mid-1990s*. Stockholm: Swedish Institute.

TUC. 1942. *Report of proceedings at the 74th annual Trades Union Congress held at Blackpool, September 7–11, 1942*. London: Trades Union Congress.

———. 1948. *Report of proceedings at a special conference of executive committees of affiliated organizations, March 24, 1948*. London: Trades Union Congress.

———. 1950. *Report of proceedings at the annual Trades Union Congress*. London: Trades Union Congress.

———. 1951. *Report of proceedings at the annual Trades Union Congress*. London: Trades Union Congress.

———. 1952. *Report of proceedings at the annual Trades Union Congress*. London: Trades Union Congress.

———. 1953. *Report of proceedings at the annual Trades Union Congress*. London: Trades Union Congress.

———. 1954. *Report of proceedings at the annual Trades Union Congress*. London: Trades Union Congress.

———. 1955. *Report of proceedings at the annual Trades Union Congress*. London: Trades Union Congress.

References

———. 1956. *Report of proceedings at the annual Trades Union Congress*. London: Trades Union Congress.

———. 1957. *Report of proceedings at the annual Trades Union Congress*. London: Trades Union Congress.

———. 1958. *Report of proceedings at the annual Trades Union Congress*. London: Trades Union Congress.

———. 1959. *Report of proceedings at the annual Trades Union Congress*. London: Trades Union Congress.

———. 1961. *Report of proceedings at the annual Trades Union Congress*. London: Trades Union Congress.

———. 1964. *Collective bargaining and the social contract*. London: TUC.

———. 1965. *Productivity, prices and incomes: Report of a conference of executive committees, April 1965*. London: TUC.

———. 1972. *Report of proceedings at the annual Trades Union Congress*. London: Trades Union Congress.

———. 1974. *Report of proceedings at the annual Trades Union Congress*. London: Trades Union Congress.

———. 1980. *Report of proceedings at the annual Trades Union Congress*. London: Trades Union Congress.

———. 1981. *Report of proceedings at the annual Trades Union Congress*. London: Trades Union Congress.

———. 1994. *Report of proceedings at the annual Trades Union Congress*. London: Trades Union Congress.

———. 1995. *Report of proceedings at the annual Trades Union Congress*. London: Trades Union Congress

———. 2000. *Annual report of the Trades Union Congress*. London: Trades Union Congress.

U.K. Central Statistical Office. 1955. *National income and expenditure*. Blue book. London: HMSO.

———. Various Years. *Annual abstract of statistics*. London: HMSO.

U.K. Department of Employment. 1983. *Democracy in trade unions*. London: HMSO.

U.K. Department of Health and Social Services. 1985. "Reform of social security." Green paper, Cmnd 9517, HMSO, London.

U.K. Department of Trade and Industry. 1998. "Fairness at work." White paper, Cmd. 3968, HMSO, London. Available at http://www.dti.gov.uk/er/fairness/index.htm

U.K. Government Statistical Service. 1988. *Social security statistics*. London: HMSO.

U.K. Parliament. 1948. "Statement on personal incomes, costs and prices." White paper, Cmd. 7321, HMSO, London.

U.K. Treasury. 1998. *Stability and investment for the long term: Economic and fiscal strategy report, 1998*. London: HMSO. Available at http://www.hm-treasury.gov.uk/Documents/UK˙Economy/Economic˙and˙Fiscal˙Strategy˙Report˙1998/ukecon˙efsr˙index.cfm

U.S. Bureau of Labor Statistics. Various Years. *Handbook of labor statistics*. Washington, DC: Bureau of Labor Statistics.

Victorin, A. 1975. *The implementation of a wage policy: Centralized collective bargaining in Sweden*. Stockholm: Almquist & Wicksell International.

Visser, J., and A. Hemerjick. 1997. *A Dutch miracle: Job growth, welfare reform and corporatism in the Netherlands*. Amsterdam: Amsterdam University Press.

———. 2000. "Change and Immobility: Three decades of policy adjustment in the Netherlands and Belgium." *West European Politics* 23: 229–56.

Volkerink, B., and J. de Haan. 2000. *Tax ratios: A critical survey*. Paris: OECD.

Volkerink, B., J.-E. Sturm, and J. de Haan. 2001. "Tax ratios in macroeconomics: Do taxes really matter?" Working paper 7/2001, European Economy Group, Madrid.

Waddington, J. 1992. "Trade union membership in Britain, 1980–1987: Unemployment and restructuring." *British Journal of Industrial Relations* 30(2): 297–323.

Wallich, H. 1955. *Mainsprings of the German revival*. New Haven, CT: Yale University Press.

Wanger, G. 1999. "Soziale Sicherung im Spannungsfeld von Demokratie und Arbeitsmarkt." In *Herausforderungen an die Wirtschaftspolitik an der Schwelle zum 21. Jahrhundert*, ed. I. Nübler and H. Trabold, pp. 77–91. Berlin: Sigma.

Weinzen, W., ed. 1986. *Wirtschafts-und Steuerpolitik: Expansive Lohnpolitik*. Berlin: DVK Verlag.

Wendl, M. 1997. "Die 'angebotspolitische Wende in der Tarifpolitik: Kritik der aktuellen Lohnpolitik der Gewerkschaften." *Prokla* 27(1): 97–111.

Wever, G., ed. 1998. *Die Ära Kohl*. Opladen, Germany: Leske und Budrich.

Whiteside, N. 1996. "Creating the welfare state in Britain, 1945–1960." *Journal of Social Policy* 25(1): 83–103.

Wickham-Jones, M. 1991. "A calendar of events." In *Labour's economic policies, 1974–1979*, ed. M. Artis and D. Cobham, pp. 278–95. Manchester: Manchester University Press.

Wilthagen, T. 1998. "Flexicurity: A new paradigm for labour market policy reform?" Discussion paper FS I 98–202, Wissenschaftszentrum Berlin, Berlin.

———, F. Tros, and H. von Lieshout. 2003. "Towards 'flexicurity'? Balancing flexibility and security in EU member states." Paper delivered at the 13th World Congress of the International Industrial Relations Association, Berlin, September.

Wood, S. 1998. "Capitalist constitutions: Supply-side reforms in Britain and West Germany." Ph.D. diss., Harvard University.

———. 2001. "Business, government and patterns of labor market policy in Britain and the Federal Republic of Germany." In *Varieties of capitalism*, ed. P. Hall and D. Soskice, pp. 247–74. New York: Oxford University Press.

Ziegler, N. 2000. *Governing ideas: Strategies for innovation in France and Germany*. Ithaca, NY: Cornell University Press.

Zolnhöfer, R. 2000. "Der lange Schatten der schönen Illusion: Finanzpolitik nach der deutschen Einheit 1990–1998." *Leviathan* 1: 14–38.

Index

Index

Calmfors, L., 9, 21, 25, 26, 63
Calmfors-Driffill model, 11, 15, 20–2, 23, 36, 62, 221, 222
  assumption about utility function of unions, 49–50
  equilibrium wage levels in, 38
  Iversen model and, 31, 33
  objections to, 25
  Soskice-Iversen model and, 29
  studies confirming, 25
  versus linear model, 22–3, 26–7
  wage bargaining centralization and, 46, 58–60, 72
Cameron, D., 8, 18, 20–1, 43, 48, 63, 64
Canada
  centralization of wage bargaining institutions, 13, 71, 74–6
  monetary regime, 67
Carlin, W., 169
Castles, F., 73
central bank independence. See also monetary nonaccommodation
  composite index of independence, 66, 67–8
  estimated effect on unemployment, 79
  unemployment and, 34–5
  unions and, 11–12
Christian Democratic coalition government, 128, 134, 160. See also Germany; Grand Coalition
  codetermination and, 133–4
  electoral promises of, 160
  fiscal consolidation and, 160–1
  German reunification and, 167–8
  social policy expansion and, 135, 138–9
  tax reforms and, 161
  welfare state reforms and, 161–4
Clark, T., 200, 201, 203, 204
Clasen, J., 2
Clegg, H. A., 180, 190
Cobham, D., 203

codetermination, 133, 134–5
collective action, 20
Colling, T., 207
comparative statics, 43, 56–8
Compston, H., 16, 219
Concerted Action (*Konzertierte Aktion*), 142–4, 147
  social symmetry, 143
Confederation of British Industry, 197
conservative governments (Sweden), 104–8. See also SAP (*Sveriges Socialdemokratiska Arbetraparti*); Sweden
  active labor market policies and, 105–6
  devaluation and, 104
  fiscal stabilization and, 117
  noninflationary policy and, 116–17
  price freeze and, 104
  social policy and, 104–5, 118–19
  tax policy and, 104, 107, 120
Conservative party, 194–9, 218. See also Britain; Labour party
  decentralization of wage bargaining and, 208–9
  deinstitutionalization of the social wage and, 206–12
  economic policies during 1950s and, 179
  efforts to weaken power of trade unions and, 195, 206–9
  electoral promises of, 195, 206, 209
  fiscal retrenchment and, 185, 196
  housing policies and, 182–3, 196
  labor market deregulation and, 209
  minimum wage policies and, 214
  monetary policies and, 198, 208
  opposition to universalistic social policies, 179
  privatization and, 207–8
  social policy and, 179–84, 187, 188, 212
  tax policies and, 196, 209
  U-turn in economic policy and, 197

Index

Index

Soskice, D., 11, 25–6, 27, 35, 64–6, 103, 169, 173, 180, 182, 217, 221, 222
Soskice-Iversen model, 15, 23–8, 29, 30, 32–4, 60, 167, 222
  Calmfors-Driffill model and, 29
  Iversen model and, 35
  limitations of, 28–30
Spain
  social pacts in, 16, 226
  wage bargaining institutions, 226, 227
Sperling, H.-J., 146
Stephens, J., 85, 105
Stewart, J., 192, 211
Strand, A., 91
Streeck, W., 26
strikes
  in Britain, 181, 207
  in Germany, 137–8, 146–7, 149
  in Sweden, 99, 107, 124, 129
Sturm, J.-F., 70
Sturm, R., 160, 161
Svenskt Näringsliv, 12, 126
Swank, D., 73, 105
Sweden, 83–127. *See also*
  Landsorganisationen i Sverige (LO);
  SAP (*Sveriges Socialdemokratiska Arbetraparti*)
  accession to European community, 116, 123
  agrarian party, 92
  conservative governments in, 104–8, 116
  economic decline in, 115–16
  employment in, 71, 126
  exports, 100, 104, 109, 115
  insurance in, 118, 127
  interunion rivalry in, 100–3, 104
  labor market policies in, 92, 93, 106
  on monetary regime index, 68
  noninflationary macroeconomic policies and, 117
  pension retrenchment in, 119
  public opinion in, 105

social services, 96, 100, 110, 114, 119–20, 122, 125
strikes in, 99, 107, 124, 129
taxes in, 111–12, 120, 121
unemployment in, 8
wages, output and productivity in, 90, 91, 94–5, 108, 114, 115, 124–5
Swedish employers. *See* SAF (*Svenska Arbetsgivareföreningen*)
Swedish employers, 63. *See* VF (*Verkstads Förening*)
Swedish unions. *See also* HAO (Union of Commercial Employees); *Landsorganisationen i Sverige* (LO); Metall (Sweden); TCO (*Tjänstermännens Centralorganisation*)
  active labor market policies and, 88–9
  centralization of wage bargaining system, 83–4, 89, 95, 122
  conservative governments and, 104–8, 116
  decentralization of wage bargaining and, 89, 100, 124
  devaluation and, 109
  Europe norm and, 123
  full employment and, 87–8
  inflation and, 87
  mediation commission and, 87, 98, 121, 122, 123
  price controls and, 84–5
  Rehn-Meidner model and, 87–9
  social democratic governments and, 92–3, 110
  social policy and, 85, 95
  solidaristic wage policy and, 88–9
  state involvement in wage-setting and, 97–8
  strikes and, 99, 107, 124, 129
  tax policy and, 85, 88, 91, 94–5, 106, 122
  wage drift and, 86, 101, 122–3
  wage freeze and, 86

263

Index

Vad, T. B., 109, 115, 116, 124
Van der Meer, M., 219
Van Reenen, J., 216
VF (*Verkstads Förening*), 113–14
Victorin, A., 95
Visser, J., 131, 147, 208, 219, 228
Volkerink, B., 70
von Lieshout, H., 230

Waddington, D., 207, 208
Wadsworth, J., 209
wage bargaining. *See also* labor market
    institutions
    centralization, 15, 33–7, 122–3. *See
      also* wage bargaining centralization
    decentralization, 100–1
    employment and, 49–50
    institutions, 8, 25–6, 36
    logic of collective action and, 20
    models, 36–49
    social policies and, 38–41
    system, 89–90, 174. *See also* wage
      bargaining centralization
    unemployment and, 20
    welfare state's effects on, 1–16
wage bargaining centralization, 15,
    33–7
    Calmfors-Driffill approach and,
      58–60
    cross-national variation in, 37
    equilibrium employment and, 37–43,
      44
    measurement of, 62–4
    predicted employment and, 44–7
    rankings and aggregate scores, 63–4,
      82
    unemployment and, i, 8–9, 22, 23,
      45–6
    unions and, 24–5, 127
    wage militancy and, 1–16, 95
    wage moderation and, 95
wage drift, 101–2
wage moderation, 3, 10, 221
    in Britain, 179–80, 188, 189–91
    economic boom and, 131

in Germany, 129–32, 141, 148–9,
    150–1, 153–4, 172
in Sweden, 85–6, 127
tax reduction and, 103
welfare state expansion as source of,
    95–6
wage policies
    in Britain, 175–7, 179, 181–2
    in Germany, 128
    in Sweden, 94–9, 115–26
    tax increases and, 101
wage restraint, 126, 177, 180–1, 182
wage setting, 27–30, 140–1
    centralization, 122–3
    process, 121–2, 181
wages
    determination in advanced
      industrialized societies, 15
    equilibrium employment and, 41–3
    union demands, 41–3, 52–6, 61, 127
    welfare state commitments and, 222
wage–social policy nexus, 15–16,
    128–41, 167. *See also* social wage
Walker, J. R., 96, 100, 112
Wallerstein, M., 26, 63, 64
Wallich, H., 133, 134
Wanger, G., 2
Webb, S., 34, 66, 67
Webber, D., 162
Weinzen, W., 132
welfare state
    design of, 136–7
    effects on employment, 1–13, 16
    fiscal consolidation and, 118–20
    growth of, 3
    labor market institutions and, 35–47
    monetary policy and, 35
welfare state commitments
    influence of existing, 10, 12
    magnitude and composition of,
      68–71
    measurement of, 62
    unemployment and, 222
    wage choices and, 222
    wage demands of unions and, 61

David C. Kang, *Crony Capitalism: Corruption and Capitalism in South Korea and Philippines*

Junko Kato, *Regressive Taxation and the Welfare State*

Robert O. Keohane and Helen B. Milner, eds., *Internationalization and Domestic Politics*

Herbert Kitschelt, *The Transformation of European Social Democracy*

Herbert Kitschelt, Peter Lange, Gary Marks, and John D. Stephens, eds., *Continuity and Change in Contemporary Capitalism*

Herbert Kitschelt, Zdenka Mansfeldova, Radek Markowski, and Gabor Toka, *Post-Communist Party Systems*

David Knoke, Franz Urban Pappi, Jeffrey Broadbent, and Yutaka Tsujinaka, eds., *Comparing Policy Networks*

Allan Kornberg and Harold D. Clarke, *Citizens and Community: Political Support in a Representative Democracy*

Amie Kreppel, *The European Parliament and the Supranational Party System*

David D. Laitin, *Language Repertories and State Construction in Africa*

Fabrice E. Lehoucq and Ivan Molina, *Stuffing the Ballot Box: Fraud, Electoral Reform, and Democratization in Costa Rica*

Mark Irving Lichbach and Alan S. Zuckerman, eds., *Comparative Politics: Rationality, Culture, and Structure*

Evan Lieberman, *Race and Regionalism in the Politics of Taxation in Brazil and South Africa*

Pauline Jones Luong, *Institutional Change and Political Continuity in Post-Soviet Central Asia*

Doug McAdam, John McCarthy, and Mayer Zald, eds., *Comparative Perspectives on Social Movements*

James Mahoney and Dietrich Rueschemeyer, eds., *Historical Analysis and the Social Sciences*

Scott Mainwaring and Matthew Soberg Shugart, eds., *Presidentialism and Democracy in Latin America*

Isabela Mares, *The Politics of Social Risk: Business and Welfare State Development*

Anthony W. Marx, *Making Race, Making Nations: A Comparison of South Africa, the United States, and Brazil*

Joel S. Migdal, *State in Society: Studying How States and Societies Constitute One Another*

Joel S. Migdal, Atul Kohli, and Vivienne Shue, eds., *State Power and Social Forces: Domination and Transformation in the Third World*

Scott Morgenstern and Benito Nacif, eds., *Legislative Politics in Latin America*

Layna Mosley, *Global Capital and National Governments*

Wolfgang C. Müller and Kaare Strøm, *Policy, Office, or Votes?*

Maria Victoria Murillo, *Labor, Unions, Partisan Coalitions, and Market Reforms in Latin America*

Ton Notermans, *Money, Markets, and the State: Social Democratic Economic Policies Since 1918*

Roger Petersen, *Understanding Ethnic Violence: Fear, Hatred, and Resentment in Twentieth-Century Eastern Europe*

Simona Piattoni, ed., *Clientelism, Interests, and Democratic Representation*

Paul Pierson, *Dismantling the Welfare State? Reagan, Thatcher, and the Politics of Retrenchment*

Marino Regini, *Uncertain Boundaries: The Social and Political Construction of European Economies*

Lyle Scruggs, *Sustaining Abundance: Environmental Performance in Industrial Democracies*

Jefferey M. Sellers, *Governing from Below: Urban Regions and the Global Economy*

Yossi Shain and Juan Linz, eds., *Interim Government and Democratic Transitions*

Beverly Silver, *Forces of Labor: Workers' Movements and Globalization Since 1870*

Theda Skocpol, *Social Revolutions in the Modern World*

Regina Smyth, *Candidate Strategies and Electoral Competition in the Russian Federation: Democracy Without Foundation*

Richard Snyder, *Politics after Neoliberalism: Reregulation in Mexico*

David Stark and László Bruszt, *Postsocialist Pathways: Transforming Politics and Property in East Central Europe*

Sven Steinmo, Kathleen Thelen, and Frank Longstreth, eds., *Structuring Politics: Historical Institutionalism in Comparative Analysis*

Susan C. Stokes, *Mandates and Democracy: Neoliberalism by Surprise in Latin America*

Susan C. Stokes, ed., *Public Support for Market Reforms in New Democracies*

Duane Swank, *Global Capital, Political Institutions, and Policy Change in Developed Welfare States*

Sidney Tarrow, *Power in Movement: Social Movement and Contentious Politics*

Kathleen Thelen, *How Institutions Evolve: The Political Economy of Skills in Germany, Britain, the United States, and Japan*

Charles Tilly, *Trust and Rule*

Joshua Tucker, *Regional Economic Voting: Russia, Poland, Hungary, Slovakia, and the Czech Republic, 1990–1999*

Ashutosh Varshney, *Democracy, Development, and the Countryside*

Stephen I. Wilkinson, *Votes and Violence: Electoral Competition and Ethnic Riots in India*

Elisabeth J. Wood, *Forging Democracy from Below: Insurgent Transitions in South Africa and El Salvador*

Elisabeth J. Wood, *Insurgent Collective Action and Civil War in El Salvador*